BLACK CHICAGO

BLACK CHICAGO
THE MAKING OF A NEGRO GHETTO
1890–1920

Allan H. Spear

THE UNIVERSITY OF CHICAGO PRESS

CHICAGO & LONDON

THE UNIVERSITY OF CHICAGO PRESS, CHICAGO 60637

The University of Chicago Press, Ltd., London

© 1967 by The University of Chicago. All rights reserved

Published 1967. Printed in the United States of America

05 04 03 02 01 00 99 98 97 96   13 14 15 16 17

ISBN: [Paperbound] 0-226-76857-0

LCN: 67-21381

∞ The paper used in this publication meets the minimum
requirements of the American National Standard for Information
Sciences–Permanence of Paper for Printed Library Materials,
ANSI Z39.48–1984.

TO MY PARENTS

PREFACE

On July 27, 1919, a seventeen-year-old Negro boy, Eugene Williams, drowned at the Twenty-ninth Street beach in Chicago. The youth had accidentally floated across the unmarked barrier that separated the white and Negro sectors of the beach and had been stoned by angry whites. Nevertheless, the policeman patrolling the beach refused to make any arrests. Negroes, infuriated by the officer's indifference, attacked the whites, and soon the bathers were engaged in a pitched battle that rapidly spilled beyond the confines of the beach. This incident, coming after months of racial tension, fomented one of the bloodiest race riots in American history. For six days, white and Negro mobs terrorized the city, clashing on street corners, murdering passersby, and destroying property. Thirty-eight died, 537 were injured, and over one thousand were rendered homeless before the state militia finally restored order. From those hot summer days until the present, racial conflict has ranked high among Chicago's unsolved municipal problems.

After the riot Illinois Governor Frank Lowden appointed a commission to study the causes of the outbreak and the general status of race relations in Chicago.[1] The commission documented, in over six hundred detailed pages, what any casual observer of city life could have seen: Chicago had in its midst a sharply delineated Negro ghetto, separated from the white community by a high though unofficial wall of segregation and discrimination. Within this wall, a quarter of a million black Chicagoans maintained a community life that, on the surface at least, seemed virtually independent of white Chicago. Negroes organized their own civic and social institutions, congregated in their own churches, operated their own businesses, and ran their own political machine. The facilities of black Chicago—institutional, economic, and political—were, almost without exception, inferior to their white counterparts. The community's deteriorating homes were inadequate and overcrowded; its welfare institutions could not begin

[1] Chicago Commission on Race Relations, *The Negro in Chicago: A Study of Race Relations and a Race Riot* (Chicago: University of Chicago Press, 1922).

to meet the problems of crime, delinquency, poverty, broken homes, alcoholism, and vice; its businesses could rarely compete with white firms and provided but a handful of jobs for its citizens; its political organization was corrupt and unresponsive to the community's most pressing needs. Negroes' attempts to escape from the constrictions of the black ghetto had led to one tragic race riot. So long as whites persisted in confining Negroes to an inferior city within a city, the potential for racial war remained.

The situation described in the Race Relations Commission report of 1922 has become a commonplace of American life in the last forty-five years. Since World War I, the Negro problem has become an urban problem. As Negroes have fled from the impoverished cotton fields and stagnating villages of the rural South to the industrial centers of the North and West, every major American city has developed its Negro ghetto. These black enclaves have become not only a major concern of municipal authorities but a favorite laboratory for social scientists. New York's Harlem, Chicago's South Side, and Detroit's Paradise Valley have been minutely described and analyzed by sociologists, anthropologists, political scientists, and social psychologists. In more recent years, creative writers, such as Richard Wright, James Baldwin, and Ralph Ellison, have interpreted the temper of life in these communities. In short, every literate, socially conscious American has been made aware of the critical problems of the Negro ghetto.

The Negro ghetto is a uniquely urban phenomenon. In the rural South, where Negroes lived interspersed among whites and were dependent upon whites for their economic and physical well-being, the opportunity for separate community development was sharply limited. Rural Negroes had their own churches, lodges, and social clubs, but for other services they were forced to rely upon the inadequate, segregated facilities provided by white businesses, welfare agencies, and recreational organizations. Often they simply got along without public institutions. Not until Negroes began to migrate to the cities of the New South and the North did they begin to form cohesive communities with their own business, civic, and welfare institutions.

This study documents the formation of a northern Negro ghetto. It examines the forces, both external and internal, that conditioned the development of separate Negro community life and it analyzes the impact of this development upon Negro racial ideology, the growth of Negro race consciousness, and the composition and outlook of the Negro leadership class. It confronts these problems by tracing the history of the Chicago Negro community in the generation prior to the great riot of 1919. This work provides, in a sense, the historical background for the conditions described in the report of the Chicago Commission on Race Relations and later analyzed in St. Clair Drake and Horace Cayton's brilliant and exhaustive survey of Chicago Negro life, *Black Metropolis*.[2] It attempts to show how, in a thirty-year period, a relatively fluid pattern of race relations gave way to a rigid pattern of discrimination and segregation. And it shows how Negro leaders, in their ideology and their program, veered away from the militant abolitionist tradition and adopted a policy that basically accepted separate Negro community life.

The Negro migration of the World War I years has been described as "after emancipation . . . the great watershed in American Negro history."[3] It signaled the onset of a great population shift that was to transfer the locus of Negro life in the United States from the rural South to the urban North and place America's race problem in a new context. It profoundly changed the psychology of Negro protest and paved the way for the Negro revolt of our own times. But in Chicago, at least, the great migration did not create the Negro ghetto.[4] The southern Negroes who flocked to Chicago to work in the packinghouses and steel mills during the wartime boom found an already well-developed black enclave on the South Side. Negroes were systematically excluded from white sections of the city, drastically limited in their choice of jobs, and barred from many places of public accommodation. In response to their deteriorating status, they had developed separate institutions in the black belt. The migration accelerated developments that had been in progress since the 1890's. But it did not basically alter the pattern of Negro community life that the first wartime migrants encountered in 1915.

[2] New York: Harcourt, Brace & Company, 1945.

[3] August Meier, *Negro Thought in America, 1880–1915* (Ann Arbor: University of Michigan Press, 1963), p. 170.

[4] In some other major cities, the ghetto also antedated the World War I migration. See, for example, Gilbert Osofsky's fine study of Negro life in New York, *Harlem: The Making of a Ghetto* (New York: Harper & Row, 1965).

The analysis pursued in this study necessarily relies heavily upon the public record. No important Negro leader left private papers; no diaries or memoirs reveal the effect of community life upon individuals. Unlike the sociologist, the historian cannot conduct surveys that shed light upon personal adjustment. Therefore, the story uncovered here is one-sided; it is primarily a discussion of institutional developments, of the external structure of the Negro ghetto. The novelists, the social psychologists, and, at their best, the sociologists have demonstrated that the ghetto has another and perhaps more important side. They have described the psychology of the ghetto, the crippling impact of ghetto constrictions upon the mind and spirit of its inhabitants. Historical materials are ill-suited for a systematic treatment of the warped personalities, thwarted ambitions, and unbearable frustrations that the ghetto has produced. The historian cannot explain Bigger Thomas, John Grimes, or the Invisible Man; he can, it may be hoped, contribute to an understanding of the community that spawned them.

Many people have assisted me, both concretely and inspirationally, in this study, and I can single out only a few for special mention. Professor Alfred H. Jones has read the manuscript at every stage of development and has continually offered candid and searching criticism. Professor August Meier has saved me from innumerable errors by sharing with me his unrivaled knowledge of Negro history. Dr. Leslie H. Fishel, Jr., first aroused my interest in Negro history and has continued to provide me with ideas and encouragement. Professors John Morton Blum and Robin W. Winks supervised this study in its original form as a doctoral dissertation and gave generously of time and advice. I have further profited from the valuable suggestions of Professors John Hope Franklin, Clarke A. Chambers, and David M. Potter. The Social Science Research Council and Yale University provided financial assistance at crucial stages in the research, and Mr. Floyd J. Miller and Miss Elizabeth Katz aided me in the final preparation of the manuscript. Finally, I am grateful to the numerous people in Chicago who graciously granted me interviews and in many cases led me to important documentary material.

CONTENTS

PLATES

(Following Page 46)

MAPS

(Following Page 14)

TABLES

INTRODUCTION

By the end of the nineteenth century, Chicago had captured the imagination of the world. It epitomized the American miracle, rising within two generations from a frontier outpost in the swamps of northern Illinois to the second city in the nation, the fifth in the world. Almost destroyed by the Great Fire of 1871, Chicago rebuilt within a few years on a grander and more ambitious scale than before. Visitors saw in Chicago the very essence of American civilization and indeed the civilization of the industrial age. "I would not want to live there for anything in the world," wrote a prominent Italian playwright after visiting the city, "[but] I think that whoever ignores it is not entirely acquainted with our century and of what it is the ultimate expression."[1]

In 1893, Chicago won out, over many rivals, as the most suitable site for the World's Columbian Exposition commemorating the four-hundredth anniversary of the discovery of America. On an unpromising lakefront tract, seven miles south of the business district, an energetic group of promoters, planners, and architects, headed by the indefatigable Daniel Burnham, erected a White City, a grandiose cluster of stuccoed temples set amidst landscaped lawns, placid lagoons, and wooded islands. The Columbian Exposition was a paean to American industrial progress. The Machinery, Electricity, Mining, and Transportation Buildings displayed the technical innovations that were pushing the United States to the economic forefront of the world. Visitors could speak

[1] Giuseppe Giacosa, "A City of Smoke," in *As Others See Chicago*, ed. Bessie Louise Pierce (Chicago: University of Chicago Press, 1933), p. 276. Chicago's growth is chronicled in detail in Bessie Louise Pierce's comprehensive *History of Chicago*, 3 vols. (New York: Alfred A. Knopf, 1937, 1940, 1957), which deals with the city's history until 1893. A good short account of the rise of Chicago appears in Constance McLaughlin Green, *American Cities in the Growth of the Nation*, paperback ed. (New York: Harper & Row, 1965), pp. 100–128. Additional material can be found in Lloyd Lewis and Henry J. Smith, *Chicago: The History of Its Reputation* (New York: Harcourt, Brace & Company, 1929), and Emmett Dedmon, *Fabulous Chicago* (New York: Random House, 1953). A revealing portrait of Chicago in the 1890's appears in Louise C. Wade, *Graham Taylor: Pioneer for Social Justice* (Chicago: University of Chicago Press, 1964), pp. 51–82.

over a long-distance telephone to New York, watch demonstrations of high-tension currents, and inspect the most advanced telescope in the world. When sated by the fair's educational attractions, they could stroll a half mile west to the gaudy Midway Plaisance, to be entertained by the gyrations of the Ferris Wheel and the undulations of Little Egypt.[2]

Few visitors in 1893, however, saw the other Chicago—the workers' city of tenements and cottages which housed those who manned Chicago's thriving industries. While tourists walked the clean, paved streets of the White City, hundreds of thousands returned each night to crowded, filthy, airless rooms. Underpaid, overworked, and subject to periodic layoffs and slowdowns, Chicago's working class testified to the social cost of Chicago's phenomenal economic and material growth. Since the depression of the 1870's, the city had been a focal point of industrial conflict in America. The railroad strike of 1877 had brought Chicago to the brink of open warfare and left a bitterness among the working people that provided fertile soil for socialist and anarchist organizers. The Haymarket episode nine years later symbolized an era in American history; it dramatized the determination of the business interests to maintain the status quo. Chicago was not, of course, the only battleground in the industrial war that gripped the United States in the late nineteenth century. But as its achievements had seemed the very consummation of the American success story, its traumas seemed to provide the supreme test for industrial relations in the United States.[3]

The lights had barely dimmed on the Midway Plaisance when Chicago found itself in the grips of industrial strife even grimmer than the conflicts of 1877 and 1886. The depression that had come in the wake of the financial panic of 1893 left thousands of Chicagoans jobless. As winter approached, unemployed men lined up at soup kitchens, and hundreds sought shelter each night in

[2] Pierce, *History of Chicago*, 3: 501–12; Pierce, *As Others See Chicago*, pp. 324–50; Lewis and Smith, *Chicago: The History of Its Reputation*, pp. 202–16; Ray Ginger, *Altgeld's America* (New York: Funk & Wagnalls, 1958), pp. 15–22.

[3] Green, *American Cities*, p. 124; Ginger, *Altgeld's America*, pp. 35–60; Pierce, *History of Chicago*, 3: 234–99. The standard account of the Haymarket affair is Henry David, *History of the Haymarket Affair*, paperback ed. (New York: Collier Books, 1964).

the corridors of City Hall.[4] In the spring, open warfare erupted at George Pullman's model company town ten miles south of the city. Pullman's paternalistic benevolence did not prevent him from cutting wages without reducing rents, and the workers, receiving no satisfaction from their protests, walked out. The strike precipitated a nationwide railroad shutdown and placed Chicago in the midst of a crisis that ended only when federal troops entered the city and the union leaders were arrested for defying a federal court injunction.[5]

The turmoil of 1893–94 ushered in a decade of feverish concern over social reform. William T. Stead, an English editor and Christian socialist, issued a challenge to Chicagoans in a speech in 1893, followed a year later by his sensational exposé of social conditions in the city, *If Christ Came to Chicago*. Stead described graphically the plight of the workers, the savage brutality with which their aspirations were crushed, and the corruption and indifference of Chicago's leaders. "If Chicago is to be the Capital of Civilization," he wrote, "it is indispensable that she should at least be able to show that every resident within her limits enjoyed every advantage which intelligent and public-spirited administration has secured for the people elsewhere."[6]

In response to the conditions that Stead revealed, Chicagoans launched a series of reform ventures designed to refurbish the city's tarnished image. The Civic Federation, headed by many of Chicago's most prominent businessmen and their wives, dabbled in genteel reform. Though committed to the city's current economic structure and to the idea of class conciliation, the Federation made noteworthy efforts to provide systematic relief for the needy, improve housing and sanitary conditions, and drive the grafters and boodlers from City Hall. Among the supporters of the Federation were a group of professional reformers more closely attuned to the plight of Chicago's masses than the Palmers, Fields, and Gages who occupied the organization's top echelons. Jane Addams, for instance, and the remarkable women she en-

[4] Green, *American Cities*, p. 122; William T. Stead, *If Christ Came to Chicago* (Chicago: Laird & Lee, 1894), pp. 31–38; Ginger, *Altgeld's America*, pp. 91–93.

[5] A full account appears in Almont Lindsey, *The Pullman Strike* (Chicago: University of Chicago Press, 1942).

[6] Stead, *If Christ Came to Chicago*, p. 336.

listed at Hull House knew through personal experience the problems of alienation and exploitation faced by Italian and Slavic immigrants who huddled in Chicago's West Side tenements. Graham Taylor of the Chicago Commons settlement house combined practical knowledge of the plight of the poor with a strong belief in the social gospel. Clarence Darrow, already known nationally as the "people's lawyer," brought to the reform movement a searching critique of the American industrial system. And at the vital, young University of Chicago Thorstein Veblen sought to revise classical economic theory and John Dewey formulated a philosophy of education designed for the new industrial age.[7]

The problems of class conflict, industrial strife, and corrupt politics that confronted Chicago's reformers at the turn of the century were complicated by the city's great ethnic diversity. Since the Civil War, the emerging metropolis had attracted peoples from every part of the world. By 1890, 77.9 per cent of its population was foreign born or of foreign parentage.[8] The Germans, Irish, and Scandinavians were still the largest ethnic groups in the city, but after 1880, increasing numbers of Poles, Lithuanians, Czechs, Italians, and Eastern European Jews entered the city, concentrating in Chicago's perennial area of first settlement—the near West Side. There, cultural alienation complicated the problems of poverty. Facing the baffling complexities of urban life and an alien culture, these new groups strove against difficult odds to maintain their own ethnic integrity. Although various immigrant groups met the problems of American life in diverse ways, all attempted, through the creation of community institutions or the preservation of a traditional family structure, to maintain enough of their heritage to provide identity and a sense of belonging.[9]

[7] Ginger, *Altgeld's America*, pp. 113–42, 193–208, 234–56. See also Jane Addams, *Twenty Years at Hull House*, paperback ed. (New York: New American Library, 1961), pp. 133–47; Wade, *Graham Taylor*, pp. 83–116.

[8] Pierce, *History of Chicago*, 3: 22.

[9] *Ibid.*, 3: 22–47. See also Paul Cressy, "The Succession of Cultural Groups in the City of Chicago," unpublished doctoral dissertation, University of Chicago, 1930; Andrew J. Townsend, "The Germans of Chicago," unpublished doctoral dissertation, University of Chicago, 1927; Philip P. Bregstone, *Chicago and Its Jews* (Chicago: privately printed, 1933); Rudolph Vecoli, "Chicago's Italians Prior to World War I: A Study of Their Social and Economic Adjustment," unpublished doctoral dissertation, University of Wisconsin, 1963.

There were, then, many Chicagos by the end of the century. The reformers faced not merely the problem of an exploited working class, but of numerous worker enclaves, each clinging proudly to its own traditions. The newcomers' ignorance of American economic and political life made them particularly susceptible to the blandishments of unscrupulous employers and political bosses. A few of the reformers, such as Jane Addams and Graham Taylor, attempted to bring the immigrants into the mainstream of the city's life while at the same time respecting and even encouraging their cultural diversity. But many old-stock Chicagoans —and this included many of the sons and daughters of the earlier immigrants—were hostile, or at best patronizing, toward the ways of the newcomers.

Of Chicago's many ethnic groups, none had a longer local history than the Negroes. According to tradition, the first permanent settler on the site of Chicago was a black trader from Santo Domingo, Jean Baptiste Pointe de Saible, who built a cabin on the mouth of the Chicago River in about 1790.[10] The beginning of Negro community life in the city can be traced to the late 1840's, when a small stream of fugitive slaves from the South and free Negroes from the East formed the core of a small Negro settlement. Soon there were enough Negroes in Chicago to organize an African Methodist Episcopal church, and within a decade several more churches and a number of social and civic clubs were flourishing. By 1860, almost a thousand Negroes lived in Chicago. A small leadership group, headed by a well-to-do tailor, John Jones, participated in antislavery activities and articulated the grievances of a people who already found themselves the victims of segregation and discrimination.[11]

Despite the presence of an active antislavery movement, Negroes in antebellum Chicago were severely circumscribed. Residents of downstate Illinois frequently characterized Chicago as a "sinkhole of abolition" and a "nigger-loving town"; yet the sympathy that many white Chicagoans expressed for the Southern slaves

[10] Milo M. Quaife, *Checagou* (Chicago: University of Chicago Press, 1933), pp. 44–46.

[11] St. Clair Drake, "Churches and Voluntary Associations in the Chicago Negro Community," Report of Official Project 465-54-3-386, Works Progress Administration, mimeographed (Chicago, 1940), pp. 34–49; St. Clair Drake and Horace Cayton, *Black Metropolis* (New York: Harcourt, Brace & Co., 1945), pp. 32–45.

was not often extended to the local Negroes. To be sure, the anti-slavery press, on occasion, noted approvingly the orderliness and respectability of the city's Negro community, but little was done to improve the status of the group. Chicago's Negroes could not vote, nor could they testify in court against whites. State law forbade intermarriage between the races. Segregation was maintained in the schools, places of public accommodation, and transportation. Chicago's abolitionists regarded these conditions as side issues and manifested little interest in them.[12]

Between 1870 and 1890, the Chicago Negro community grew from less than four thousand to almost fifteen thousand and developed a well delineated class structure and numerous religious and secular organizations. After the fire of 1871, the community became more concentrated geographically. Most Negroes lived on the South Side, but were still well interspersed with whites. Although a majority of the city's Negroes worked as domestic and personal servants, a small business and professional class provided community leadership. St. Clair Drake and Horace Cayton described the Chicago Negro community of this period as

a small, compact, but rapidly growing community divided into three broad social groups. The "respectables"—church-going, poor or moderately prosperous, and often unrestrained in their worship—were looked down upon somewhat by the "refined" people, who, because of their education and breeding, could not sanction the less decorous behavior of their racial brothers. Both of these groups were censorious of the "riffraff," the "sinners"—unchurched and undisciplined.[13]

During the postwar years, the formal pattern of segregation that had characterized race relations in antebellum Chicago broke down. By 1870, Negroes could vote. In 1874, the school system was desegregated. A decade later, after the federal civil rights bill was nullified by the United States Supreme Court, the Illinois legislature enacted a law prohibiting discrimination in public places.[14] Despite these advances, however, the status of Negroes in Chicago remained ambiguous. They continued to face dis-

[12] Pierce, *History of Chicago*, 2: 12; Drake and Cayton, p. 41; for a general discussion of the status of Negroes in the antebellum North, see Leon Litwack, *North of Slavery* (Chicago: University of Chicago Press, 1961).

[13] Drake and Cayton, *Black Metropolis*, p. 48.

[14] *Ibid.*, p. 50; Pierce, *History of Chicago*, 3: 49–50.

crimination in housing, employment, and, even in the face of the civil rights law, public accommodations. But they were not confined to a ghetto. Most Negroes, although concentrated in certain sections of the city, lived in mixed neighborhoods. Negro businessmen and professional men frequently catered to a white market and enjoyed social, as well as economic, contacts with the white community. And although Negro churches and social clubs proliferated, there were still few separate civic institutions. Local Negro leaders were firmly committed to the ideal of an integrated community in which hospitals, social agencies, and public accommodations would be open to all without discrimination.[15]

From the beginning, the experience of Chicago's Negroes had been, in significant ways, separate from the mainstream of the city's history. No other ethnic group had been legally circumscribed; no white minority had been forced to fight for legal recognition of citizenship rights. In 1890, despite the improvement in the Negroes' status since 1865, many of their problems were still unique. In a chiefly industrial city, they worked principally in domestic and service trades, almost untouched by labor organization and industrial strife. The political and economic turmoil of the late nineteenth century seemed to have little effect on the city's Negroes. No Jane Addams or Graham Taylor sought to bring them within the reform coalition that was attempting to change the life of the city. Generally ignored by white Chicagoans, Negroes were viewed neither as a threat to the city's well-being nor as an integral part of the city's social structure. Most responsible whites probably held the view quoted by Ray Stannard Baker: "We have helped the Negro to liberty; we have helped to educate him to stand on his own feet. Now let's see what he can do for himself. After all, he must survive or perish by his own efforts."[16]

Still, the story of Chicago's Negroes in the late nineteenth and early twentieth centuries is interwoven with the general history of the city. As their numbers increased between 1890 and 1910, Negroes became ever more conspicuous, and the indifference with which they had been regarded in the nineteenth century changed

[15] The ambiguity of the Negro's status in late nineteenth-century Chicago is discussed in detail in chapters 1, 2, and 3.

[16] Ray Stannard Baker, "The Color Line in the North," *American Magazine,* 65 (February, 1908): 349.

to hostility. Labor strife, ethnic tension, political corruption, and inefficiency—the problems of greatest concern to white Chicagoans—all helped determine the status of the city's Negroes. So too did the rise of racist doctrines that many old-stock Chicagoans applied indiscriminately to Negroes and the "new" immigrants. The virulently anti-Negro works of Thomas Dixon, the Chautauqua addresses of South Carolina's Senator Benjamin Tillman, as well as the anti-immigrant propaganda of Prescott Hall, Henry Pratt Fairchild, and Madison Grant epitomized an age of race chauvinism in which Anglo-Americans strove to preserve a mythical racial purity.[17]

The profound changes that took place in the Chicago Negro community between the 1890's and 1920 had both internal and external dimensions. On the one hand, they were the result of the mounting hostility of white Chicagoans. Whites grew anxious as a growing Negro population sought more and better housing; they feared job competition in an era of industrial strife when employers frequently used Negroes as strikebreakers; and they viewed Negro voters as pawns of a corrupt political machine. All of these fears were accentuated by the rise of a racist ideology that reinforced traditional anti-Negro prejudices. On the other hand, Negroes were not passive objects in the developments of the early twentieth century. Their response to discrimination and segregation, the decisions their leaders made, and the community activities in which they engaged all helped to shape the emerging Negro ghetto. The rise of Chicago's black ghetto belongs to both urban history and Negro history; it was the result of the interplay between certain trends in the development of the city and major currents in Negro life and thought.

[17] For a detailed discussion of anti-Negro propaganda in the early twentieth century, see I. A. Newby, *Jim Crow's Defense* (Baton Rouge: Louisiana State University Press, 1965); the best treatment of the anti-immigrant campaign is in John Higham, *Strangers in the Land* (New Brunswick, N.J.: Rutgers University Press, 1955).

PART I

THE RISE OF THE GHETTO, 1890–1915

CHAPTER 1

THE PHYSICAL GHETTO

Between 1890 and 1915, the Negro population of Chicago grew from less than fifteen thousand to over fifty thousand. Although this growth was overshadowed by the massive influx of Negroes during and after World War I, this was nevertheless a significant increase. By the eve of World War I, although Negroes were still a minor element in the city's population, they were far more conspicuous than they had been a generation earlier. The population increase was accompanied by the concentration of Negroes into ever more constricted sections of the city. In the late nineteenth century, while most Negroes lived in certain sections of the South Side, they lived interspersed among whites; there were few all-Negro blocks. By 1915, on the other hand, the physical ghetto had taken shape; a large, almost all-Negro enclave on the South Side, with a similar offshoot on the West Side, housed most of Chicago's Negroes.

Migration was the major factor in the growth of the Negro community, and most migrants were coming from outside of the state. Over 80 per cent of Chicago's Negro population in 1900 was born in states other than Illinois. The largest portion of these migrants originated in the border states and in the Upper South: Kentucky, and Missouri, in particular, had sent large groups of Negroes to Chicago. The states of the Deep South were, as yet, a secondary source of Chicago's Negro population; only 17 per cent had come from these states as opposed to 43 per cent from the Upper South. The states located directly south of Chicago supplied a larger segment of the population than the southeastern states, but there were sizable groups born in Virginia and Georgia.[1]

From the beginning of Chicago's history, most Negroes had lived on the South Side. As early as 1850, 82 per cent of the Negro population lived in an area bounded by the Chicago River on the

[1] See Table 2.

north, Sixteenth Street on the south, the South Branch of the river on the west, and Lake Michigan on the east.[2] The famous South Side black belt was emerging—a narrow finger of land, wedged between the railroad yards and industrial plants just west of Wentworth Avenue and the fashionable homes east of Wabash Avenue. By 1900, the black belt stretched from the downtown business district as far south as Thirty-ninth Street. But there were also sizable Negro enclaves, usually of a few square blocks each, in several other sections of the city.[3] The Thirteenth Ward Negro

TABLE 1

NEGRO POPULATION OF CHICAGO
1850–1930

DATE	TOTAL POPULATION	NEGRO POPULATION	PER CENT NEGRO	PER CENT INCREASE	
				Total Population	Negro Population
1850......	29,963	323	1.1	....	....
1860......	109,260	955	0.9	265	196
1870......	298,977	3,691	1.2	174	286
1880......	503,185	6,480	1.1	68	75
1890......	1,099,850	14,271	1.3	119	120
1900......	1,698,575	30,150	1.9	54	111
1910......	2,185,283	44,103	2.0	29	46
1920......	2,701,705	109,458	4.1	24	148
1930......	3,376,438	233,903	6.9	25	114

SOURCE: *U.S. Census Reports*, 1850–1930.

community stretched along West Lake Street from Ashland to Western. The Eighteenth Ward Negroes lived in the old immigrant neighborhood on the Near West Side near Hull House. On the Near North Side, Negroes had begun to settle in the Italian Seventeenth Ward. And on the South Side, beyond the black belt,

[2] Pierce, *History of Chicago*, 2: 11.

[3] Census figures for 1900 are available only on a ward basis. Because of the size of the subdivisions, these statistics must be used with caution. In Wards 31 and 34, for instance (see Map 1), the Negro population is concentrated in the extreme northern parts of the wards; thus, despite the appearance of the map, there are, with the exception of small communities in Roseland and Morgan Park, few Negroes south of Sixty-ninth Street.

TABLE 2

STATE OF BIRTH OF NATIVE NON-WHITES
CHICAGO, 1900

Area of Birth	Number Per State	Totals	Per Cent
Illinois...................	5,875	5,875	19.8
Middle West (except Illinois)[a]			
Ohio.....................	1,808		
Indiana..................	1,052		
Iowa....................	280		
Michigan................	605		
Kansas..................	331		
Wisconsin	204		
Minnesota...............	56		
Nebraska................	54		
North Dakota............	4		
South Dakota............	7		
Region.................	....	4,401	14.8
Northeast			
Pennsylvania.............	442		
New York................	427		
Massachusetts............	98		
New Jersey..............	54		
Connecticut..............	28		
Rhode Island.............	10		
Maine...................	13		
New Hampshire..........	4		
Vermont.................	8		
Region.................	....	1,084	3.6
Upper South and Border			
Tennessee...............	3,216		
Kentucky................	4,411		
Missouri.................	2,222		
Virginia.................	1,701		
North Carolina...........	431		
Maryland................	425		
District of Columbia......	232		
West Virginia............	105		
Oklahoma................	3		
Delaware................	6		
Indian Territory..........	9		
Region.................	....	12,761	42.9
Lower South			
Mississippi...............	1,148		
Alabama.................	1,181		
Georgia.................	1,092		
Louisiana...............	618		
Arkansas................	291		
South Carolina...........	276		
Texas...................	282		
Florida..................	98		
Region.................	....	4,986	16.8

SOURCE: *U.S. Twelfth Census*, 1900, vol. 1, *Population*, part 1, pp. 706–25. Derived by adding figures in Tables 31 and 32 and subtracting from figures in Table 30.

[a] Middle West totals (including Illinois): 10,276 and 34.5 per cent.

TABLE 2—*Continued*

Area of Birth	Number Per State	Totals	Per Cent
West			
Colorado.................	35		
California.................	69		
Washington..............	19		
New Mexico..............	6		
Montana.................	8		
Idaho....................	1		
Arizona..................	2		
Oregon..................	7		
Nevada..................	1		
Wyoming................	2		
Utah....................	11		
Region..................	....	161	0.5
Not specified and born abroad	....	475	....
Total native non-white...	....	29,743	....

Summary

Born in Illinois............	....	5,875	19.8
Born outside Illinois.......	....	23,393	78.7
Total native non-white...	....	29,743	....

communities of upper- and middle-class Negroes had emerged in Hyde Park, Woodlawn, Englewood, and Morgan Park.[4]

Despite this concentration of Negroes in enclaves, the Negro population of the city was still relatively well distributed in 1900. Nineteen of the city's thirty-five wards had a Negro population of at least .5 per cent of the total population of the ward and fourteen wards were at least 1 per cent Negro. Only two wards had a Negro population of more than 10 per cent. In 1898, just over a quarter of Chicago's Negroes lived in precincts that were more than 50 per cent Negro, and over 30 per cent lived in precincts

[4] Richard R. Wright, Jr., "The Industrial Condition of Negroes in Chicago," unpublished B.D. thesis, University of Chicago Divinity School, 1901, pp. 7–8; on the West Side, see *Defender*, March 22, 1913, p. 4; on Morgan Park, see E. Franklin Frazier, *The Negro Family in Chicago* (Chicago: University of Chicago Press, 1932), p. 94, and Chicago Commission on Race Relations, *The Negro in Chicago: A Study of Race Relations and a Race Riot* (Chicago: University of Chicago Press, 1922), pp. 137–38.

MAPS

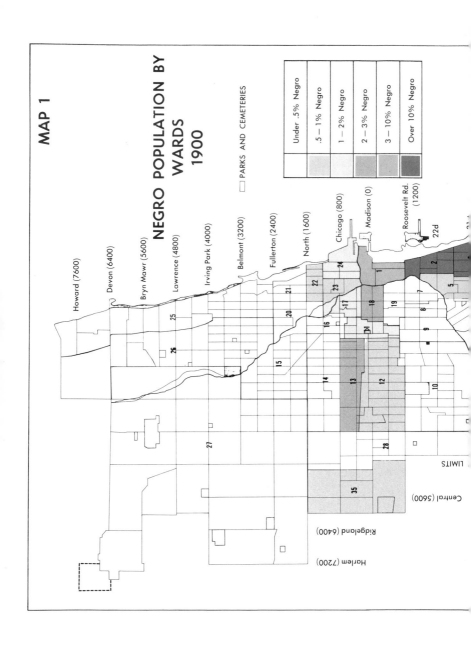

MAP 1

NEGRO POPULATION BY
WARDS
1900

☐ PARKS AND CEMETERIES

	Under .5% Negro
	.5 – 1% Negro
	1 – 2% Negro
	2 – 3% Negro
	3 – 10% Negro
	Over 10% Negro

Howard (7600)
Devon (6400)
Bryn Mawr (5600)
Lawrence (4800)
Irving Park (4000)
Belmont (3200)
Fullerton (2400)
North (1600)
Chicago (800)
Madison (0)
Roosevelt Rd. (1200)
22d

Harlem (7200)
Ridgeland (6400)
Central (5600)
LIMITS

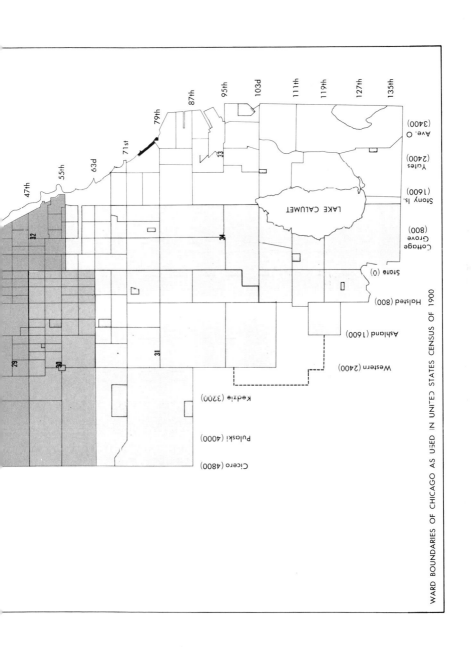

WARD BOUNDARIES OF CHICAGO AS USED IN UNITED STATES CENSUS OF 1900

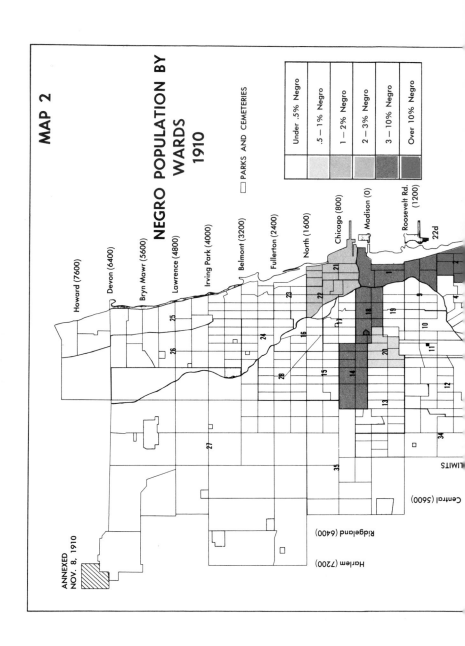

MAP 2

NEGRO POPULATION BY WARDS
1910

☐ PARKS AND CEMETERIES

	Under .5% Negro
	.5 – 1% Negro
	1 – 2% Negro
	2 – 3% Negro
	3 – 10% Negro
	Over 10% Negro

Howard (7600)
Devon (6400)
Bryn Mawr (5600)
Lawrence (4800)
Irving Park (4000)
Belmont (3200)
Fullerton (2400)
North (1600)
Chicago (800)
Madison (0)
Roosevelt Rd. (1200)
22d

Central (5600)
Ridgeland (6400)
Harlem (7200)

LIMITS

ANNEXED
NOV. 8, 1910

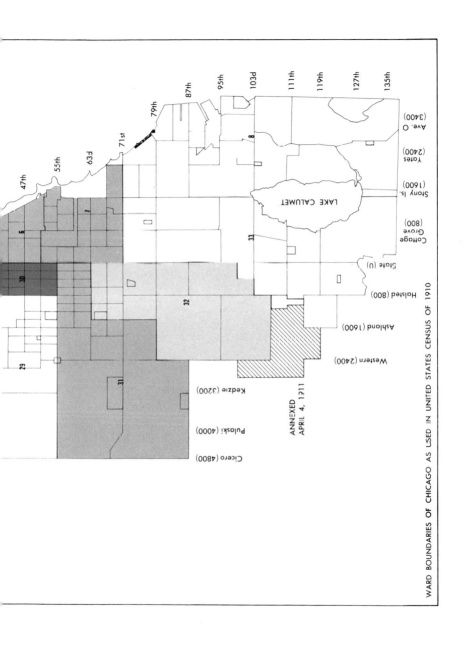

WARD BOUNDARIES OF CHICAGO AS USED IN UNITED STATES CENSUS OF 1910

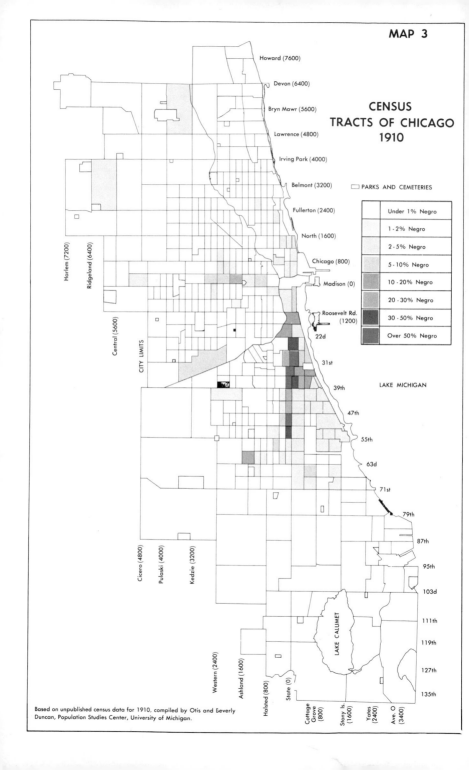

MAP 3

CENSUS
TRACTS OF CHICAGO
1910

Howard (7600)

Devon (6400)

Bryn Mawr (5600)

Lawrence (4800)

Irving Park (4000)

Belmont (3200)

Fullerton (2400)

North (1600)

Chicago (800)

Madison (0)

Roosevelt Rd. (1200)

22d

31st

39th

47th

55th

63d

71st

79th

87th

95th

103d

111th

119th

127th

135th

☐ PARKS AND CEMETERIES

Under 1% Negro

1 - 2% Negro

2 - 5% Negro

5 - 10% Negro

10 - 20% Negro

20 - 30% Negro

30 - 50% Negro

Over 50% Negro

LAKE MICHIGAN

LAKE CALUMET

Harlem (7200)

Ridgeland (6400)

Central (5600)

CITY LIMITS

Cicero (4800)

Pulaski (4000)

Kedzie (3200)

Western (2400)

Ashland (1600)

Halsted (800)

State (0)

Cottage Grove (800)

Stony Is. (1600)

Yates (2400)

Ave. O (3400)

Based on unpublished census data for 1910, compiled by Otis and Beverly
Duncan, Population Studies Center, University of Michigan.

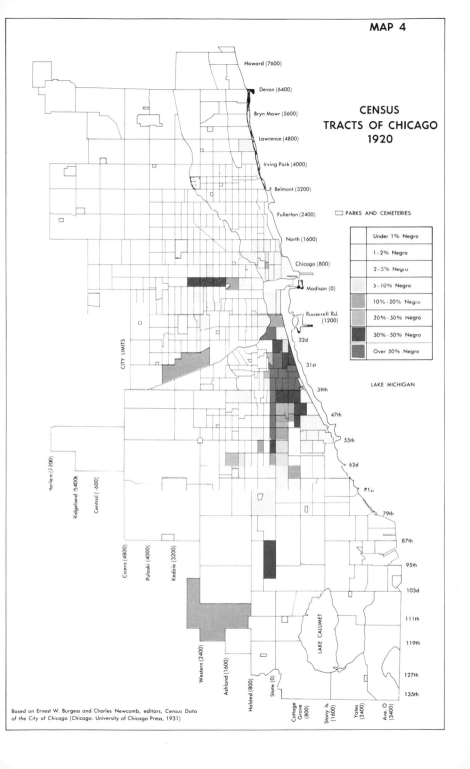

MAP 4

CENSUS
TRACTS OF CHICAGO
1920

Howard (7600)

Devon (6400)

Bryn Mawr (5600)

Lawrence (4800)

Irving Park (4000)

Belmont (3200)

Fullerton (2400)

North (1600)

Chicago (800)

Madison (0)

Roosevelt Rd.
(1200)

22d

31st

39th

47th

55th

63d

71st

79th

87th

95th

103d

111th

119th

127th

135th

CITY LIMITS

LAKE MICHIGAN

LAKE CALUMET

Harlem (7200)

Ridgeland (5400)

Central (-600)

Cicero (4800)

Pulaski (4000)

Kedzie (3200)

Western (2400)

Ashland (1600)

Halsted (800)

State (0)

Cottage Grove (800)

Stony Is. (1600)

Yates (2400)

Ave. O (3400)

☐ PARKS AND CEMETERIES

	Under 1% Negro
	1 - 2% Negro
	2 - 5% Negro
	5 - 10% Negro
	10% - 20% Negro
	20% - 30% Negro
	30% - 50% Negro
	Over 50% Negro

Based on Ernest W. Burgess and Charles Newcomb, editors, *Census Data
of the City of Chicago* (Chicago: University of Chicago Press, 1931)

that were at least 95 per cent white.[5] As late as 1910, Negroes were less highly segregated from native whites than were Italian immigrants.[6]

[5] Paul Cressy, who compiled these figures, used a school census of uncertain accuracy for his 1898 tabulations. But in the absence of statistics for subdivisions smaller than wards in any federal census prior to 1910, these data are the best available. Cressy, "The Succession of Cultural Groups in the City of Chicago," unpublished doctoral dissertation, University of Chicago, 1930, p. 93.

[6] Stanley Lieberson, "Comparative Segregation and Assimilation of Ethnic Groups," unpublished doctoral dissertation, University of Chicago, 1960, pp. 176–79.

TABLE 3

NEGRO POPULATION BY WARD
CHICAGO, 1900 AND 1910

WARD NUMBER[a]	1900			1910		
	Total Population	Negro Population	Per Cent Negro	Total Population	Negro Population	Per Cent Negro
1......	24,274	1,528	6.3	29,528	2,603	8.8
2......	28,547	4,752	16.6	42,801	10,709	25.0
3......	32,989	7,518	22.8	46,131	11,081	24.0
4......	37,029	3,370	9.0	....	....	....
5......	43,315	339	0.8	....	....	....
6[b].....	....	....	....	75,121	1,962	2.6
7......	....	....	....	90,423	1,903	2.1
11......	37,533	410	1.1	....	....	....
12......	75,507	396	0.5	....	....	....
13......	47,527	1,250	2.6	....	....	....
14......	....	....	....	52,770	2,409	4.6
17......	20,713	288	1.4	....	....	....
18......	20,503	483	2.4	26,137	798	3.1
20......	....	....	....	61,708	369	0.6
21......	....	....	....	47,906	721	1.5
22......	32,767	286	0.9	49,324	524	1.1
23......	33,424	267	0.8	....	....	....
24......	35,830	550	1.5	....	....	....
29......	41,214	868	2.1	....	....	....
30......	106,124	3,246	3.1	51,308	6,431	12.5
31......	56,576	596	1.1	78,571	1,806	2.3
32......	69,202	1,439	2.1	70,408	514	0.7
34......	91,145	1,176	1.3	....	....	....
35......	11,795	88	0.7	....	....	....

SOURCES: *U.S. Twelfth Census*, 1900, Bulletin no. 72, July 13, 1901, p. 8; *U.S. Thirteenth Census*, 1910, *Statistics for Illinois*, pp. 644–46.

[a] Figures for 1900 and for 1910 are not comparable on a one-to-one basis because of changes in the ward boundaries (see Maps 1 and 2).

[b] Table includes data only for those wards with at least 0.5 per cent Negro population. Blank spaces indicate wards with under 0.5 per cent Negro population.

The decade 1900 to 1910 saw several significant changes in the population pattern of Negroes in Chicago. The growth rate, which had far outpaced the white growth rate in the 1890's, declined from 111 per cent to 46 per cent, and the proportion of Negroes in the population increased from 1.9 per cent to only 2 per cent. Yet despite this stabilization, the Negro population was still composed largely of migrants. Over 77 per cent of Chicago's Negroes were born outside of Illinois. This represents only a slight drop from 1900 and was almost five times as great as the corresponding

TABLE 4

CONCENTRATION OF NEGROES IN CHICAGO
1898–1920

PERCENTAGE OF NEGRO POPULATION IN THE RESIDENCE AREA[a]	PERCENTAGE OF TOTAL NEGRO POPULATION		
	1898[b]	1910	1920
Less than 5......	31.3	24.1	7.4
5– 9..........	9.7	8.2	2.6
10– 19..........	7.8	4.4	6.9
20– 49..........	23.3	32.5	32.6
50– 74..........	17.1	30.8	14.8
75–100..........	10.8	....	35.7

SOURCES: Paul Cressy, "The Succession of Cultural Groups in the City of Chicago," unpublished doctoral dissertation, University of Chicago, 1930, p. 93; unpublished census data for the city of Chicago, 1910, compiled by Otis and Beverly Duncan, Population Studies Center, University of Michigan; Ernest W. Burgess and Charles Newcomb, editors, *Census Data of the City of Chicago, 1920,* Chicago, University of Chicago Press, 1931.

a Residence areas in 1898 refer to precincts; in 1910 and 1920 to census tracts.

b 1898 figures are based on a school census.

figure for white Chicagoans.[7] Only three major Negro communities in the country—Los Angeles, Denver, and Oklahoma City, all young Western cities with highly mobile populations—had higher proportions of out-of-state migrants than Chicago. Even such burgeoning industrial centers as Detroit, Pittsburgh, and Cleveland had a lower percentage of Negroes born in other states.[8]

[7] See Table 5.

[8] U.S. Bureau of the Census, *Negro Population in the United States, 1790–1915* (Washington, D.C.: Government Printing Office, 1918), p. 74. The 1910 census tabulations do not permit a breakdown of the Chicago Negro population by state of birth. The only materials available are state of birth

The concentration of Negroes in enclaves was clearly increasing throughout this period. By 1910, over 30 per cent lived in predominantly Negro sections of the city and over 60 per cent in areas that were more than 20 per cent Negro. Whereas in 1900 nineteen of thirty-five wards had been over .5 per cent Negro, this figure was reduced to thirteen in 1910. Furthermore, the second and third wards, which included the heart of the black belt, were now 25 per cent Negro, while in 1900 only one ward had even approached that figure.[9]

Negro residential patterns for 1910 can be seen most clearly through the use of census tract data.[10] Of 431 census tracts in the city, Negroes could be found in all but ninety-four; eighty-eight were at least 1 per cent Negro. Four tracts were over 50 per cent Negro, but no tract was more than 61 per cent Negro. Despite greater concentration, therefore, there were still few all-Negro neighborhoods in Chicago.

The eight or nine neighborhoods that had been distinguishable as areas of Negro settlement in 1900 remained the core of the Chicago Negro community in 1910. The principal South Side black belt was slowly expanding to accommodate the growing population. Not only did Negroes push steadily southward, but the narrow strip of land that made up the black belt began to widen as Negroes moved into the comfortable neighborhood east of State Street. By the end of the decade, Negroes could be found as far east as Cottage Grove Avenue.[11]

Statistical data, then, reveal several definite trends in the pattern of Negro population in Chicago in the early twentieth century. The growth rate between 1900 and 1910 had decreased from the previous decade, but was still 50 per cent greater than that of whites. Most of the population increase was the result of migration, particularly from the nearby border states. Negroes could be

---

data for the Illinois Negro population (see Table 5). A considerably higher percentage of Chicago Negroes was born outside of Illinois than was true of Negroes in the state at large: 77.1 per cent for Chicago, 64.9 per cent for Illinois. But, in all probability, data on the origins of out-of-state Negroes in Chicago would closely resemble the statewide figures.

[9] Statistics for 1900 and 1910 are, however, difficult to compare because ward lines were altered during this decade.

[10] See Map 3.

[11] *Chicago Defender*, May 30, 1914.

TABLE 5
STATE OF BIRTH OF ILLINOIS NEGROES
1900–1910

AREA OF BIRTH	1900			1910		
	Number Per State	Totals	Per Cent	Number Per State	Totals	Per Cent
Illinois...............	30,022	30,022	35.5	35,917	35,917	33.2
Middle West *(except Illinois)*[a]						
Ohio.................	2,284			2,766		
Indiana..............	1,958			2,731		
Iowa.................	580			797		
Michigan.............	712			750		
Kansas...............	497			728		
Wisconsin............	369			285		
Minnesota............	75			120		
Nebraska.............	96			105		
North Dakota........	7			12		
South Dakota........	12			5		
Region.............	....	6,509	7.8	....	8,299	7.7
Northeast						
Pennsylvania.........	589			765		
New York............	527			524		
Massachusetts........	117			140		
New Jersey...........	76			82		
Connecticut..........	36			45		
Rhode Island........	14			24		
Maine...............	19			20		
New Hampshire.......	5			5		
Vermont.............	177			5		
Region.............	....	1,560	1.8	....	1,610	1.5
Upper South and Border						
Tennessee............	10,232			15,303		
Kentucky............	10,587			13,314		
Missouri.............	8,185			9,732		
Virginia.............	3,473			3,326		
North Carolina.......	1,073			1,175		
Maryland............	693			643		
District of Columbia...	308			268		
West Virginia........	190			229		
Oklahoma............	34[b]			126		
Delaware............	8			24		
Region.............	....	34,738	41.2	....	44,140	40.8

SOURCES: *U.S. Twelfth Census*, 1900, vol. 1, *Population*, part 1, pp. 702–705; U.S. Bureau of the Census, *Negro Population in the United States*, Washington, Government Printing Office, 1918, pp. 75–79.

[a] Middle West totals (including Illinois): 1900—36,612 and 43.3 per cent; 1910—44,216 and 40.9 per cent.

[b] Includes Indian Territory.

TABLE 5—*Continued*

Area of Birth	1900			1910		
	Number Per State	Totals	Per Cent	Number Per State	Totals	Per Cent
Lower South						
Mississippi...........	3,116			4,612		
Alabama.............	2,387			3,208		
Georgia..............	1,674			2,874		
Louisiana.............	1,073			1,609		
Arkansas.............	902			1,354		
South Carolina........	649			1,217		
Texas................	430			789		
Florida...............	147			243		
Region...............	....	10,378	12.3	....	15,906	14.7
West						
Colorado.............	51			80		
California............	57			77		
Washington..........	23			32		
New Mexico..........	9			18		
Montana.............	13			13		
Idaho................	1			8		
Arizona..............	3			8		
Oregon..............	4			6		
Nevada..............	5			6		
Wyoming............	3			4		
Utah................	12			8		
Region...............	....	181	0.2	....	269	0.2
Not specified and born abroad.............	....	154	1.1	....	1,980	1.8
Total Negro........	....	85,078	....	....	109,049	....

Summary

Born in Illinois........	....	30,022	35.5	....	35,917	33.2
Born outside Illinois...	....	53,493	63.4	....	70,224	64.9
Total Negro........	....	85,078	....	....	109,049	....

found throughout much of the city and the Negro neighborhoods were by no means exclusively black. But the concentration of Negroes in two enclaves on the South and West Sides was increasing. As the population grew, Negroes were not spreading throughout the city but were becoming confined to a clearly delineated area of Negro settlement.

The increasing physical separation of Chicago's Negroes was but one reflection of a growing pattern of segregation and discrimination in early twentieth-century Chicago. As the Negro community grew and opportunities for interracial conflict increased, so a pattern of discrimination and segregation became ever more pervasive. And perhaps the most critical aspect of interracial conflict came as the result of Negro attempts to secure adequate housing.

The South Side black belt could expand in only two directions in the early twentieth century—south and east. To the north lay the business district, which was moving south; in fact, commercial and light industrial concerns were pushing Negroes out of the area between Twelfth and Twenty-second Streets. West of Wentworth Avenue was a district of low-income immigrant homes, interspersed with railroad yards and light industry; the lack of adequate housing made this area undesirable for Negro expansion. East of State Street, on the other hand, was a neighborhood suitable for Negro residential requirements. This area, bounded by Twelfth and Thirty-ninth Streets, State Street and Lake Michigan, had, in the 1880's and early 1890's, included the most fashionable streets in the city—Prairie and Calumet Avenues. But by 1900, the wealthy residents were moving to the North Side, leaving behind them comfortable, if aging, homes. South of Thirty-ninth Street was an even more desirable residential area—Kenwood and Hyde Park—and across Washington Park from the southern extremity of the black belt were the new and attractive communities of Woodlawn and Englewood. In these areas, between 1900 and 1915, the lines were drawn in the struggle for housing that would subsequently lead to full-scale racial war. If no major battle was fought before 1915, there were at least several preliminary skirmishes that set the pattern for future, and more serious, confrontations.[12]

Negro expansion did not always mean conflict, nor did it mean that a neighborhood would shortly become exclusively black. In 1910, not more than a dozen blocks on the South Side were entirely Negro,[13] and in many mixed areas Negroes and whites lived

[12] On the character of the neighborhoods surrounding the black belt, see Chicago Commission on Race Relations, pp. 108–11, 113–17, 205–9, 212–13.

[13] Otis D. Duncan and Beverly Duncan, *The Negro Population of Chicago* (Chicago: University of Chicago Press, 1957), p. 89.

together harmoniously.[14] But as Negroes became more numerous east of State and south of Fifty-first, friction increased and white hostility grew. When a Negro family moved into a previously all-white neighborhood, the neighbors frequently protested, tried to buy the property, and then, if unsuccessful, resorted to violence to drive out the interlopers. In many cases, the residents organized to urge real estate agents and property owners to sell and rent to whites only. The whites often succeeded in keeping Negroes out, at least temporarily. When their efforts failed, they gradually moved out, leaving the neighborhood predominantly, although rarely exclusively, Negro.

Such incidents occurred with only minor variations throughout the prewar period. In 1900, three Negro families brought about "a nervous prostration epidemic" on Vernon Avenue.[15] Five years later, an attempt to oust Negroes from a Forrestville Avenue building landed in court.[16] In 1911, a committee of Champlain Avenue residents dealt with a Negro family in the neighborhood by the "judicious use of a wagon load of bricks"; the Record-Herald described the affair as "something as nearly approaching the operations of the Ku Klux Klan as Chicago has seen in many years."[17] Englewood residents, two years later, did not have to go quite so far; the objectionable party, this time a white man with a Negro wife, agreed to sell his property to a hastily organized "neighborhood improvement association."[18] A Negro who moved into a home on Forrestville Avenue in 1915, on the other hand, termed an offer of this type "blackmail," but after several days of intimidation, he too submitted and sold his property.[19]

Perhaps the most serious incident, and the one which provides the most insight into the nature of the housing conflict, occurred in Hyde Park—Chicago's most persistent racial trouble spot—in 1909. A separate town until 1892, Hyde Park was still an area of pleasant, tree-shaded streets, large, comfortable homes, and a vigorous cultural life centered on the campus of the new but thriving University of Chicago. Negroes were no strangers to the

[14] See, for instance, Chicago Commission on Race Relations, pp. 108–13.

[15] Chicago Inter-Ocean, August 19, 1900.

[16] Chicago Record-Herald, March 9, 1905.

[17] Ibid., February 7, 1911.   [18] Defender, May 10, 1913.

[19] Chicago Tribune, May 3, May 4, May 5, 1915; Defender, May 8, 1915.

community: for many years a few families, mostly house servants and hotel employees who worked in the neighborhood, had clustered on Lake Avenue[20] near Fifty-fifth Street, on the eastern edge of Hyde Park. Now this community began to expand and Negroes occupied homes in nearby white blocks.[21]

White Hyde Parkers responded to the Negro "invasion" with a concerted drive to keep Negroes out of white areas. The Hyde Park Improvement Protective Club was organized in the autumn of 1908; headed by a prominent attorney, Francis Harper, it soon boasted 350 members, "including some of the wealthiest dwellers on the South Side."[22] In the summer of 1909, the Club issued a manifesto: Negro residents of Hyde Park must confine themselves to the "so-called Districts," real estate agents must refuse to sell property in white blocks to Negroes, and landlords must hire only white janitors. To implement this policy, the Club appointed a committee to purchase property owned by Negroes in white blocks and to offer bonuses to Negro renters who would surrender their leases. Moreover, the Club threatened to blacklist any real estate firm that defied its edict. "The districts which are now white," said Harper, "must remain white. There will be no compromise."[23]

Despite the efforts of the Negro residents of Hyde Park to counter the activities with indignation meetings and boycotts, the white campaign continued. The neighborhood newspaper supported the Improvement Club, and Harper maintained that he had "received hosts of letters commending the course of the organization."[24] When the Club was unable to persuade a Negro family to move voluntarily, the neighbors used more direct tactics: vandals broke into a Negro home on Greenwood Avenue one night and broke all the windows; the family left the next day.[25] In September, the Club announced a boycott of merchants who sold goods to Negroes living in white neighborhoods. It urged separate playgrounds and tennis courts for Negroes in Washington Park,

[20] Lake Avenue was the former name for the present Lake Park Avenue.

[21] *Record-Herald*, August 22, 1909; Chicago Commission on Race Relations, p. 114.

[22] *Record-Herald*, August 21, 1909.

[23] *Ibid.*; *Broad Ax* (Chicago), August 28, 1909.

[24] *Record-Herald*, August 22, August 23, 1909.

[25] *Ibid.*, August 22, 1909; *Broad Ax*, August 28, 1909.

and, in its annual report, advocated segregation of the public schools. "It is only a question of time," a Club spokesman predicted, "when there will be separate schools for Negroes throughout Illinois."[26] The group operated more quietly after 1909, but it had achieved its major goal. The little Negro community on Lake Avenue dwindled in size and the rest of Hyde Park remained white for forty years.[27]

The Hyde Park episode well illustrates the intensification of anti-Negro feeling in the early twentieth century. This feeling could even create strong sentiment among whites for a return to formalized segregation—separate schools and recreation facilities. Some white Chicagoans spoke of the necessity for a residential segregation ordinance.[28] The incident also provided an early example of techniques that were to become increasingly important as whites continually tried to stem the tide of Negro residential "invasion": the neighborhood improvement association, the community newspaper, the boycott, and in the last resort, violence. Furthermore, the episode was significant because it occurred in a middle- and upper-class community, and its victims were middle- and upper-class Negroes attempting to find comfortable homes among people of their own economic status.[29] The housing problem for Negroes was not restricted to the poor; even the affluent were blocked in their quest for a decent place to live.

The unwillingness of whites to tolerate Negroes as neighbors had far-reaching results. Because Negroes were so limited in their choice of housing, they were forced to pay higher rents in those buildings that were open to them. Real estate agents frequently converted buildings in marginal neighborhoods from white to Negro and demanded rents 10 to 15 per cent higher than they had previously received.[30] Sophonisba Breckinridge of Hull House es-

[26] *Broad Ax,* September 18, 1909; *Record-Herald,* October 10, 1909.

[27] Chicago Commission on Race Relations, p. 114.

[28] *Record-Herald,* April 5, 1911.

[29] The Negro class structure, however, does not always correspond with the white class structure. The Negro upper class, for instance, includes professional people, whose white counterparts are usually considered middle class. At the same time, postal clerks, Pullman porters, waiters and other occupational groups that would belong to the upper lower class among whites have traditionally formed the core of the Negro middle class.

[30] Louise De Koven Bowen, *The Colored Population of Chicago* (Chicago: Juvenile Protective Association, 1913), [n. p.].

timated that a Negro family "pays $12.50 for the same accommo-
dations the Jew in the Ghetto received for $9 and the immigrant
for $8."[31] One realty company inserted two advertisements for the
same apartment in a daily newspaper: one read, "seven rooms,
$25"; the other, "seven rooms for colored people, $37.50."[32] High
rents often forced Negro families to take in lodgers. A 1912 survey
of 1,775 South Side Negroes reported that 542, or 31 per cent,
lived as lodgers in the homes of others.[33]

Living conditions in much of the black belt closely resembled
conditions in the West Side ghetto or in the Stockyards district.
Although Negroes could find some decent homes on the fringes of
the Negro section, the core of the black belt was a festering slum.
Here was an area of one- and two-story frame houses (unlike the
older Eastern cities Chicago had, as yet, few large tenements),
usually dilapidated with boarded-up porches and rickety wooden
walks. Most of the buildings contained two flats and, although less
crowded than houses in the Jewish, Polish, and Bohemian slums,
they were usually in worse repair. The 1912 survey revealed that
in a four-block area in the black belt, only 26 per cent of the
dwellings were in good repair—as compared to 71 per cent in a
similar sampling in a Polish neighborhood, 57 per cent among
Bohemians, and 54 per cent in the ethnically mixed Stockyards
district.[34] "Colored tenants," the survey reported, "found it impossible to persuade their landlords either to make the necessary repairs or to release them from their contracts; . . . it was so hard to
find better places in which to live that they were forced to make
the repairs themselves, which they could rarely afford to do, or to
endure the conditions as best they might."[35]

White real estate agents, insensitive to class differences among
Negroes, made no attempt to uphold standards in middle-class
Negro neighborhoods as they did in comparable white districts.
They persistently rented flats in "respectable" Negro neighbor-
hoods to members of the "sporting element," thus forcing middle-

[31] Sophonisba P. Breckinridge, "The Color Line in the Housing Problem,"
Survey (New York), 40 (February 1, 1913): 575–76.

[32] Quoted in *Defender,* February 3, 1912.

[33] Alzada P. Comstock, "Chicago Housing Conditions; VI: The Problem
of the Negro," *American Journal of Sociology* (Chicago), 18 (September,
1912):244–45.

[34] *Ibid.*, pp. 246–55.   [35] *Ibid.*, p. 248.

class Negroes to move continually in search of decent areas to live and rear families. As a result, neighborhood stability was at best temporary. The streets east of State, which had become the mecca of the Negro middle class in the late 1890's, began to decline by 1905. A few years later the district was characterized by "men and women half clothed hanging out of a window," "rag-time piano playing . . . far into the night," and "shooting and cutting scrapes."[36]

Municipal policy regarding vice further complicated the situation. City authorities, holding that the suppression of prostitution was impossible, tried to confine it to certain well-defined areas where it could be closely watched. The police frequently moved the vice district so as to keep it away from commercial and white residential areas. Invariably they located it in or near the black belt, often in Negro residential neighborhoods. The chief of police declared that so long as prostitutes confined their activities to the district between Wentworth and Wabash, they would not be apprehended.[37] Neighborhood stability, then, was threatened not only by the influx of Negro "shadies," but by the presence of an officially sanctioned vice district catering primarily to whites.

Periodic attempts to clean up the red-light district received little support from Negro leaders who believed that such campaigns would merely drive the undesirables deeper into Negro residential neighborhoods. When legal prostitution was finally abolished in 1912, these fears were fully realized; vice in Chicago continued to be centered in the black belt.[38] Fannie Barrier Williams, a prominent Negro civic leader, summed up the plight of the middle- and upper-class Negro: "The huddling together of the good and the bad, compelling the decent element of the colored people to witness the brazen display of vice of all kinds in front of their homes and in the faces of their children, are trying conditions under which to remain socially clean and respectable."[39]

[36] *Defender*, May 30, 1914, p. 8.

[37] Vice Commission of Chicago, *The Social Evil in Chicago: A Study of Existing Conditions with Recommendations* (Chicago: Gunthorp-Warren, 1911), pp. 38–39.

[38] *Defender*, October 12, 1912; Drake and Cayton, *Black Metropolis*, p. 56.

[39] Fannie Barrier Williams, "Social Bonds in the Black Belt of Chicago," *Charities* (New York), 15 (October 7, 1905):40–41.

The pattern of Negro housing, then, was shaped by white hostility and indifference: limited in their choice of homes, Negroes were forced to pay higher rents for inferior dwellings and were frequently surrounded by prostitutes, panderers, and other undesirable elements. This, together with the poverty of the majority of Chicago Negroes, produced in the black belt the conditions of slum-living characteristic of American cities by the end of the nineteenth century.

The most striking feature of Negro housing, however, was not the existence of slum conditions, but the difficulty of escaping the slum. European immigrants needed only to prosper to be able to move to a more desirable neighborhood. Negroes, on the other hand, suffered from both economic deprivation and systematic racial discrimination. "The problem of the Chicago Negro," wrote Sophonisba Breckinridge,

> is quite different from the white man and even that of the immigrants. With the Negro the housing dilemma was found to be an acute problem, not only among the poor, as in the case of the Polish, Jewish, or Italian immigrants, but also among the well-to-do. . . . Thus, even in the North, where the city administration does not recognize a "Ghetto" or "pale", the real estate agents who register and commercialize what they suppose to be a universal race prejudice are able to enforce one in practice.[40]

The development of a physical ghetto in Chicago, then, was not the result chiefly of poverty; nor did Negroes cluster out of choice. The ghetto was primarily the product of white hostility. Attempts on the part of Negroes to seek housing in predominantly white sections of the city met with resistance from the residents and from real estate dealers. Some Negroes, in fact, who had formerly lived in white neighborhoods, were pushed back into the black districts. As the Chicago Negro population grew, Negroes had no alternative but to settle in well-delineated Negro areas. And with increasing pressure for Negro housing, property owners in the black belt found it profitable to force out white tenants and convert previously mixed blocks into all-Negro blocks. The geographical dimensions of Black Chicago in the early twentieth century underwent no dramatic shift similar, for instance, to Negro New

[40] Breckinridge, "The Color Line," pp. 575–76.

York, where the center of Negro life moved to previously all-white Harlem in less than a decade.[41] Negroes in Chicago were not establishing new communities. But to meet the needs of a growing population, in the face of mounting white resistance, Negro neighborhoods were becoming more exclusively Negro as they slowly expanded their boundaries.

[41] Gilbert Osofsky, *Harlem: The Making of a Ghetto* (New York: Harper & Row, 1965), pp. 105–23.

CHAPTER 2

JIM CROW'S TRIUMPH

As white hostility almost closed the housing market to Negroes and created a physical ghetto, it also limited the opportunities for Negroes to secure desirable jobs and gain access to public facilities. Chicago Negroes in the early twentieth century were confined to the domestic and personal service trades and were unable to gain even a foothold in industry and commerce. In 1900, almost 65 per cent of the Negro men and over 80 per cent of the Negro women worked as domestic and personal servants, while only 8.3 per cent of the men and 11.9 per cent of the women were engaged in manufacturing (and most of the women so employed worked in their own homes as dressmakers and seamstresses). In 1910 the basic pattern remained the same. Over 45 per cent of the employed Negro men worked in just four occupations—as porters, servants, waiters, and janitors—and over 63 per cent of the women were domestic servants or laundresses. In both 1900 and 1910, more Negroes were engaged in the professions than their numbers would warrant, but these were concentrated in professions that required relatively little formal training—music, the theater, and the clergy. Relatively few Negroes could be found in the legal, medical, and teaching professions. A large portion of those Negroes employed in manufacturing, trade, and transportation were unskilled laborers.[1]

[1] See Tables 6 and 7. Because of major changes in occupational classifications, these tables cannot always be directly compared. In 1900, for instance, all unclassified laborers were included as domestic and personal servants while porters were classified under trade and transportation. In 1910, on the other hand, laborers were divided among the various subdivisions with which they were associated—e.g., transportation laborers, manufacturing laborers, and so forth—and porters were listed under domestic and personal service. These changes may account partially for the increase, between 1900 and 1910, of the percentage of Negro men listed under manufacturing.

TABLE 6

Males and Females over Ten Engaged in Selected Occupations
Chicago, 1900

Selected Occupations	Total Number of Jobs	Number of Jobs Held by Negroes	Percentage of Total Jobs Held by Negroes	Percentage of Negro Labor Force in Particular Occupations
Males				
Manufacturing				
All categories............	204,867	1,079	0.5	8.3
Occupational total......	204,867	1,079	0.5	8.3
Trade and Transportation				
Teamsters..............	23,203	557	2.4	4.3
Retail dealers...........	23,240	145	0.6	1.1
Clerks..................	39,006	271	0.7	2.1
Porters and helpers[a]......	2,733	1,360	49.8	10.0
Salesmen...............	22,012	39	0.2	0.3
Occupational total......	196,163	2,965	1.5	22.8
Professional				
Lawyers................	4,241	46	1.1	0.4
Physicians..............	3,646	45	1.2	0.3
Clergymen..............	1,549	63	4.1	0.5
Teachers...............	1,591	20	1.3	0.2
Actors.................	1,599	150	9.4	1.2
Musicians..............	2,692	207	7.7	1.6
Occupational total......	30,301	602	1.9	4.6
Domestic and Personal				
Barbers and hairdressers..	4,628	362	7.8	2.8
Bartenders..............	4,414	116	2.7	0.9
Janitors................	4,023	686	17.1	5.3
Laborers, unspecified[b].....	73,597	2,251	3.1	17.3
Servants and waiters......	11,674	4,514	38.8	34.6
Occupational total......	117,853	8,381	7.0	64.4
Total employed........	555,515	13,065	2.3	100.0

Source: *U.S. Twelfth Census*, 1900, *Special Reports: Occupations*, pp. 516–23.

a Includes porters in stores.

b Includes elevator operators, longshoremen, and unskilled workers.

TABLE 6—*Continued*

Selected Occupations	Total Number of Jobs	Number of Jobs Held by Negroes	Percentage of Total Jobs Held by Negroes	Percentage of Negro Labor Force in Particular Occupations
		Females		
Manufacturing				
Dressmakers and seam- stresses..............	21,083	547	2.6	11.3
Occupational total......	46,719	585	1.3	11.9
Trade and Transportation				
All categories...........	36,371	143	0.4	2.9
Occupational total......	36,371	143	0.4	2.9
Professional				
Actresses...............	621	51	8.2	1.0
Musicians..............	2,035	40	2.4	1.0
Teachers...............	7,200	38	0.5	0.8
Occupational total......	12,340	194	1.6	3.9
Domestic and Personal				
Barbers and hairdressers...	475	76	16.0	1.6
Boardinghouse keepers....	2,151	104	4.8	2.1
Housekeepers...........	2,963	152	5.1	3.1
Laundresses.............	6,636	918	13.8	18.7
Servants and waitresses...	35,340	2,541	7.2	51.6
Occupational total......	54,045	3,998	7.4	81.2
Total employed........	149,867	4,921	3.3	100.0

Negroes entered occupations that were not desirable enough to be contested by whites. When white workers sought jobs in trades dominated by Negroes, they were usually able to drive the Negroes out. In the nineteenth century, for instance, many Negroes had worked as barbers and coachmen, but by the early twentieth century, whites had replaced most of them in these capacities.[2] Hence Negroes "were constantly driven to lower kinds of occupa-

[2] Richard R. Wright, Jr., "The Industrial Condition of Negroes in Chicago," unpublished B.D. thesis, University of Chicago Divinity School, 1901, p. 24; *Chicago Tribune,* September 25, 1900.

TABLE 7

MALES AND FEMALES OVER TEN ENGAGED IN SELECTED OCCUPATIONS CHICAGO, 1910

Selected Occupations	Total Number of Jobs	Number of Jobs Held by Negroes	Percentage of Total Jobs Held by Negroes	Percentage of Negro Labor Force in Particular Occupations
		Males		
Manufacturing				
41 specified trades[a]........	201,974	1,467	0.7	7.9
Semi-skilled, unspecified....	39,833	148	0.3	0.8
Laborers, unspecified.......	55,091	1,458	2.2	7.9
Transportation				
Chauffeurs...............	2,215	220	9.9	1.2
Teamsters...............	20,201	566	2.8	3.1
Laborers[b].................	26,780	603	2.2	3.3
Longshoremen............	598	149	24.9	0.8
Mail carriers.............	2,248	99	4.4	0.5
Engineers, firemen, motor- men, switchmen.........	14,726	20	0.1	0.1
Trade				
Store clerks[c].............	15,779	58	0.4	0.3
Deliverymen.............	11,813	266	2.3	1.4
Laborers[d].................	8,934	586	6.6	3.2
Laborers, stockyards.......	3,041	179	5.9	1.0
Retail dealers............	34,493	218	0.6	1.2
Salesmen in stores[c]........	29,820	52	0.2	0.3
Professional				
Lawyers.................	3,866	44	1.1	0.2
Physicians...............	4,032	109	2.7	0.6
Clergymen...............	1,693	76	4.5	0.4
Teachers................	1,867	11	0.6	0.1
Actors..................	1,375	78	5.7	0.4
Musicians...............	3,442	216	6.3	1.2
Public Service[e]				
All categories............	15,173	224	1.5	1.2
Domestic and Personal Service				
Barbers and hairdressers...	5,681	319	5.6	1.7
Bartenders..............	5,489	137	2.5	0.7
Elevator operators........	2,373	306	12.9	1.7
Janitors.................	6,792	1,358	20.0	7.4
Domestic laborers........	1,264	136	10.8	0.7
Laundry operatives.......	1,754	103	5.9	0.6
Porters[f].................	5,608	3,828	68.3	20.8
Servants................	6,787	1,488	21.6	8.1
Waiters.................	5,334	1,648	30.9	8.9

SOURCE: *U.S. Thirteenth Census,* 1910, vol. 4, *Population: Occupation Statistics,* pp. 544–47.

NOTE: The 1910 census report does not provide subtotals for Negro workers. The table accounts for 92.6 per cent of Negro male employees and 92.4 per cent of Negro female employees.

[a] Includes officials, foremen, apprentices.

[b] Includes road building, steam and street railway laborers.

[c] These classifications undoubtedly overlap.

[d] Includes laborers in coal and lumber yards, stores; includes porters in stores.

[e] Policemen, firemen, guards, watchmen, officials, public service laborers.

[f] Not including porters in stores.

TABLE 7—*Continued*

Selected Occupations	Total Number of Jobs	Number of Jobs Held by Negroes	Percentage of Total Jobs Held by Negroes	Percentage of Negro Labor Force in Particular Occupations
Males				
Clerical				
Bookkeepers, cashiers, accountants, stenographers.	18,561	53	0.3	0.3
Office clerks..............	43,978	572	1.3	3.1
Messengers..............	8,425	131	1.6	0.7
Total employed........	759,778	....	2.4	100.0
Females				
Manufacturing				
Dressmakers and seamstresses[g].............	15,099	867	5.7	9.9
Milliners................	5,461	62	1.1	0.7
Trade				
Store clerks[o].............	10,925	43	0.4	0.5
Saleswomen[o].............	11,632	21	0.2	0.2
Professional				
Actresses................	1,147	54	4.7	0.6
Musicians................	3,241	136	4.2	1.5
Teachers.................	8,573	53	0.6	0.6
Nurses...................	2,488	42	1.7	0.5
Domestic and Personal Service				
Barbers and hairdressers...	1,789	316	17.7	3.6
Boardinghouse keepers.....	5,000	267	5.3	3.0
Charwomen...............	1,152	98	8.5	1.1
Housekeepers.............	3,594	191	5.3	2.2
Laundresses[h].............	7,122	2,115	29.7	23.8
Laundry operatives........	4,466	184	4.1	2.1
Servants.................	34,437	3,512	10.2	39.5
Waitresses................	3,319	141	4.2	1.6
Clerical				
Bookkeepers, cashiers, accountants, stenographers.	31,646	110	0.3	1.2
Office clerks..............	11,072	45	0.4	0.5
Total employed........	236,811	....	3.7	100.0

[g] Not in factories.

[h] Not in laundries.

tions which are gradually being discarded by the white man."[3]
These jobs were generally low-paying, carried the stigma of servility, and offered few opportunities for advancement. Porters in hotels, stores, and railroads, and janitors in apartment buildings and
business houses had no chance to move up to better positions because these concerns hired Negroes in no other capacities. Among
the service trade employees, only waiters could look forward to
promotions; the job of headwaiter, which paid as much as one
hundred dollars a month, was perhaps the most lucrative to which
Negroes could aspire.[4] Negro women were particularly limited in
their search for desirable positions. Clerical work was practically
closed to them and only a few could qualify as school teachers.
Negro domestics often received less than white women for the
same work, and they could rarely rise to the position of head serv-
ant in large households—a place traditionally held by a Swedish
woman.[5]

Several factors combined to keep Negroes out of industry and
trade—especially the skilled and semiskilled jobs. First, most employers were simply disposed against hiring Negroes so long as an
adequate supply of white labor was available—and with open immigration from Europe there was seldom a labor shortage. These
employers feared that their white employees would object to
working with Negroes, and many believed that Negro workers
were less efficient.[6] Secondly, many Negroes with skills had acquired them in the South and were often unable to meet Northern
standards. Moreover, they were seldom able to acquire skills in
the North: apprentice programs were usually open to whites only,
and Negroes had little desire to learn a trade so long as its job
prospects remained uncertain.[7] Finally, the refusal of most trade
unions to admit black workers on an equal basis kept Negroes out

[3] Louise De Koven Bowen, *The Colored Population of Chicago* (Chicago:
Juvenile Protective Association, 1913) [n. p.].

[4] Wright, "The Industrial Condition of Negroes in Chicago," pp. 21–23.

[5] "Employment of Colored Women in Chicago," *Crisis* (New York), 1
(January, 1911):24–25; Wright, "The Industrial Condition of Negroes in
Chicago," p. 23.

[6] See the results of surveys by Wright, "The Industrial Condition of Negroes in Chicago," pp. 27–31, and Bowen, *The Colored Population of Chicago.*

[7] *Chicago Defender,* January 20, 1910; Bowen, *The Colored Population
of Chicago.*

of many trades. Some unions completely excluded Negroes through clauses in their constitutions; others admitted Negroes, but then either segregated them in separate, subordinate locals, excluded them from specific projects, or simply made no effort to find jobs for them.[8]

Civil service jobs were theoretically open to all without discrimination. State law required competitive examinations and appointment on the basis of merit for a wide range of municipal jobs.[9] Yet, in 1910, only 224 or 1.5 per cent of the public service jobs were held by Negroes; by 1913, Negroes held 1.9 per cent of these positions, but this figure was still lower than the proportion of Negroes in the total work force.[10] The inability of many Negroes, especially recent migrants from the South, to compete successfully on the examinations partially explains this lag. But, despite the law, personal prejudice also played a part. Appointing officers found numerous devices to circumvent legal regulations: they held examinations infrequently, filled vacancies with temporary appointments that were repeatedly renewed, and showed favoritism in the examining process. As one Negro employee explained, "Civil Service is run by friendship . . . and under that sort of arrangement, Negroes won't come out on top."[11] One Negro, certified for a civil service job in 1906, told how a head clerk exerted pressure and coercion to persuade him that the job would not satisfy him.[12] Once appointed, Negroes often faced segregated working conditions and discrimination in promotion. This was most flagrant in the fire department, which openly maintained Jim Crow units until the 1930's.[13] In other departments, Negroes rarely advanced beyond menial positions. An exception was the police department where, at the onset of World War I, there were about fifty Negro officers. But most Negro policemen were assigned only

[8] Erie W. Hardy, "Relation of the Negro to Trade Unionism," unpublished master's thesis, University of Chicago, 1911, *passim;* Oscar D. Hutton, "The Negro Worker and the Labor Unions in Chicago," unpublished master's thesis, University of Chicago, 1939, pp. 3–10.

[9] Harold Gosnell, *Negro Politicians: The Rise of Negro Politics in Chicago* (Chicago: University of Chicago Press, 1935), p. 219.

[10] Bowen, *The Colored Population of Chicago;* and see Table 7.

[11] Gosnell, *Negro Politicians,* p. 220. [12] *Ibid.,* pp. 226–27.

[13] *Defender,* January 26, 1929, October 11, 1930; Gosnell, *Negro Politicians,* pp. 229–30.

to Negro neighborhoods and few could aspire to become sergeants, lieutenants, or detectives.[14]

In the postal service, where similar civil service regulations applied, Negroes fared better. By 1910, over five hundred Negroes worked in the Chicago Post Office.[15] Negroes rarely complained of discrimination in securing postal jobs. This was primarily the result of Congressman Martin Madden's position on the House of Representatives Post Office Committee. Even during the Wilson administration, when the federal government sought to reduce the number of Negroes in the postal service, Madden, who represented a predominantly Negro district on Chicago's South Side, protected his Negro constituents.[16] Promotions, however, which depended only upon the discretion of the postmaster, came slowly; only two Negroes held supervisory positions before the War.[17] Nevertheless, the postal service provided Negroes with almost their only opportunity for clerical work and carried considerable prestige among Chicago Negroes. Several post office clerks became community leaders, and an organization of Negro postal employees, the Phalanx Forum, was a major political and social force in prewar Black Chicago.[18]

The only opportunity Negroes had to enter basic trades in early twentieth-century Chicago was as strikebreakers. The use of Negro scab labor heightened anti-Negro feeling in the city and left a legacy of bitterness and distrust between white and black workers. In the 1904 stockyards strike and the 1905 teamsters strike, the importation of non-union Negro labor set off the most serious racial conflicts of the prewar period.

The use of scabs to break strikes was nothing new in the meatpacking industry, but the 1904 strike was the first in which Negroes played a major role in crushing the union. From the packers' point of view, Negroes were ideal strikebreakers. They generally had no scruples about working as scabs: those brought in from

[14] Gosnell, *Negro Politicians*, pp. 247–50, 253, 258, 263.

[15] *Ibid.*, p. 302. The census did not include postal workers under public service employees, but classified them according to the nature of their work.

[16] Henry W. McGee, "The Negro in the Chicago Post Office," unpublished master's thesis, University of Chicago, 1961, pp. 9–10; Gosnell, *Negro Politicians*, p. 307.

[17] Gosnell, *Negro Politicians*, p. 314.

[18] McGee, "The Negro in the Chicago Post Office," pp. 16–17, 70–71.

the South were almost totally ignorant of the principles of trade unionism, while those who had had experience with unions had generally found them discriminatory. Moreover, the importation of Negroes in large numbers created panic and fear within union ranks.[19]

Throughout the summer of 1904, as the strike wore on, the strikers focused their hostility upon the most visible symbol of their frustration—the Negro scabs. During the first weeks, as the packers announced the gradual resumption of operations with non-union men, the strikers began attacking the scabs as they entered the plants. Almost all of the victims were Negroes.[20] The most serious incident occurred when a mob, estimated at between two and five thousand, stoned two hundred Negroes who, with police protection, were attempting to leave the Hammond Company packing plant.[21] The packers then set up makeshift housing for the workers within the plants, and trainloads of Negro laborers poured in from the South. Relatively few local Negroes were employed; the companies instead sent agents south to lure workers to Chicago with the prospect of $2.25-a-day wages plus room and board. The strikers and their sympathizers characterized the Southern workers as "big, ignorant, vicious Negroes, picked up from the criminal elements of the black belts of the country."[22] The antipathy toward the importation of Southern Negroes helped create support for the union cause. The Ashland Avenue Business Men's Association, for instance, protested to the mayor about the strikebreakers: "These men and women," the group stated, "are a menace to the city of Chicago; for to any responsible man it is plain that such people cannot permanently be retained by the trust and hence must be poured out upon the city at the beginning of the winter season; they are a menace as future paupers."[23]

Nevertheless, the strikebreakers proved to be an effective weap-

[19] Alma Herbst, *The Negro in the Slaughtering and Meat Packing Industry in Chicago* (New York: Houghton, Mifflin & Company, 1932), pp. 19–20, 24–25.

[20] *Tribune,* July 11, July 12, July 15, July 17, July 18, July 24, 1904.

[21] *Ibid.,* July 22, 1904; *Chicago Record-Herald,* July 22, 1904.

[22] "Harry Rosenberg on Packing Industry and Stockyards," unpublished memorandum in Mary McDowell papers (Chicago Historical Society, Chicago, Illinois), cited hereafter as McDowell Papers.

[23] *Ibid.*

on. The industry was sufficiently mechanized to allow the packers to increase their operations to nearly full capacity while using unskilled scab labor. A few Negroes, to be sure, deserted the packers. A union man, for example, who boarded a labor train as it entered the city, persuaded a hundred Negroes from Cincinnati to leave their jobs before they had even begun work.[24] And two days later, three hundred Negroes left the Armour and Morris plants, protesting they could not cash their paychecks because of the tense conditions.[25] But most of the strikebreakers remained loyal and provided the packers with the tool that they needed to defeat the union.[26]

Negroes made few permanent gains as a result of the strike. While the Poles, who had first entered the stockyards as strikebreakers in 1886, remained to form an important segment of the labor force, most of the Negro workers were discharged once the strike was settled.[27] Although an estimated two thousand Negroes were hired by the packers during the strike, by 1910 only 365 of the 16,367 workers classified by the census as stockyards and packinghouse operatives were Negroes.[28] The strike did, however, induce the union to take greater cognizance of Negro workers. The Amalgamated Meat Cutters and Butcher Workmen admitted those Negroes who remained in the yards, and by the time the packers began to employ large numbers of black workers, it had become one of the few large unions to welcome Negroes as members.[29] But the major legacy of the strike was an intensified anti-Negro

[24] *Tribune*, July 29, 1904. Arna Bontemps and Jack Conroy describe a similar incident during a strike at the Latrobe Steel and Coupler Company in 1901. Then, company efforts to use Negro strikebreakers were completely thwarted by a group of union men who persuaded the Negroes to return to Birmingham. *They Seek a City* (Garden City, N.Y.: Doubleday, Doran & Company, 1945), pp. 110–12.

[25] *Tribune*, July 31, 1904.

[26] *Ibid.*, August 17, August 26, 1904; Herbst, *The Negro in the Slaughtering and Meat Packing Industry in Chicago*, p. 23; "Harry Rosenberg on Packing Industry and Stockyards," in McDowell Papers.

[27] Herbst, *The Negro in the Slaughtering and Meat Packing Industry in Chicago*, pp. xviii–xix, 24–25.

[28] *Appeal* (St. Paul), August 20, 1904; and see Table 9.

[29] Chicago Commission on Race Relations, *The Negro in Chicago: A Study of Race Relations and a Race Riot* (Chicago: University of Chicago Press, 1922), pp. 412–13.

sentiment on the part of white Chicagoans. Ben Tillman, speaking in Chicago shortly after the end of the strike, reminded a stockyards district audience of something they would not soon forget. "It was the niggers," he said, "that whipped you in line. They were the club with which your brains were beaten out."[30]

Eight months after the stockyards union surrendered, Chicago found itself in the grips of the most violent labor disturbance since the Pullman strike of 1894. In April, 1905, the Teamsters Union called a sympathy strike at Montgomery Ward's—in support of a group of striking garment workers. The owners of the major downtown department stores charged the union with breach of contract, announced that they would not renew their union contracts when they expired, and vowed a war of extermination against the teamsters. By the end of the month, the strike had spread to every leading employer in Chicago. Business came to a virtual standstill and pitched battles, claiming as many as a hundred casualties in a single day, raged throughout the city.[31]

On the first of May, the merchants brought in a trainload of Negro teamsters under the leadership of a professional strikebreaker. As in the case of the stockyards strike, the importation of Negroes created widespread alarm. The appearance of a Negro driver on the streets of Chicago signaled violent attacks and rioting.[32] The city council asked the corporation counsel for an opinion "as to whether the importation of hundreds of Negro laborers is not a menace to the community and should not be restricted."[33] Local Negroes, too, objected to the importation of strikebreakers. The *Broad Ax*, a Negro weekly, said that the employers

> are not justified in bringing hundreds and hundreds of colored men here from the remote parts of the South—many of them representing the lowest and toughest element of the race . . . to temporarily serve as strikebreakers for such Negrohating concerns as Marshall Field and Company, Mandel Brothers and Montgomery Ward and Company, who have no use for Negroes in general except to use them as brutish clubs to beat their white help over the head. . . . The presence of

[30] *Broad Ax* (Chicago), October 15, 1904.

[31] *Tribune,* April 7–May 3, 1905.

[32] For typical incidents, see *Ibid.*, May 1–May 5, 1905.

[33] *Ibid.*, May 2, 1905.

this class of Negro in Chicago at the present time makes it much more difficult for the respectable colored people in this community to get along.[34]

The employers' association finally agreed to stop bringing in Negro teamsters from outside the city, but refused to discharge strikebreakers and continued to hire local Negroes.[35]

Unlike the stockyards strike, when anti-Negro violence was generally confined to attacks on actual strikebreakers, the teamsters strike brought Chicago to the brink of a race riot. Hostility toward Negro scabs was easily translated into general antipathy toward Negroes. Several Negro leaders, alarmed by the rising tide of anti-Negro feeling, protested police brutality toward Negroes and condemned the daily newspapers for "the hostile attitude they have assumed against all Afro-Americans" during the strike.[36] Nowhere in the city was hostility toward Negroes more intense than in the working-class neighborhood just west of the black belt. Every day, the residents—many of them striking teamsters—saw Negroes driving the wagons of the nearby Peabody Coal Company. Then, on May 16, a Negro shot and killed an eight-year-old boy who had shouted insults at him as he passed through the streets. During the following week, hysteria gripped the neighborhood. Negroes were dragged from streetcars and beaten, and even heavy police guards, posted throughout the area, could not protect Negroes from white attacks. The climax came on May 21 when a white bartender shot a Negro to death in a saloon brawl. Negroes retaliated and in the course of the day, two people were killed and twelve were injured. It was the bloodiest racial conflict in the city before the riot of 1919.[37]

The merchants, like the packers, used Negro workers to serve their purposes and then discharged them. The census reported fewer Negro teamsters in 1910 than in 1900.[38] Not until Chicago's major employers found themselves confronted with a real labor shortage were Negroes able to gain a foothold in the basic industries and trades.

The Negro's status in the job market, then, differed widely from

[34] *Broad Ax*, May 6, 1905.

[35] *Tribune*, May 6, 1905.   [36] *Broad Ax*, May 13, 1905.

[37] *Tribune*, May 17–May 22, 1905; *Broad Ax*, May 20, May 27, 1905.

[38] See Tables 6 and 7.

that of most white ethnic minorities. Excluded from the major industries where the possibility of decent wages and advancement was greatest, Negroes had little chance to escape poverty. European immigrants secured steady jobs in the stockyards or steel mills and could advance to skilled or supervisory capacities; their sons entered clerical and managerial occupations. But as porters and servants and janitors who entered industry only to serve as the unwitting tools of beleaguered employers, Negroes had few such opportunities.

The law prohibited racial discrimination in public accommodations, municipal services, and schools in Chicago and prescribed punishments for violators. The Illinois Civil Rights Law, enacted in 1885, provided "that all persons . . . shall be entitled to the full and equal enjoyment of the accommodations, advantages, facilities and privileges of inns, restaurants, eating houses, barber shops, theatres, and public conveyances on land and water . . . and all other public accommodations."[39] When the state supreme court held in 1896 that the last clause was too vague to be enforced,[40] the legislature promptly amended the law to cover explicitly hotels, soda fountains, saloons, bathrooms, skating rinks, concerts, cafés, bicycle rinks, elevators, ice cream parlors, railroads, omnibuses, stages, streetcars, and boats.[41] Violation of the law could result in forfeiture of from $25 to $500 to be paid to the aggrieved party, plus a fine of up to $500 and imprisonment of up to one year.[42]

Despite the law and the city's official color blindness in providing municipal services, numerous incidents testified to a persistent, although not rigid, pattern of discrimination in these areas. A Negro could never be certain of what awaited him when he entered a store, restaurant, saloon, or hotel outside of the black belt. Most

[39] Illinois, *Laws* (1885), p. 64; discussed in *Smith-Hurd Illinois Annotated Statutes* (Chicago: Burdette-Smith, 1935), chap. 38, "Criminal Code," no. 125, p. 163.

[40] *Cecil* v. *Green*, 60 Ill. App. 61, 161 Ill. 265, 43 Northeast 1105 (1896); Gilbert T. Stephenson, *Race Distinctions in American Law* (New York: D. Appleton & Company, 1910), pp. 133–34.

[41] Illinois, *Laws* (1897), p. 137; *Smith-Hurd Illinois Annotated Statutes*, chap. 38, no. 125, p. 164.

[42] *Smith-Hurd Illinois Annotated Statutes*, chap. 3, no. 125, p. 164.

proprietors would accommodate a Negro if they thought refusal would create a major controversy; Booker T. Washington, for instance, stayed regularly at the plush Palmer House when he visited Chicago.[43] But less prominent Negroes were often harassed or simply refused service in downtown establishments. The La Salle Hotel turned away a luncheon meeting of one thousand clubwomen because their number included several Negro members.[44] Many theaters seated Negroes only in the balcony, and bartenders frequently refused to serve Negro patrons.[45] In 1913, a theater opened on the very edge of the black belt and announced that Negroes would not be seated on the main floor.[46] Leading department stores were also wont to discriminate, but their policy was erratic. Negroes frequently complained of discourteous treatment at Marshall Field's, but in one incident when a prominent Negro woman spoke to the manager about such treatment, the salesperson involved was immediately discharged.[47]

Although the state civil rights law seemed explicitly to forbid discriminatory practices, it was difficult to obtain a conviction under it. In 1905, a jury refused to award damages to a Negro politician who was denied service at a bar, and a 1910 jury decided in favor of a theater that had turned down a Negro who was trying to buy tickets for the main floor.[48] Even when Negroes won such suits, the punishment was often minimal: one bartender found guilty of violating the civil rights law was fined $5 and costs.[49]

Businessmen not covered by the civil rights law could discriminate more openly. An osteopath on the edge of the black belt displayed a sign reading "white patients only," and a cemetery ran a display advertisement announcing that their grounds "are exclusively for the white race."[50] Another form of discrimination—anal-

[43] Emmett J. Scott to S. Laing Williams, March 29, 1904, and J. A. Hertel to Booker T. Washington, January 19, 1905, in Booker T. Washington Papers (Library of Congress, Washington, D.C.).

[44] *Defender,* April 5, 1913; *Crisis,* 6 (May 11, 1913): 15.

[45] For typical incidents, see *Record-Herald,* July 14, 1905, June 10, 1910, February 8, February 10, 1911; *Broad Ax,* May 28, 1910; *Defender,* June 11, 1910.

[46] *Defender,* September 16, 1913.   [47] *Ibid.,* June 20, 1914.

[48] *Record-Herald,* July 14, 1905; *Broad Ax,* May 28, 1910.

[49] *Record-Herald,* February 11, 1911.

[50] *Defender,* March 4, 1910.

ogous to that found in the housing field—was the practice of charging Negroes higher prices. This was widespread in the insurance business. While some companies refused to sell life insurance policies to Negroes, others offered policies to Negroes at higher premiums, arguing that this was necessary because of their higher death rate.[51] Price differentials were so common in the cemetery business that, in 1911, Edward Green, a Negro member of the state legislature, secured passage of an amendment to the civil rights law forbidding discriminatory rates in the sale of cemetery plots.[52]

Official city agencies never, of course, openly admitted discriminatory practices. There were, however, persistent charges that a "color line" was drawn in the Cook County Jail. The *Broad Ax* maintained that "white and black prisoners are kept apart as much as possible," and the *Defender* insisted that Negro inmates were allowed to exercise in the bullpen only when whites were not there and that meal service was segregated.[53] Publicly supported hospitals were also charged with discrimination. The Cook County Hospital, while admitting Negro patients, refused to hire Negro nurses, arguing that "white nurses refuse to work with colored."[54] The director of the Hospital for Contagious Diseases, a branch of the county hospital, maintained privately that white patients would walk out if placed in the same room with Negroes and that the idea of having Negro nurses for white patients was "absolutely impossible."[55] "You see," said Celia Parker Woolley, a prominent white progressive, "how far it is from being true that segregation could never be practiced in institutions supported by public money."[56]

[51] *Broad Ax*, February 17, 1912. This was a major factor in the rise of Negro insurance companies. See below, chaps. 6 and 9.

[52] *Ibid.*, April 29, 1911; *Smith-Hurd Illinois Annotated Statutes*, chap. 38, no. 125, p. 164.

[53] *Broad Ax*, April 23, October 18, 1902; *Defender*, July 6, 1912.

[54] Celia Parker Woolley to Charlotte Johnson, November 27, 1912, copy in Julius Rosenwald Papers (University of Chicago Library), cited hereafter as Rosenwald Papers.

[55] William C. Graves to Julius Rosenwald, December 13, 1912, Rosenwald Papers.

[56] Celia Parker Woolley to Julius Rosenwald, November 27, 1912, Rosenwald Papers.

The police and the courts were also charged with hostility toward Negroes. The strike disturbances of 1904 and 1905 gave rise to numerous charges of discrimination. A decade later, Louise De Koven Bowen, a white reform leader, stated that Negroes were frequently arrested "on charges too flimsy to hold a white man" and were often "convicted on inadequate evidence." She cited the case of one George W., a nineteen-year-old Negro arrested for rape in 1912. The police, she said, beat and kicked George until he confessed, and his lawyer advised him to plead guilty even when he insisted on his innocence. Although the judge referred to the evidence as flimsy in his instructions to the jury, the youth was found guilty and sentenced to fourteen years in prison. One witness, asked why he had not been more explicit in his testimony in the defendant's behalf, reportedly answered, "Oh well, he's only a nigger anyway."[57] The police were also criticized for their attitude toward prostitutes and saloons. Not only was the segregated vice district always located in the black belt, but, according to the *Tribune*, the police raided so-called "black and tan resorts" because they were frequented by an interracial clientele. The police chief allegedly ordered that "colored saloonkeepers must keep white men out of their saloons and that white saloonkeepers are to prevent colored men from entering their places of business."[58]

The public school system had been legally integrated since 1874, but here, too, there were frequent instances of discrimination and interracial friction after 1890. Much of it came from white students and their parents rather than from school officials. Changes in school boundary lines or pupil transfers, resulting in newly integrated schools, often led to white protests. In 1905, a group of white children rioted when they were transferred to a predominantly Negro school, and in 1908, over one hundred and fifty students stayed home when they were transferred to a school attended by Negroes. A year later, two Negro children, enrolling in a previously all-white school, were insulted and beaten by their classmates.[59] Wendell Phillips High School, the city's first predom-

[57] Bowen, *The Colored Population of Chicago.*

[58] *Tribune,* November 11, 1905; *Broad Ax,* September 30, 1905.

[59] *Record-Herald,* September 26, 1908, November 11, 1909; report on Negro education in "The Negro in Illinois," a file of reports and interviews compiled by the Illinois Writers Project of the Works Progress Administration (George Cleveland Hall Branch of the Chicago Public Library), cited hereafter as Illinois Writers Project Files.

inantly Negro high school, was the scene of frequent racial conflicts. In 1912, for instance, several white students attacked a Negro boy who had allegedly insulted a white girl: the resulting
melee was described by the *Tribune* as a "miniature race war."[60]
School officials frowned upon these manifestations of white hostility. After the 1908 "school strike," the president of the board of
education commented, "a clean colored boy is, in my opinion, far
better than a dirty white boy. . . . The parents of some of the
colored children who attend the Keith School are far above parents of some of the white children there."[61] But the board was
forced to acknowledge that the "color line is a source of continual
strife."[62]

White groups asked periodically for formal segregation of the
Chicago school system. Between 1900 and 1915, such proposals
were discussed openly in the press and at school board meetings,
causing sufficient alarm to induce Negro leaders to lodge formal
protests against any possible public school segregation. In 1906,
reports that whites would attempt to insert a clause in the new
city charter, permitting segregated schools, aroused Negro leaders
to conduct a successful campaign to place a Negro on the charter
commission.[63] Four years later, the Southern Society of Chicago
urged Negroes to join them in supporting separate schools, emphasizing the greater opportunity this would provide for Negro
teachers.[64] The Hyde Park Improvement Protective Club, which
had suggested the desirability of separate schools during the 1909
housing quarrel, continued to campaign for this policy. In 1912, it
petitioned the mayor in favor of segregation and held a meeting
to discuss the proposal.[65] But few responsible Chicagoans seriously entertained these suggestions. School superintendent Ella
Flagg Young, a friend of John Dewey and Jane Addams and a
prominent member of Chicago's progressive intellectual circle,
persistently quashed any attempt at discrimination. When, for instance, Wendell Phillips High School set up separate social activities for white and Negro students in 1915, Mrs. Young declared that

[60] *Tribune,* November 1, 1912.

[61] *Record-Herald,* September 26, 1908.

[62] *Ibid.,* October 14, 1908.

[63] *Appeal,* June 30, 1906; and see also October 24, 1903.

[64] *Defender,* November 12, 1910.

[65] *Ibid.,* February 24, June 22, 1912.

if the school continued this policy, all social affairs would be canceled.[66]

Private educational and social welfare institutions developed widely varying policies, but few were completely free of discrimination. The University of Chicago and Northwestern University admitted Negroes without apparent discrimination, but both institutions experienced minor disturbances when Negro students entered the dormitories.[67] Catholic parochial schools, on the other hand, were openly segregated: all Negro students attended St. Monica's School.[68] Most private welfare institutions were closed to Negroes. Only after vigorous protest from Negro leaders did the Juvenile Protective Association admit Negroes to its Hyde Park center.[69] When a small Negro orphanage closed its doors in 1913, the officials of the white Park Ridge School helped transfer them to another Negro home, but strongly resisted the suggestion that they be admitted to Park Ridge. "These girls," wrote a Park Ridge official privately, "when put with or even *near* the same class of white girls . . . exercise a very deleterious influence on each other."[70]

Although Negroes had participated in the activities of the Young Men's Christian Association in the late nineteenth century, they met mounting discrimination after 1900. By 1910, they found themselves completely shut out of the white YMCA, and as a result, the all-Negro Wabash Avenue YMCA was opened in 1913.[71] Ida Wells-Barnett, a prominent Negro civic leader, described the plight of Negroes, barred from white social agencies:

> While every other class is welcome in the Y.M.C.A. dormitories, Y.W.C.A. homes, the Salvation Army and the Mills

[66] *Ibid.*, January 23, April 17, 1915; *Crisis,* 9 (March, 1915): 220. On Mrs. Young, see J. T. McManis, *Ella Flagg Young and a Half-Century of the Chicago Public Schools* (Chicago: A. C. McClurg, 1916), and Charles H. Judd, "Ella Flagg Young," *Dictionary of American Biography* (New York: Charles Scribner's Sons, 1936), 20:126–27.

[67] *Tribune,* September 6, November 5, 1902; report on Negro education in Illinois Writers Project Files.

[68] *Defender,* March 18, April 5, 1913.   [69] *Ibid.,* June 25, 1910.

[70] Esther W. S. Brophy to Julius Rosenwald, December 7, 1913, Rosenwald Papers; *Broad Ax,* December 20, 1913.

[71] See chap. 5.

An oil painting (by Aaron E. Darling, about 1865) of John Jones, the undisputed leader of Chicago's Negro community until his death in 1879.

Robert S. Abbott, who built the *Chicago Defender* into the most important Negro newspaper in the country.

3

4

Ferdinand and Ida Barnett, prominent members of the militant wing of Chicago's Negro leaders.

Olivet Baptist church in 1904-5, housing the largest Negro congregation in Chicago.

6

Robert Mott's theater cafe about 1920. The Pekin featured a lively fare of ragtime, cakewalks, and "coon" songs.

7

A packinghouse official leads a group of Negro women strikebreakers into a plant during the 1904 strike.

Negro strikebreakers at Swift & Company during the 1904 stockyards strike.

A rear view, taken about 1920, of tenements on Federal Street, in the heart of the Negro slum.

Homes owned by middle-class Negroes on South Park Boulevard, about 1920.

A Negro family, just arrived in Chicago from the South, during the World War I migration.

Alderman Oscar DePriest posts bond after being charged with bribery in 1917.

13

14

During the 1919 race riots, a white mob chases a Negro into his home—and then stones him to death with bricks. He is dead by the time the police arrive.

16

A policeman escorts a Negro couple to safety during the 1919 race riots.

17

The state militia stands guard in the black belt, after the 1919 riots.

hotels, not one of these will give a negro a bed to sleep in or permit him to use their reading rooms and gymnasiums. Even the Women's Model Lodging House announces that it will give all women accommodations who need a place to sleep except drunkards, immoral women and negro women. What, then, is the negro to do? Those of us who realize the condition of this great, idle, proscribed class and view with pain and shame this increasing criminal record have absolutely no money to use in helping to change these conditions.[72]

Although race relations before World War I were peaceful by 1919 standards, an ominous, if muted, current of racial violence was manifest. The stockyards and teamsters strikes and the disputes over housing occasioned the most serious outbreaks, but they were not the only ones. Negro criminals—or suspected criminals—were frequently threatened by lynch mobs. In 1900, a crowd of angry whites stoned a Clark Street building in an attempt to capture a Negro who had been arrested for attacking a seven-year-old white girl.[73] On another occasion, five thousand whites left a sandlot baseball game to chase six Negroes who were fighting with white men. Four of the Negroes were arrested, and the mob, shouting "lynch them," then tried unsuccessfully to wrest them from the police.[74]

More serious was the wave of violence that came in the wake of the 1908 Springfield race riot. News of racial warfare in the state capital inspired many Chicago whites to attack Negroes. A mob attempted to lynch two Negro murder suspects, even though the victims, in both cases, were also Negroes.[75] Violence erupted on a Chicago River dock, where several white laborers declared that they would leave their jobs unless their Negro coworkers were fired.[76] For several weeks, armed posses hunted Negroes who were supposed fugitives from Springfield and, in at least two cases, planned lynchings.[77] The police, however, took special measures to prevent a general outbreak. The authorities mobilized special mounted forces and drill squads, and police

[72] Letter to the editor, *Record-Herald*, January 26, 1912.

[73] *Tribune*, November 21, 1900.

[74] *Record-Herald*, June 13, 1910.

[75] *Ibid.*, August 17, 1908.

[76] *Ibid.*, August 21, 1908.

[77] *Ibid.*, September 2, 1908.

officers were ordered to intervene quickly in any quarrels between Negroes and whites. With the cooperation of Negro leaders, who organized a law and order league on the South Side, a major riot was averted.[78]

Most observers—both Negro and white—agreed that the status of Negroes in Chicago was deteriorating, and some saw parallels between developments in Chicago and the hardening of Jim Crow patterns in the South. Two white commentators noted that "in the face of increasing manifestations of race prejudice, the Negro has come to acquiesce silently as various civil rights are with-held him in the old 'free North.' "[79] A Negro columnist, in 1914, took an even more pessimistic position. He noted that "Afro-American people in increasing numbers are refused the accom-modations of public places . . . in . . . violation of the laws of the state of Illinois," that "discrimination is manifesting itself more and more in the courts of Chicago," and that "the police depart-ment is especially filled with the wicked and unlawful determina-tion to degrade Afro-Americans and fix upon them the badge of inferiority." He concluded that Negroes "are more and more be-ing reduced to a fixed status of social and political inferiority."[80]

To compare the evolution of the Negro's status in Chicago with the crystallization of the caste system in the South during the same period was an exaggeration. Discrimination in Chicago re-mained unofficial, informal, and uncertain; the Negro's status did not become fixed. Nevertheless, as Negroes became more numer-ous and conspicuous, white hostility increased and Negroes en-countered an ever more pervasive pattern of exclusion. Edward E. Wilson, a Negro attorney, noted that the growth of the Negro community "brought [Negroes] into contact with whites who hardly knew that there were a thousand Colored people in Chi-cago." Moreover, "Colored children have appeared in numbers in many schools," and "Colored men have pushed their way into many employments." "All these things," he concluded, "have a tendency to cause the whites to resort to jim crow tactics."[81]

[78] *Ibid.*, August 17, August 19, 1908.

[79] Sophonisba Breckinridge and Edith Abbott, "Editors' Notes; Chicago Housing Conditions," reprinted from *American Journal of Sociology.*

[80] *Defender,* October 3, 1914.   [81] *Broad Ax,* December 31, 1910.

By 1915, Negroes had become a special group in the social structure of prewar Chicago. They could not be classified as merely another of Chicago's many ethnic groups. The systematic proscription they suffered in housing and jobs, the discrimination they often—although not always—experienced in public accommodations and even municipal services, the violence of which they were frequently victims, set them apart from the mainstream of Chicago life in significant ways. They were forced to work out their destiny within the context of an increasingly biracial society.

CHAPTER 3

CHICAGO'S NEGRO ELITE

The late nineteenth and early twentieth centuries were un-
happy years for American Negroes. In the South, state after state
wrote disfranchisement provisions into their constitutions and
established formal and rigid systems of segregation. In the northern cities, as the Negro population grew, discrimination became
ever more prevalent. The deterioration in the Negro's status
forced Negro leaders to reassess their assumptions about their
goals and the means by which these goals could be attained.[1]

The traditional approach of Negro leaders in the North called
for a relentless crusade against the biracial system itself. As the
abolitionists had fought slavery without compromise, so post-
Civil War Negro leaders leveled a broadside attack against all
forms of segregation and discrimination. The ultimate goal was
unquestioned: the integration of Negroes into the mainstream of
American life. The means of attack, too, were well-established: a
continual barrage of law suits against the vestiges of formal
segregation, political pressure to secure broader civil rights legislation, and frequent protests and indignation meetings to voice
the Negro's discontent over any violation of his rights. To the
integrationists, any type of separate Negro institution smacked of
segregation and represented a compromise of principle. At times,
a Negro institution might be necessary as a temporary expedient,
but it could never be regarded as a substitute for the ultimate
goal of integration.

[1] The best account of Negro leadership and conflicting racial ideologies in
the late nineteenth and early twentieth centuries is in August Meier, *Negro
Thought in America, 1880–1915* (Ann Arbor: University of Michigan Press,
1963). For my appraisal of Chicago Negro leadership, I am heavily indebted
to the ideas developed by Meier in his book, in his doctoral dissertation,
"Negro Racial Thought in the Age of Booker T. Washington," Columbia
University, 1957, and in his article, "Negro Class Structure and Ideology in
the Age of Booker T. Washington," *Phylon* (Atlanta) 23 (Fall, 1963): 258–66.

Before 1900, most Chicago Negro leaders accepted these doctrines as articles of faith. Their major civic undertakings were designed to secure equal rights for Negroes. Between 1865 and 1900, Negro leaders were absorbed in campaigns to secure the ballot, assure an integrated school system, pass and then broaden the Civil Rights Act, and finally bring suits under the Act. The typical nineteenth-century organization was the Vigilance Committee, which flourished in the 1870's for the purpose of seeking redress when Negro rights were violated.[2] If a lynching occurred in the South, or if a Negro suffered a slight in Chicago, the community leaders responded with an indignation meeting to draft a petition laying their grievances at the foot of the President or the governor or the mayor.

Any attempt to organize a separate Negro institution met with stiff opposition from those who regarded it as a form of self-segregation. Ida Wells-Barnett, who came to Chicago at the time of the Columbian Exposition, "was very much surprised to find fear of the color line hampering an attempt to supply the need of the Negro community." She tried to organize a kindergarten for Negro children, but "there seemed to be a united front against the establishment of a kindergarten on the ground that it would be drawing the color line and thus make it impossible for Negro children to be accepted at Armour Institute kindergarten."[3] A proposal to establish a Negro YMCA in 1889 met with loud cries of protest and after a spirited indignation meeting the idea was shelved.[4] Some Negro organizations refused to support Colored American Day at the Columbian Exposition; they regarded it as a form of segregation, although other ethnic groups also had special "days" at the fair.[5] Even Provident Hospital, an avowedly interracial enterprise, aroused the hostility of several Chicagoans

[2] St. Clair Drake, "Churches and Voluntary Associations in the Chicago Negro Community," Report of Official Project 465-54-3-386, Works Progress Administration, mimeographed (Chicago, 1940), p. 62.

[3] Alfreda Barnett Duster, untitled and unpublished manuscript on the life of Ida Wells-Barnett, in the possession of Mrs. Duster, Chicago, Illinois, chap. 8, p. 5.

[4] *Appeal* (St. Paul), November 30, December 7, December 22, 1889.

[5] Arna Bontemps and Jack Conroy, *They Seek a City* (Garden City, N.Y.: Doubleday, Doran & Company, 1945), p. 69.

who opposed the establishment of any institution under specifically Negro auspices.[6]

Even in this period, however, when the ideal of integration was ascendant, Chicago Negroes found some separate institutions necessary. This was most apparent in church life, where Negroes had had their own institutions since before the Civil War. In some cases, Negroes even expressed preference for churches of their own. Both Negro Episcopalians and Roman Catholics broke away from white churches to form separate congregations.[7] For the most part, though, Negro leaders were reluctant to encourage any form of separate institutional development. Frequently compelled to act as a group apart, they still regarded such actions as mere expedients, and they never raised the idea of separate development to the level of a racial ideology. Ferdinand L. Barnett, editor of the *Conservator*, Chicago's first Negro newspaper, probably spoke for most Chicago Negroes when he wrote in the late 1880's: "As a race let us forget the past so far as we can, and unite with other men upon issues liberal, essential, and not dependent upon color of skin or texture of hair for its [sic] gravamen."[8]

After 1900, however, Chicago Negro leaders increasingly gave voice to a new ideology that challenged the assumptions of the old civil rights creed. Their new approach was a northern variation of the philosophy of racial solidarity and self-help that had emerged in the post-Reconstruction South and had found its greatest vogue in the teachings of Booker T. Washington.[9] As

[6] Helen Buckler, *Doctor Dan* (Boston: Little, Brown & Company, 1954), p. 71.

[7] See chap. 5.

[8] Quoted by St. Clair Drake and Horace Cayton, *Black Metropolis* (New York: Harcourt, Brace & Company, 1945), p. 51.

[9] This philosophy has been a continual theme in the history of Negro racial thought, one that has come to the fore in periods of discouragement. Meier writes: "On the one hand white hostility has led Negroes to regard the creation of their own institutions as either necessary or wise; on the other hand these institutions reinforce and perpetuate thinking favorable to group separatism. Segregated institutions, of course, have appeared most desirable in the periods of greatest oppression and discouragement, and it has been in such periods that this desirability was most often expounded overtly and became the core of a dominant ideological orientation" (*Negro Thought in*

Washington and other southern Negro leaders responded to segregation and disfranchisement by urging Negroes to develop skills and organize their own economic and civic institutions, Chicago leaders responded to growing white hostility, not with direct counterattack, but by trying to build a Negro community that would itself provide all of the advantages of white Chicago. While the ultimate goal of complete integration was never abandoned in Chicago, it was temporarily relegated to the background. Negro leaders now showed a willingness to work within the framework of a biracial institutional structure and encourage the semiautonomous development of the Negro community. They emphasized self-reliance and racial cooperation rather than protests against mounting injustices.

The exponents of the old creed did not give up without a fight; frequently, they reminded the new leaders that parallel development was not a permanent solution and that it could often lead to a sacrifice of basic rights. The lines between the two ideological camps were not always clearly drawn; alliances shifted on different issues and often strong currents of integrationism and radical solidarity combined in the same man. At times, the issues were clearly spelled out; at other times, they were only implicit. But regardless of the many variations and complexities, Chicago's Negro leaders were engaged in a significant debate over the future course of Negro development in Chicago. Its most important expression was found in the very pattern of Negro community life in the early twentieth century—in civic institutions, politics, and business.

The ideological debate reflected a gradual but profound change in the social makeup of Chicago's Negro leadership. Before 1900, the community was dominated by a small group of upper-class Negroes, usually descendents of free Negroes and often of mixed stock, who had direct links with the abolitionist movement. Concentrated in the service trades and the professions, they usually had economic ties with the white community and numbered among their associates white men of comparable social position.

America, pp. 13–14). Thus, Negro thought had been primarily integrationist during the Reconstruction era, when Negro hopes were high, but began to turn toward separatism in the disheartening days after 1876.

The unchallenged leader of Chicago's Negroes from the 1850's until his death in 1879 was John Jones. Of mixed free Negro and white parentage, Jones came to Chicago in 1845, opened a downtown tailoring shop, and soon built up a thriving business making clothes for wealthy white Chicagoans. He worked actively with the abolitionist movement and frequently played host to Frederick Douglass, when the eminent Negro leader visited Chicago. After the war, Jones entered politics and was elected, with white support, to the Cook County Board of Commissioners.[10] Jones saw no conflict between the fight for equal rights and Negro racial solidarity. Chicago's Negro community was too small to support separate institutions and businesses, and Jones depended upon the white community for his economic and political success. He stressed the importance of economic advance as the keystone of Negro progress, but did not envisage it within the context of a separate Negro community. In his civic activities, such as the Vigilance Committee, he worked to secure equal rights for Negroes. "All that we ask is to be paid the regular price for our work," he said in 1874, eschewing special pleading, but "we must also have our civil rights, . . . they are essential to our complete freedom."[11]

After Jones's death, no single man assumed his mantle; Chicago's Negro community was already too diversified to recognize one man as its leader. Instead, a group of younger men emerged to carry on the type of leadership that Jones had exemplified. The majority of these leaders were long-time Chicago residents or had been born elsewhere in the North, although a few were of southern origin. Most of them worked in professions that brought them into close contact with whites. Some devoted themselves primarily to their professional careers while others were noted principally as civic or social leaders. Almost all of them

[10] For biographical data on Jones, see *Chicago Tribune*, March 12, 1875, May 22, 1879 (obituary); Drake and Cayton, *Black Metropolis*, pp. 41, 49; Harold Gosnell, *Negro Politicians: The Rise of Negro Politics in Chicago* (Chicago: University of Chicago Press, 1935), pp. 81–82; Bessie Louise Pierce, *A History of Chicago* (New York: Alfred A. Knopf, 1957), 3:48; Bontemps and Conroy, *They Seek a City*, pp. 28–36; Frederick Douglass, *The Life and Times of Frederick Douglass, Written By Himself* (New York: Collier Books, 1962), p. 454.

[11] *Tribune*, January 2, 1874.

were well-educated and had usually attended predominantly white institutions. Proud of their cultural attainments, they maintained high standards of respectability in their personal and civic lives. Until after the turn of the century, they formed a coherent elite group and set the tone of the social, intellectual, and civic life of the Negro community.

This social and cultural elite was, by and large, antagonistic to the ideology of self-help and racial solidarity popularized by Booker T. Washington and his followers. As direct heirs of the abolitionist tradition, they held fast to the old creed of militant protest for the attainment of equal rights. As educated, cultured men and women who enjoyed close relationships with their white counterparts, they leaned toward assimilationist views and envisioned an integrated society as their ultimate goal. Many of them identified with the Niagara movement, an organization of Negro militants, led by W. E. B. Du Bois, which first met in Niagara Falls, Ontario, in 1905, and for the next five years vigorously opposed Washington's accommodationism. After 1910, many of the old elite became active in the militant National Association for the Advancement of Colored People. Yet the problems they faced were more complex than those confronted by John Jones, and they were often aware of the contradictions inherent in a philosophy that espoused both integration and Negro economic and cultural advancement. To achieve the latter, Negro leaders were forced to make concessions to the ideology of separate development. Moreover, as accommodationism and self-help became the dominant national ideology among Negroes, the Chicago leaders, like it or not, were often forced to go along. Then, too, the Chicago Negro community was growing rapidly and could now support separate institutions that would have been inconceivable in John Jones's day. The old elite, then, fought to maintain the militant tradition, but between 1900 and 1915, it frequently found itself out of step with the times.

The most eminent member of Chicago's Negro elite was Daniel Hale Williams, the best-known Negro physician in the country and one of the outstanding surgeons of his day. Born in Pennsylvania of a family that had been free for generations, Williams came to Chicago in 1880 from Janesville, Wisconsin. After graduating from Chicago Medical College, where he received the best training available to a prospective physician in the late nineteenth century, he rose rapidly in his profession and developed close and lasting associations with the leading medical men in the city. The high regard in which he was held by his colleagues was amply justified by a distinguished medical career that included the first successful suture of the human heart. In 1891, he headed the group that founded Provident Hospital, and he insisted that the hospital—although established under Negro auspices—have an interracial staff chosen solely on the basis of ability.[12]

Williams devoted most of his energy and talent to his medical career and rarely articulated his views on racial matters. His publications were limited exclusively to articles in the medical journals. But a man of his prominence could hardly avoid the maelstrom of conflicting ideologies that troubled the Negro leaders of the day. For several years, Williams was a warm supporter of Booker T. Washington. He sent money to Tuskegee, offered to help Washington establish a hospital and training school, and used his influence to persuade the editor of the *Conservator* to cease his attacks on Washington's leadership. In 1904, he worked with Washington in founding the National Medical Association, an organization of Negro physicians, who, excluded from white medical societies and hospitals, banded together for mutual support and cooperation. But in 1907, Williams went over to the opposition when Washington refused to press for the reorganization of the Freedmen's Hospital in Washington, D.C., under a competent medical staff. After that, Williams regarded Washington as a political manipulator who failed to appreciate the importance of professional training. He identified with the Niagara group not because of their protest ideology, but because he found in the idea of the "talented tenth," espoused by Du Bois and his followers, an echo of his own strong beliefs in the necessity for an educated Negro leadership.[13]

Williams' closest associate on the Provident staff was Charles E. Bentley, a Negro dentist, whose background and interests led him into an alliance with Williams in civic as well as professional affairs. Bentley was born in Ohio and educated at the Chicago College of Dental Surgery. Like Williams, he was well-known in his profession: he was the founder and first president of the

[12] Buckler, *Doctor Dan,* pp. 67–68 and *passim.* On Provident Hospital, see chap. 5.

[13] *Ibid.,* pp. 191–94, 231–51.

Odontographic Society, held a professorship in oral surgery at Harvey Medical College, and headed the dental clinics at the 1903 St. Louis World's Fair.[14]

Bentley played a more active role in Negro affairs than Williams. From the first, he allied himself with the militants. In 1903, he helped organize the Equal Opportunity League and then brought W. E. B. Du Bois to Chicago to speak to the group. Two years later, he was one of two Chicagoans to attend the first Niagara Conference, and according to Du Bois "planned the method of organization" of the conference.[15] Returning to local affairs, Bentley organized a Chicago chapter of the Niagara movement and appeared before the Charter Convention in 1906 to advocate a clause in the new city charter prohibiting segregation in the public schools.[16] In 1912, he helped organize the Chicago branch of the NAACP and served on its first board of directors.[17]

The only other Chicagoan to journey to Niagara Falls in 1905 was James B. Madden, another of the city's Negro elite who became an outspoken militant. Madden had been active in social and civic affairs since the 1880's. He was a charter member of the Prudence Crandall Club, an exclusive literary society, and one of the original trustees of Provident Hospital. Like many members of the old elite, Madden had economic ties with the white community: he was the first Negro to work as a bookkeeper for a white firm in Chicago.[18]

Ferdinand and Ida Barnett were leaders of a somewhat different order. Publicists by trade, they were not torn between professional and civic duties as were Williams and Bentley; in this

[14] "Some Chicagoans of Note," *Crisis* (New York), 10 (September, 1915): 239–40; *Appeal,* April 2, 1892; Buckler, *Doctor Dan,* pp. 55, 76, 232.

[15] *Broad Ax* (Chicago), December 19, 1903, January 21, 1905; Meier, "Negro Racial Thought," p. 529; Buckler, *Doctor Dan,* pp. 69, 256; S. Laing Williams to Booker T. Washington, July 21, 1905, in Booker T. Washington Papers (Library of Congress, Washington, D.C.), cited hereafter as Washington Papers.

[16] *Appeal,* June 30, 1906.

[17] *Chicago Defender,* January 20, 1912; William C. Graves to Julius Rosenwald, April 18, 1914, in Julius Rosenwald Papers (University of Chicago Library), cited hereafter as Rosenwald Papers.

[18] Buckler, *Doctor Dan,* pp. 69, 256; S. Laing Williams to Booker T. Washington, July 21, 1905, Washington Papers; *Appeal,* January 7, 1888.

sense, they foreshadowed the professional Negro leaders who were to emerge in the World War I period. Ida Wells-Barnett was born in Mississippi and went to Memphis at the age of fourteen. There she taught school and edited a militant Negro weekly, *Free Speech*. Her uncompromising opposition to lynching aroused the ire of her white neighbors, who attacked and burned the *Free Speech* print shop and forced the young editor to flee for her life. In the tradition of the Negro abolitionists, Miss Wells embarked on a speaking tour to present the Negro's case before audiences in the North and in England. Visiting Chicago for an appearance at the Columbian Exposition, she decided to settle in the city and, in 1895, married Ferdinand L. Barnett.[19]

A militant long before militancy found a national spokesman in W. E. B. Du Bois, Mrs. Barnett was a natural leader of the anti-Tuskegee group on both the national and local levels. By the turn of the century, she had emerged as the leading militant in the Afro-American Council. The Council was the successor to the Afro-American League, which had been organized in Chicago in 1890 as a national protest organization. The League was defunct by 1893, but was revived as the Afro-American Council five years later. At its first convention in 1898, it tried to maintain a precarious balance between militant northern Negroes and more cautious southerners.[20] Nevertheless, Mrs. Barnett, uncompromising by nature, attacked Booker T. Washington's accommodationism in a sharply worded and coolly received address. Washington, she declared, was seriously mistaken in his notion that Negroes could gain their rights merely by economic advancement. "We must educate the white people out of their 250 years of slave history," she declared.[21] Washington, still basking in the

---

[19] Duster, manuscript on the life of Ida Wells-Barnett, *passim;* interview with Alfreda Barnett Duster, July 3, 1962; report on Ida Wells-Barnett in "The Negro in Illinois," a file of reports and interviews compiled by the Illinois Writers Project of the Works Progress Administration (George Cleveland Hall Branch of the Chicago Public Library), cited hereafter as Illinois Writers Project Files; *Defender,* April 28, 1931 (obituary); Bontemps and Conroy, *They Seek a City,* pp. 77–82.

[20] Emma Lou Thornbrough, "The National Afro-American League, 1887–1908," *Journal of Southern History* (Houston), 27 (November, 1961): 494–512; Meier, *Negro Thought in America,* pp. 172–74.

[21] *Colored American* (Washington), January 7, 1899.

glory of his famous Atlanta address three years earlier, enjoyed the confidence of most Negro leaders. But Mrs. Barnett had enough support within the Council to be elected secretary and later chairman of the Council's Anti-Lynching Bureau. She remained active until 1903, when the organization fell under the complete control of the Tuskegee machine.[22]

After 1903, Ida Barnett increasingly devoted her energy to local affairs. When a Negro was lynched in southern Illinois in 1909, she journeyed to Springfield to urge Governor Charles Deneen to reinstate the sheriff who had tried unsuccessfully to prevent the lynching. The governor complied and Illinois experienced no more lynchings. Mrs. Barnett's interests also led her into the woman's suffrage movement, women's club activities, social settlement work, and progressive politics. In these activities she developed close relations with white reformers, particularly Jane Addams. Mrs. Barnett was the only Chicago Negro to sign the call for the conference that led to the establishment of the NAACP in 1909.[23]

Ferdinand L. Barnett had been a prominent figure in Chicago for twenty years when he married Ida Wells. He founded the city's first Negro newspaper, the *Conservator*, in 1878. Continually in the vanguard of militant protest leaders, Barnett encouraged racial solidarity not as a basis for accommodation but as the means by which Negroes could combine in the struggle for equal rights. "Race elevation can be attained only through race unity," he told the National Conference of Colored Men in 1879. "White people will grant us few privileges voluntarily. We must wage continued warfare for our rights."[24] After leaving the *Conservator*, Barnett went into private law practice and entered politics. He served as assistant state's attorney for a decade, and in 1906 was almost elected to the municipal court. A member of the Equal Opportunity League and a firm opponent of Booker T. Washing-

[22] Meier, "Negro Racial Thought," pp. 180, 462, 472.

[23] Illinois Writers Project Files; Mary White Ovington, *How the National Association for the Advancement of Colored People Began* (New York: National Association for the Advancement of Colored People, 1914); for Mrs. Barnett's civic and philanthropic work, see chap. 5.

[24] National Conference of Colored Men of the United States, *Proceedings*, Nashville, Tennessee, May 6-9, 1879 (Washington: Rufus H. Darby, 1879), p. 85.

ton, he nevertheless maintained political contacts sufficient to secure his appointment, over Washington's opposition, as head of the Chicago branch of the Negro Bureau in the 1904 Republican presidential campaign.[25]

Another member of the Chicago elite who achieved national prominence as a militant was attorney Edward H. Morris. Born in Kentucky, Morris came to Chicago at an early age, studied law, and was elected to the state legislature. A successful corporation lawyer and attorney for Cook County, he maintained professional and social relations with white attorneys. Morris allied himself with the Negro militants both in Chicago and nationally. In 1903, he played a leading role at the organizational meeting of the Equal Rights League of Illinois at Springfield. After speaking strongly in favor of a report censuring Washington, he was elected chairman of the executive committee.[26] That same year, he told the Chicago *Inter-Ocean,* a white daily, that Washington was "largely responsible for the lynching in this country," and that "he teaches that Negroes are fit only for menial positions." "As far as the good of the colored race is concerned," he continued, "I prefer a radical like Senator Tillman of South Carolina to Booker T. Washington. . . . The colored people think it doesn't matter so much what he says . . . [but they] believe and do what [Washington] tells them. Then they don't insist upon being treated the equals of whites."[27] Morris repeated his attack a year later in Washington, D.C., in a speech that became a rallying point in the growing opposition to the Tuskegee brand of leadership.[28]

Edward E. Wilson, another attorney and politician, was not as well-known nationally as Morris, but locally he was one of the most articulate and perceptive critics of accommodationism

[25] Gosnell, *Negro Politicians,* pp. 85, 155; *Chicago Bee,* May 22, 1936 (obituary); interview with Mrs. Duster; Booker T. Washington to S. Laing Williams, August 9, 1904, and Williams to Washington, November 16, 1906, Washington Papers.

[26] *Appeal,* October 17, 1903.

[27] Quoted in *Cleveland Gazette,* August 8, 1903.

[28] For biographical data on Morris, see Gosnell, *Negro Politicians,* pp. 66, 111; Chicago Commission on Race Relations, *The Negro in Chicago: A Study of Race Relations and a Race Riot* (Chicago: University of Chicago Press, 1922), p. 652; Meier, *Negro Thought in America,* pp. 154, 178; Meier, "Negro Racial Thought," p. 766; Bontemps and Conroy, *They Seek a City,* p. 83.

and separate development. Wilson came to Chicago after studying at Oberlin and Williams Colleges and succeeded Barnett as assistant state's attorney. He wrote in 1910:

> Separation, where it does not bring a lessening of one's rights and privileges, is not to be frowned upon; but this so seldom happens that it is a dangerous experiment; and wherever there is a tendency to the curtailment of civic rights, or where such separation is an entering wedge for further discriminations, it should be fought without apology and without truce.[29]

Wilson vigorously attacked those local Negroes who argued that separate schools would provide more work for Negro teachers: "For a few jobs, some Negroes are willing to be cooped off by themselves with inferior advantages and with a door left open for further invasions of their rights." He was one of the few Chicago Negroes to oppose the plan of Julius Rosenwald, the white philanthropist, for the construction of a Negro YMCA. Wilson characterized the project as a means "for travelling to heaven by a back alley." "One could not be sure," he added, "that after a long and weary journey along a jim-crow route to glory, that he would not find a jim-crow Paradise awaiting him beyond."[30]

Probably the most uncompromising integrationist in Chicago was still another attorney and politician, John G. Jones,[31] whose long record of militant protest activities earned him the nickname, "Indignation" Jones. An "old settler," he never deviated from his faith in the equal rights creed. From the 1880's, when he shared a law office with Ferdinand Barnett, until the early twentieth century, when he was elected to the state legislature, he fought every infringement on Negro rights and every move toward separatism. Jones led the protests against the establishment of a Negro YMCA in 1889 and against Provident Hospital in 1891. When a coroner's jury handed down a verdict critical of integrated employment in a Chicago firm, Jones called an indignation meeting and declared that the jury and the coroner should be tarred and feathered. Dan Williams felt the lash of the impetuous Jones when he remarked in an interview that Negroes were fond of secret societies and bright regalia. Jones called a meeting to censure

[29] *Broad Ax,* December 31, 1910.

[30] *Ibid.;* see also Gosnell, *Negro Politicians,* pp. 206–7.

[31] Not to be confused with the pioneer Negro leader, John Jones.

Williams for slandering the Negro people, but he could muster no support against the prestigious doctor. Naturally, Jones became a vitriolic critic of Booker T. Washington. As chairman of the Equal Rights League convention in Springfield in 1903, he called Washington's methods detrimental to the race and urged the assembly to censure him. Two years later, he and Edward Morris used their influence to block a federal appointment for Washington's friend, S. Laing Williams.[32]

Three clergymen, with widely differing outlooks, were also prominent members of the Chicago elite. Reverdy Ransom was an active proponent of the social gospel, an ardent reformer and an articulate spokesman for the Negro militants. Born in a Quaker settlement in Ohio and educated at Wilberforce and Oberlin, Ransom came to Chicago in 1896 to become minister of Bethel A.M.E. Church. He expanded the program of the church to include a Men's Sunday Club, the first of the Sunday forums that were to become popular in Negro churches, and he worked actively in politics to secure needed public improvements for the burgeoning black belt. Immersing himself in reform activities, even dabbling at times with socialism, Ransom met such prominent white reformers as Jane Addams, Mary McDowell, Clarence Darrow, and Graham Taylor and, with their help, established the Institutional Church and Social Settlement in 1900. The first attempt to provide a full program of social services among Chicago Negroes, Institutional attracted not only the poor who were to benefit from its activities, but sophisticated, upper-class Negroes who found Ransom's social gospel more attractive than the traditional type of Negro religion. Ransom continued to play an active role in civic reform. In 1903, he denounced the policy racket in a series of sermons that led to the dynamiting of his church, and during the 1904 stockyards strike he attempted to mediate between the Negro strikebreakers and the angry white strikers. Ransom left Chicago in 1904 for a long career as orator, writer, reformer, and leader in the Niagara movement.[33]

[32] *Appeal*, February 11, March 10, 1888, December 7, 1889, April 18, 1891, October 17, 1903; Buckler, *Doctor Dan*, pp. 71–72; John G. Jones to Senator A. J. Hopkins, December 9, 1905, Washington Papers; I. C. Harris, *Colored Men's Professional and Business Directory of Chicago* (Chicago: I. C. Harris, 1885), p. 22.

[33] Reverdy Ransom, *The Pilgrimage of Harriet Ransom's Son* (Nashville, Tenn.: Sunday School Union [1950?]), pp. 15–17, 33, 81–135; Buckler, *Doctor*

In 1909, Ransom's Institutional Church called to its pulpit Archibald J. Carey. Born in Georgia in 1868 of a "household slave" family, Carey received a liberal education at Atlanta University and came to Chicago in 1896 to become pastor of Quinn Chapel A.M.E. Church, the oldest in the city. Like Ransom, Carey was deeply concerned with civic and political matters and both at Quinn Chapel and Institutional he used his pulpit as a forum for matters of community concern. He carried on Ransom's social welfare program, brought in prominent white and Negro leaders to speak to the Sunday Forum, and gathered around him a qualified staff of trained social workers.[34]

Carey participated in partisan politics more fully than Ransom and successfully used his congregation as a base for personal political power. Although a Republican, he frequently supported Democrats on the state and local level. Governor Edward Dunne, a Democrat, named him chairman of the organizing committee of the Emancipation Golden Jubilee in 1913, a position that gave him considerable patronage. A year later, Democratic Mayor Carter Harrison II appointed Carey to the motion-picture censorship board where he successfully led the fight to suppress the anti-Negro film, *The Birth of a Nation,* in 1915. When his long-time friend, William Hale Thompson, was elected mayor of Chicago as a Republican in 1915, Carey was among the most powerful Negro political figures in the city.[35]

Unlike Ransom, Carey remained nominally neutral in the debate over Negro racial ideology, but his views more closely coincided with the militants' than with Washington's. For a brief period, just after 1900, he edited the *Conservator* and followed a policy described as "more or less hostile" to Washington.[36] When a white speaker at a Lincoln centennial celebration in 1909 told a Negro audience not to "trouble yourselves too much about politics," but

---

Dan, pp. 223–25; *Chicago Inter-Ocean,* July 29, 1900; *Broad Ax,* May 9, 1903; *Appeal,* May 9, 1903; for a discussion of Institutional Church, see chap. 5.

[34] Joseph Logsdon, "Reverend A. J. Carey and the Negro in Chicago Politics," unpublished master's thesis, University of Chicago, 1961, pp. 5–18; *Defender,* March 7, March 14, 1914, April 28, 1931 (obituary).

[35] Logsdon, "Reverend A. J. Carey," pp. 23–50; Gosnell, *Negro Politicians,* pp. 49–51.

[36] S. Laing Williams to Booker T. Washington, July 6, 1909, Washington Papers.

to "try to get ahead in the material things of life," Carey, who was chairing the meeting, immediately arose to reply and called the ballot the Negro's "only weapon of defense."[37] In 1913, Carey secured an appointment as orator at the Centennial of the Battle of Lake Erie at Put-In-Bay, and he used the occasion to deliver an impassioned plea for Negro rights.[38]

J. B. Massiah, rector of the fashionable St. Thomas Episcopal Church, also ministered to Chicago's Negro elite. Born in Barbados, he received his training at Oxford University and at the General Theological Seminary in New York. He served in Chicago from 1906 until his death in 1916. Unlike Ransom and Carey, Massiah generally eschewed racial and political affairs, but in 1912, while the Tuskegee-dominated National Negro Business League was meeting in Chicago, he delivered a ringing denunciation of the accommodationist approach:

> I cannot refrain from deploring the failure of the race, in the north especially, to continue to agitate against infringement of the constitutional rights of our people in the south. We should not cease to agitate, even for the sake of trying the policy of conciliation, which is proving too plainly, even in the north, that bank accounts and property are not changing the black man's skin or the white man's spotted prejudice.[39]

Although most of Chicago's old established leaders retained their commitment to the equal rights ideology and rejected compromise, there were some exceptions. A few members of the Negro elite completely avoided involvement in racial affairs. Charles J. Smiley, for instance, perhaps the wealthiest Negro in Chicago after the death of John Jones, devoted his energies exclusively to his successful catering business that served affluent white Chicagoans.[40] Julius Avendorph, the "Ward McAllister of the South

[37] Nathan W. MacChesney, ed., *Abraham Lincoln, The Tribute of a Century* (Chicago: A. C. MacClurg, 1910), pp. 102–12.

[38] Logsdon, "Reverend A. J. Carey," pp. 18–23; Gosnell, *Negro Politicians,* p. 50; *Defender,* September 20, 1913.

[39] *Defender,* August 13, 1912; for biographical data on Massiah, see "A Preacher of the Word," *Crisis,* 11 (April, 1916):290; and *Defender,* January 15, 1916 (obituary).

[40] Richard R. Wright, Jr., "The Industrial Condition of Negroes in Chicago," unpublished B. D. thesis, University of Chicago Divinity School, 1901, pp. 16–18, 19; Drake and Cayton, *Black Metropolis,* p. 49; Buckler, *Doctor Dan,* pp. 75, 156, 256.

Side," limited his activities to social affairs. As assistant to the president of the Pullman Company, he became "personally acquainted with more millionaires than any other Colored man in Chicago." He served as master of ceremonies at every major Negro social event and was considered "Chicago's undisputed social leader from 1886 up until 1910."[41] If Avendorph never participated in protest activities, he clearly articulated the elitist social views of many who considered themselves the cream of Negro society in Chicago. Writing in 1917, he deplored the blurring of class lines that had occurred since the turn of the century. "22 years ago," he said, "Chicago could rightfully claim a social set that stood for high ideals and did not hesitate to draw a line of demarcation. . . . Society must stand for something and its cardinal principle ought to be class distinction."[42]

Several members of the old elite went beyond neutrality and actually joined the Tuskegee camp. One of these was Lloyd Wheeler, a friend of Dan Williams and one of the founders of Provident Hospital. Wheeler married John Jones's adopted daughter and became manager of Jones's tailoring establishment. Socially prominent, he was known as a "good dresser" and "an elegant Mixer"; but he differed from most of his friends on racial matters. Wheeler helped to establish a Chicago branch of the National Negro Business League, and after suffering business misfortunes in Chicago, he moved to Tuskegee to take a job at the Institute.[43]

S. Laing Williams and his wife, Fannie Barrier Williams, were more important exceptions to the thesis that the old elite remained racial militants. Born in Georgia, S. Laing Williams came to Chicago in the mid-1880's after graduating from the University of Michigan and the Columbian Law School in Washington, D.C. He was admitted to the Illinois bar and for a short time shared a law office with Ferdinand Barnett.[44] Williams immediately became a leader in Chicago Negro society. In 1887, he organized the

[41] *Defender,* August 10, 1918, May 12, 1923 (obituary); *Appeal,* December 4, 1897, October 6, 1900.

[42] *Defender,* October 6, 1917.

[43] Buckler, *Doctor Dan,* pp. 69–70, 232, 256; I. C. Harris, *Colored Men's Professional and Business Directory,* pp. 25–26, 28; *Appeal,* April 27, 1901.

[44] George W. Ellis, "The Chicago Negro in Law and Politics," *Champion Magazine* (Chicago), 1 (March, 1917): 349; report on Williams in Illinois Writers Project Files; Meier, *Negro Thought in America,* p. 238.

Prudence Crandall Club, a literary society, and attracted to it a membership that included nearly every socially prominent Negro in the city.[45] Yet from an early date, Williams was a warm supporter and personal friend of Booker T. Washington. He delivered the commencement address at Tuskegee in 1895 and, by the turn of the century, was Washington's closest aide in Chicago. He arranged for Washington's periodic visits to the city, kept him advised of political maneuvers in Chicago, and acted as a liaison between Tuskegee and the Chicago Negro press. In 1904, Washington hired him to ghostwrite his biography of Frederick Douglass.[46]

Williams dutifully informed Washington of the activities of the Niagara group in Chicago and faithfully echoed the Tuskegee line. Edward Morris and Ferdinand Barnett, he told Washington in 1904, were aspiring to gain control of the Negro Bureau of the Republican presidential campaign and "would certainly use the position for personal gains and for revenging their spleen or spite."[47] The next year, he kept Washington advised of the movement of Chicago Negroes in relation to the Niagara conference and commented that the Niagara proclamation "contains nothing new or constructive" but "is a mere harking back to old methods of protest and complaint."[48] When the NAACP began to organize in 1910, he wrote to Emmett Scott, Washington's secretary, that despite several meetings in Chicago, "I cannot see any evidence of paramount interest in the thing." The NAACP leaders, he said, were "at heart . . . hostile [to Washington] but they are menaced by the overwhelming sentiment of the country that Dr. Washington is everlastingly right in his views and work."[49]

[45] *Appeal*, January 7, 1888; and see chap. 5.

[46] *Appeal*, June 1, 1895; Emmett J. Scott to S. Laing Williams, July 20, 1904; E. P. Oberholzer to Booker T. Washington, July 14, 1904; Williams to Washington, June 7, 1904; Washington to Williams, June 12, 1904; Williams to Scott, July 26, 1904—Washington Papers.

[47] S. Laing Williams to Emmett J. Scott, July 8, 1904; Williams to Booker T. Washington, July 14, 1904; Williams to Charles Anderson, July 8, 1904—Washington Papers.

[48] S. Laing Williams to Booker T. Washington, July 21, 1904, and Williams to Emmett J. Scott, July 10, 1905, Washington Papers.

[49] S. Laing Williams to Emmett J. Scott, October 25, 1910, Washington Papers.

As a reward for his loyalty to Washington, Williams sought a federal appointment, but his activities as a spy for Tuskegee had earned him the enmity of many Chicagoans. In 1904, he expected to be appointed head of the Chicago branch of the Republican Party's Negro Bureau, but even Washington's intervention could not prevent the job from going to Ferdinand Barnett, Williams' old law partner and now a bitter ideological foe.[50] Williams, nevertheless, worked diligently for the party and after the Republican victory confidently awaited a federal appointment, perhaps even the Haitian ministry or the Registry of the Treasury, the highest positions to which a Negro could aspire. But now Edward Morris and John G. Jones used their influence against him.[51] Finally, Washington secured for Williams an appointment in 1908 as Assistant U.S. District Attorney for Illinois and Eastern Wisconsin. He was discharged a year later, but Washington arranged for his reappointment. In 1912, he lost the job permanently because he was "short on energy and practicability."[52]

Despite Williams' close involvement with Washington and his continual reiteration of the Tuskegee ideology, there remained a certain ambiguity in his position. From time to time it seemed that his natural instincts were with his former friends, Morris, the Barnetts, and Madden. When the militant Equal Opportunity League brought Du Bois to Chicago in 1903, Williams appeared on the program. A decade later, he was vice-president of the Chicago branch of the NAACP which he had previously dismissed as

[50] Booker T. Washington to S. Laing Williams, July 14, 1904; Washington to Williams, July 21, 1905; Williams to Washington, July 27, 1904; Williams to Washington, August 6, 1904; Williams to Washington, August 8, 1904; Washington to Williams, August 9, 1904; Washington to Williams, August 14, 1904; Williams to Washington, August 17, 1904; Washington to Williams, September 7, 1904—Washington Papers.

[51] S. Laing Williams to Booker T. Washington, December 31, 1904; Washington to Williams, May 20, 1905; Williams to Washington, May 17, 1905; Williams to Washington, May 25, 1905; Williams to Theodore Roosevelt, November 20, 1905; John G. Jones to Senator A. J. Hopkins, December 9, 1905; Edward Morris to Hopkins, December 9, 1905; Washington to Williams, January 13, 1906—Washington Papers; *Broad Ax*, January 13, 1906; Chicago *Record-Herald*, December 10, 1905.

[52] Booker T. Washington to S. Laing Williams, March 30, 1908; Williams to Washington, June 30, 1909; Williams to Washington, October 1, 1909; P. W. Tyler to Washington, December 12, 1912; Tyler to Washington, December 16, 1912—Washington Papers.

being unconstructive.[53] By 1914, Williams was devoting a portion of his practice to civil rights cases and giving legal assistance to the NAACP grievances committee.[54] As early as 1895, while speaking at Tuskegee, he could not accept the Washington ideology without reservations. He praised industrial education for Negroes, but added that "I would be equally as earnest in my wish to shorten the way for every superior man or woman that leads to the classic halls of Harvard, Yale or Ann Arbor."[55] Like many other Negro leaders during the era of Washington's preeminence, Williams found it personally advantageous to associate himself with Tuskegee and undoubtedly he agreed with many of Washington's ideas. But he never became an accommodationist, and when he no longer depended upon Tuskegee for his job, he participated fully in the activities of the militants.

Fannie Barrier Williams occupied an even more ambiguous position than her husband. Born in Brockport, New York, of a prominent free Negro family, she came to Chicago in the 1880's. Married in 1887, she soon won a reputation as an able speaker, writer, and organizer. She worked with Dan Williams in establishing Provident Hospital and was chosen to deliver two addresses at the Columbian Exposition—one before the World's Congress of Representative Women, the other at the World's Parliament of Religions.[56] Fannie Williams' speeches in 1893 reflected the traditional views of the Negro elite. While favoring union and organization among Negroes for purposes of race advancement, she reminded her white audience that slavery was responsible for "every moral imperfection that mars the character of the colored American" and that by continuing to deny equal opportunity to Negroes, "the American people are but repeating the common folly of history in thus attempting to repress the yearnings of common humanity." She expressed indignation that "colored women can find no employment in this free America" and she saw as the only solution to the Negro's plight "opportunities untrammeled by prejudice" and "the right of the individual to be judged, not by tradition and race

[53] *Broad Ax*, December 19, 1903; *Crisis*, 5 (April, 1913): 297; *Crisis*, 6 (May, 1913): 38–39.

[54] William C. Graves to Julius Rosenwald, April 18, 1914, Rosenwald Papers.

[55] *Appeal*, June 1, 1895.

[56] *Defender*, July 26, 1914; Buckler, *Doctor Dan*, pp. 71, 73, 83.

estimate, but by the present evidence of individual worth."[57] After Mrs. Williams finished one address, Frederick Douglass, the venerable champion of Negro militancy, stepped forward and, overcome with emotion, hailed the dawn of a "new earth . . . in which all discriminations . . . is passing away."[58]

Perhaps Fannie Williams never completely lost her faith in equal rights and equal opportunity; but by 1900, she had become a leading exponent of the doctrine of self-help and racial solidarity, actively writing and speaking in behalf of Booker T. Washington. In 1904, she attacked "the man who is always complaining and [who] fails to cultivate strength against adversity and wrongdoing." Disfranchising the Negro in the South, she continued, "has been a great blessing in disguise; since he is not permitted to vote, he is acquiring land and money."[59] In another article, she lauded the Negro's faith "that emancipation from the ills of poverty and ignorance and race prejudice is through co-operation."[60] It is, of course, possible that Mrs. Williams simply changed her mind. Yet, it can hardly be coincidental that her most active work for the Tuskegee cause came at the very time her husband was seeking a federal job. Contemporaries credited her with playing a major role in winning favor for her husband.[61] Even more than S. Laing Williams, perhaps, Fannie Williams' background, instincts, and general inclinations disposed her toward the equal rights school of racial thought, but the Negro power structure of the day forced her into the Tuskegee camp.

[57] Fannie B. Williams, "The Intellectual Progress of the Colored Women of the United States since the Emancipation Proclamation," *The World Congress of Representative Women,* ed. May Wright Sewall (Chicago: Rand, McNally & Company, 1894), pp. 703, 705, 707. See also Mrs. Williams' "Religious Duty to the Negro," *The World's Congress of Religions,* ed. J. W. Hanson (Chicago: W. B. Conkey, 1894), pp. 893–97.

[58] Williams, "The Intellectual Progress," p. 717.

[59] Fannie B. Williams, "The New Negro," *Record-Herald,* October 9, 1904; see also Mrs. Williams' "The Club Movement among Colored Women in America," *A New Negro for a New Century,* ed. J. E. MacBrady (Chicago: American Publishing House, [1900?]), p. 417; and S. Laing Williams to Booker T. Washington, February 24, 1908, Washington Papers.

[60] Fannie B. Williams, "Social Bonds in the Black Belt of Chicago," *Charities* (New York), 15 (October 7, 1905): 40–41.

[61] *Broad Ax,* January 13, 1906.

CHAPTER 4

THE NEW LEADERSHIP

The old elite dominated Negro community life until the first decade of the twentieth century. They ran the social affairs, organized the civic ventures, and acted as spokesmen for Chicago's Negroes in matters of group concern. But between 1900 and 1910, new names became increasingly prominent—the names of men who were not accepted socially by the old elite but whose economic or political attainments gave them status in the community. Prominent among the new leadership group were South Side businessmen, professional men with business interests, and a new brood of professional politician. All of these leaders were dependent upon the Negro community for support—whether economic or political—and did not maintain close ties with white colleagues, as had the old elite. In background, these men were a varied lot: most of them were relative newcomers to Chicago, but like their predecessors they came from both northern and southern communities. The majority of them lacked the educational and cultural attainments of the older group. Most were self-made men with no more than rudimentary formal educations—even the professional men among them often had sub-standard training. And while the old elite had scrupulously maintained high standards of respectability and gentility, the new leaders often associated with the "shady" elements of both Negro and white society.

The new leaders were less wont to articulate a racial ideology than the old elite, and many of them shunned racial activities altogether. These were self-styled men of affairs, who left their mark not by writing or speaking but in business ventures, institutions, and organizational politics. Yet, implicit in their activities were a view of racial affairs and a vision of the Negro's future in Chicago that differed markedly from the militant integrationism of their predecessors. As men who had their primary economic and social ties in the black belt, they contributed to the development of a

71

separate institutional life for Chicago Negroes. They established Negro businesses, built a Negro political machine, and participated in the organization of Negro social agencies. To the extent that they were involved in the ideological battles of the day, they gravitated to Booker T. Washington's philosophy of self-help. But the Tuskegee ideology did not determine their action; it merely justified what they were already doing.

If there was a counterpart to Daniel Hale Williams among the new leadership class, it was his long-time professional rival, George Cleveland Hall. The most articulate of the business leaders, Hall typified, in his professional and civic activities, the outlook and aspirations of the rising Negro middle class. Hall came to Chicago from Michigan in the late 1880's and received his medical training at Bennett College, a school operated by the Eclectics, one of the many dubious medical sects that proliferated in the nineteenth century.[1] When Hall tried to secure a position on the Provident Hospital staff, Dan Williams sought unsuccessfully to block it on the grounds that Hall was inadequately trained. Hall interpreted Williams' action as a personal affront and charged that Williams preferred white doctors to Negroes. The ensuing conflict raged for more than a decade and spilled over into many areas of community life.[2]

While Hall and Williams vied for professional eminence, their wives carried on a feud that delineated the social difference between the old elite and the new business class. According to Williams' biographer, the women of the Negro elite—Mrs. Williams, Mrs. Charles Bentley, Mrs. Julius Avendorph—"did not ordinarily welcome the aspiring Mrs. George Hall, whose laughter and clothes were both apt to be a little loud." Once Mrs. Hall appeared uninvited at a ladies' gathering in the Avendorph home. Most of the women were cool toward her; Mrs. Williams walked out.[3]

[1] For biographical data on Hall, see *Chicago Defender,* June 21, 1930 (obituary); *Broad Ax* (Chicago), February 17, 1912; "Some Chicagoans of Note," *Crisis* (New York), 10 (September, 1915): 241; Helen Buckler, *Doctor Dan* (Boston: Houghton, Mifflin & Company, 1954), p. 77.

[2] Buckler presents a detailed account of the Hall-Williams feud, written from Williams' point of view. *Doctor Dan,* pp. 175–76. For the impact of the feud on the development of Provident Hospital, see chap. 5.

[3] Buckler, *Doctor Dan,* pp. 189, 228. Buckler obtained this material through interviews and it is, therefore, hard to verify.

From an early date, Hall aligned himself with Booker T. Washington. In 1899, he told the Bethel Church Sunday Forum that "the race is not progressing as rapidly in all those things which must necessarily be acquired before we can become substantial and highly respected individuals and citizens." He specifically criticized Negroes for their reluctance to support Negro businesses, newspapers, and institutions.[4] Hall himself became a leading promoter of Negro business and in 1912 assumed the presidency of the Chicago branch of Washington's National Negro Business League. A personal friend of Washington, he and Mrs. Hall frequently visited the principal and his wife in Tuskegee.[5] Yet like many of Washington's northern supporters, Hall was no accommodationist. Although an exponent of self-help and racial solidarity, he also felt that Negroes had to fight white prejudice and discrimination directly. He stated:

> Those of the race who are desirous of improving their general condition are prevented to a great extent by being compelled to live with those of their color who are shiftless, dissolute and immoral. . . . Prejudice of landlords and agents render it almost impossible for [the Negro] to take up his residence in a more select quarter of the city . . . no matter . . . how much cultivation and refinement he may possess.[6]

Hall evidently found no contradiction in serving as a member of the NAACP's committee on grievances just a year after he assumed the presidency of the Negro Business League.[7]

[4] *Broad Ax*, October 28, 1899.

[5] S. Laing Williams to Booker T. Washington, July 12, 1909, Booker T. Washington Papers (Library of Congress, Washington, D.C.), cited hereafter as Washington Papers; *Broad Ax*, August 24, 1912; Buckler, *Doctor Dan*, pp. 250–51.

[6] Speech before the Frederick Douglass Center, reprinted in the *Broad Ax*, December 31, 1904. August Meier remarks that "large numbers of those who supported Washington did not personally follow his accommodating tactic." *Negro Thought in America, 1880–1915* (Ann Arbor: University of Michigan Press, 1963), p. 167. This was especially true in northern cities. Some supported Washington for personal reasons without any genuine commitment to his policies. Others—and Hall was probably among these—agreed with Washington's emphasis on self-help and racial solidarity but thought that his accommodationist methods and views were improper in the North.

[7] *Crisis*, 6 (May 1, 1913): 38–39.

The core of the new leadership was made up of businessmen. Theodore W. Jones, the Canadian-born owner of a large South Side express company was, together with S. Laing Williams, Booker T. Washington's contact man in Chicago and an officer of the National Negro Business League.[8] A supporter of the Tuskegee philosophy, he said in 1906 that "the Southern Negro's interest in the ballot is on the wane" and that "in those states where the disfranchisement laws are the most rigid, there thrift and repeated success has more than crowned the efforts of the Negro."[9] But Jones rapidly fell from leadership and left Chicago under clouded circumstances. In 1908, he was reported in Kansas, facing a bigamy charge.[10]

Another businessman who espoused the self-help ideology was Sandy W. Trice. Born in Tennessee, Trice came to Chicago in 1886 and worked for the Pullman Company and later for the Illinois Central Railroad. From 1905 until 1909, he operated a clothing store on State Street which, for a few years at least, enjoyed a measure of success.[11] Trice supported the Negro Business League and assisted Washington in trying to secure favorable press coverage in Chicago. In 1908, Trice acquired an interest in the faltering *Conservator* and ousted its anti-Tuskegee editor, J. Max Barber, previously junior editor of the militant, Atlanta-based *Voice of the Negro*. A year later, when the *Conservator* fell back into hostile hands, Trice appealed to Washington, through S. Laing Williams, for assistance in another attempt to secure a friendly editorial policy. Washington, however, preferred to allow the ailing newspaper to die a natural death.[12]

By 1910, Chicago's leading Negro businessman was Jesse Binga,

[8] Reverdy Ransom, *The Pilgrimage of Harriet Ransom's Son* (Nashville: Sunday School Union, [1950?]), pp. 81–82.

[9] Quoted in *Broad Ax*, January 27, 1906; see also S. Laing Williams to Booker T. Washington, October 4, 1905, Washington Papers; Harold Gosnell, *Negro Politicians: The Rise of Negro Politics in Chicago* (Chicago: University of Chicago Press, 1935), pp. 82–83; Buckler, *Doctor Dan*, pp. 69–70; and *Appeal* (St. Paul), April 27, May 4, August 24, 1901.

[10] *Chicago Record-Herald*, October 11, 1908.

[11] *Chicago Whip*, July 17, 1920; and see chap. 6.

[12] S. Laing Williams to Booker T. Washington, March 10, 1908; Washington to Williams, March 16, 1908; Williams to Washington, July 6, 1909; Williams to Washington, September 9, 1909; Washington to Williams, September 15, 1909—Washington Papers. On Barber, see Meier, *Negro Thought*

a prosperous real estate agent and banker. Binga was to hold his position of preeminence for another twenty years and to become, more than any other Chicagoan, a symbol of the new business class. Born in Detroit in 1865, he left high school in his third year and wandered through the West as an itinerant barber before settling in Chicago in the mid-1890's. For a short time he worked as a huckster. In 1898, he opened a real estate office on State Street and within a few years became one of the wealthiest Negroes in the city. In 1908, he established the Binga Bank, which was to become one of the most celebrated Negro business ventures in the United States.[13]

Jesse Binga, a bluff, rough-hewn, single-minded businessman, had neither the time nor the inclination to involve himself in conflicts over racial ideology. His civic activities were mere extensions of his business interests. He belonged to the Negro Business League but had little interest in its self-congratulatory testimonial meetings. In his one major effort for the League, he chaired the Grand August Carnival and Negro Exposition in 1912, designed to "show our possibilities both industrially and otherwise."[14] In the same year, Binga added to his personal fortune by marrying Eudora Johnson, who had inherited $200,000 from her brother, John "Mushmouth" Johnson, the first of Chicago's long line of Negro gambling lords. The wedding demonstrated the extent to which the new businessmen were replacing the old elite as Chicago's social leaders. The affair was described as "the most elaborate and the most fashionable wedding ever held in the history of the Afro-American race in this city . . . or in any other section of the country. . . . The old settlers and society belles and matrons vied with each other in admiration of the grandeur of the surroundings and occasion."[15]

---

in America, pp. 211–12. The *Conservator* died a lingering death between 1900 and 1910. None of its editors lasted more than a few months and its editorial policy veered wildly from one position to another. Unfortunately, only scattered copies from this period are extant.

[13] Inez V. Cantey, "Jesse Binga," *Crisis*, 34 (December, 1927): 329, 350, 352; Junius B. Wood, *The Negro in Chicago* (Chicago: *Chicago Daily News*, 1916), pp. 11–12; *Chicago Defender*, November 5, 1910; *Broad Ax*, November 3, 1907.

[14] *Broad Ax*, August 10, August 17, August 31, 1912.

[15] *Defender*, February 24, 1912; *Broad Ax*, February 24, 1912.

The Binga-Johnson marriage also illustrated the rising status of another segment of Chicago Negro society—the "shadies," of whom "Mushmouth" Johnson was the first to rise to prominence. A native of St. Louis with little formal education, Johnson began his career about 1880 as a porter in a white gambling house. After learning the business, he opened his own establishment on State Street and made a fortune. "While my family went in for religion and all that," he said, "I didn't exactly fancy so much book learning and went out to see where the money grew. Some of those who know me say that I found it."[16] Despite his preoccupation with making money, Johnson supported "race advancement" and contributed to many Negro causes. His unsavory reputation and uncouth demeanor, however, offended the more respectable leaders, especially the old elite, and he was forced to carry on most of his civic work through others. His mother, for instance, contributed money for him to the Baptist Church, and other relatives used part of his fortune to aid in the establishment of the Old Peoples Home.[17] Johnson died in 1907, five years before his sister's brilliant marriage.

Johnson's successors, and even some of his contemporaries, had less difficulty in gaining respectability. Pony Moore, for instance, whose elegant saloon and gambling house on East Twenty-first Street flourished until 1905, participated regularly in the activities of the Negro Business League.[18] Robert T. Motts, who succeeded "Mushmouth" Johnson as gambling lord of the South Side, was openly regarded as a community leader. During a police crackdown on gambling in 1905, Motts expanded his operations by opening the Pekin Theater, which featured a lively fare of ragtime, cakewalks, and "coon songs." Proudly billed as "the only Negro owned theater in the world," the Pekin became one of the show places of the South Side.[19] Like all gambling lords, Motts developed a close working relationship with the police and the politicians and used his influence to secure jobs for Negroes. His

[16] Quoted by Gosnell, *Negro Politicians*, p. 126.

[17] Gosnell, *Negro Politicians*, pp. 125–27; *Broad Ax*, November 7, 1903.

[18] *Broad Ax*, November 18, 1905, August 10, 1907.

[19] *Whip*, May 8, May 15, May 22, 1920.

death in 1911 occasioned community-wide mourning: four thousand attended his funeral.[20]

After 1911, the leader of the South Side's flourishing gambling industry was a resourceful saloonkeeper, Henry "Teenan" Jones. Born in Alabama, Jones grew up in downstate Illinois and came to Chicago at the age of sixteen. After drifting from one odd job to another, he established a saloon and gambling house in Hyde Park in 1895. His Lakeside Club, catering primarily to whites, prospered for fifteen years before being driven out of business by a neighborhood reform group. Jones then moved his operations to the black belt where his two State Street saloons, the Elite #1 and the Elite #2, became centers of Negro night life between 1910 and 1915. Like his predecessors, he was active in civic and political affairs. He patronized Negro cultural and athletic enterprises and used both his influence and his financial resources to help aspiring Negro politicians. Although he was suspended by the Masons for his "shady" activities, he generally enjoyed the esteem of the community. Clearly, the standards of respectability of an earlier era were falling before the new ideal of economic achievement.[21]

The politicians shared many of the characteristics of the business leadership. Prior to the 1890's, there was no separate Negro political organization, nor was the Negro community large enough to serve as a base for electoral support. John Jones, Edward Morris, Ferdinand Barnett, and Theodore Jones won political office by working within the general Republican organization and enlisting white support. These men were not primarily politicians, but businessmen and lawyers who engaged in politics as a sideline. As community leaders, they treated politics as an extension of their civic activities.

Between 1900 and 1915, however, a new group of political leaders emerged—the men who were to dominate Negro political life

[20] Gosnell, *Negro Politicians*, pp. 127–28; *Broad Ax*, July 15, 1911 (obituary); Arna Bontemps and Jack Conroy, *They Seek a City* (Garden City, N.Y.: Doubleday, Doran & Company, 1945), pp. 96–97.

[21] *Defender*, May 8, 1915; Henry Brown, "Chicago's Night Life of Former Years," *Abbott's Monthly* (Chicago), 4 (July, 1930): 4–6, 45; Gosnell, *Negro Politicians*, pp. 128–30; Proceedings of the 44th Annual Communication of the Most Worshipful Prince Hall Grand Lodge Ancient, Free and Accepted Masons of the State of Illinois and Jurisdiction, Peoria, 1910, pp. 62–63.

in Chicago until the 1930's. Unlike their predecessors, they were professional politicians, who made their reputations in politics and devoted all of their talent and energy to political careers. They built a political machine based in the Negro community and dealt with white politicians, not as party retainers seeking favors, nor as spokesmen for a special interest group, but as political powers in their own right. The Negro political machine emerged fully during and after World War I, but it made a significant beginning during the prewar years.

Foremost among the professional politicians of the early twentieth century was Edward H. Wright, later Chicago's first Negro ward committeeman. Born in New York, Wright came to Chicago in the mid-1880's at the age of twenty. He had enough influence in the Republican party by 1894 to play an instrumental role in securing the nomination of Theodore Jones for county commissioner. Two years later, Wright himself was elected to the commission, a post he held for two terms. He made an unsuccessful bid for election to the city council in 1910, but polled enough votes to demonstrate the potential strength of a Negro candidate on the South Side. Wright used this demonstration of power as a springboard from which to launch a campaign for Negro representation that culminated in the election of a Negro alderman in 1915 and Wright's own election as Second Ward committeeman in 1920.[22] Wright was a full-time politician who rarely involved himself in civic affairs outside politics. His one major avocational interest was the Appomattox Club, which he founded in 1900 as a rendezvous for Negro Republican politicians.[23]

No one benefited more from Wright's pioneer efforts than Oscar De Priest, Chicago's first Negro alderman and later the first Negro to be elected to the United States Congress from the North. De Priest's career was a classic case of the poor southern Negro migrant who made good in the North. Born in Alabama, he came to Chicago in 1889 and worked as a house painter. Like Wright, he entered politics at the bottom, but by 1904 he had worked his way up to the county commission. From 1908 until 1915, he built up support in the Second Ward Republican organization and was

[22] Gosnell, *Negro Politicians*, pp. 153–56; *Broad Ax*, December 27, 1902; *Appeal*, November 12, 1898.

[23] *Whip*, July 6, 1929; *Defender*, June 26, 1920.

rewarded with an aldermanic nomination. De Priest was first of all a politician, but he also operated a lucrative real estate business and participated in the organization of the Chicago branch of the Negro Business League.[24]

At least two other politicians of note emerged before World War I. Robert R. Jackson, a lifelong Chicagoan, was born in 1870, left school in the eighth grade to work successively as a newsboy, bootblack, and postal employee, and finally established his own printing and publishing business. Ed Wright gave him his start in politics. By 1912, he had enough influence to win the nomination —and ultimately the election—to the state legislature.[25] Beauregard F. Moseley was also an active politician from an early age, but he remained a lawyer and businessman and a warm supporter of cooperative business ventures. Born in Georgia, he came to Chicago just after 1890. He lived in a predominantly white section of the city, but drew heavily upon the Negro community for his law practice and was retained as chief counsel by Olivet Baptist Church, the largest Negro congregation in the city. A charter member of the Appomattox Club, Moseley was a frequent speaker at Republican gatherings, a frequent and usually unsuccessful candidate for public office, and in 1912, one of the few Chicago Negroes to support the Progressive party.[26]

The newspaper editors also usually allied themselves with the new business class. Unlike other businessmen and unlike the politicians, the editors were compelled by the nature of their occupation to speak out on racial affairs, but they were not of one voice on matters of racial ideology. Like all Negro newspapermen, the Chicago editors faced a peculiar dilemma. As businessmen catering to a Negro market, they sympathized with those leaders who called upon Negroes to stand together in support of race enterprises. Yet the raison d'être of the Negro press was to protest prejudice and oppression. As a result, many editors combined the

[24] Gosnell, *Negro Politicians*, pp. 163–72; *Appeal*, August 24, 1901.

[25] *Whip*, July 6, 1929; transcript of interview with Jackson in "The Negro in Illinois," a file of reports and interviews compiled by the Illinois Writers Project of the Works Progress Administration (George Cleveland Hall Branch of the Chicago Public Library), cited hereafter as Illinois Writers Project Files.

[26] *Broad Ax*, March 30, 1901, December 27, 1902, June 22, August 3, 1912; Gosnell, *Negro Politicians*, p. 130.

doctrine of self-help with the militant protest technique of the old elite.

Two leading Chicago journalists stood squarely in the Tuskegee camp. Cyrus Field Adams was a close associate of Booker T. Washington. Born in Louisville, Adams moved to St. Paul in 1885 to help his brother, John Quincy Adams, edit a weekly newspaper, the *Western Appeal*. In 1888, the brothers opened a Chicago office of their journal with Cyrus as its manager. The *Appeal* maintained its Chicago office until 1913 and, although it remained a St. Paul newspaper, printed Chicago news, sought subscriptions and advertisements in Chicago, and for a few years billed itself as a joint Chicago–St. Paul publication.[27]

The *Appeal*, always pro-Washington, hailed the Tuskegee leader as "the Moses of his people" as early as 1897.[28] Cyrus Adams participated in Washington-dominated organizations on both the national and local levels. He served as transportation agent of the National Negro Business League and president of the National Afro-American Press Association. As secretary of the Afro-American Council in 1903, he worked for the Tuskegee forces in their successful battle to maintain control of the organization and to re-elect T. Thomas Fortune as president. With Washington's support, he secured an appointment as Assistant Registrar of the Treasury in 1901.[29] Yet Adams also had occasional praise for Du Bois and insisted that "there is no contradiction between Washington's theories and the words of the cultivated advocate of higher education." He felt that "Washington's teachings have evidently been misunderstood" by Du Bois, for "nowhere has Mr. Washington advised his people to give up their rights."[30]

W. Allison Sweeney, a peripatetic journalist who had edited the Indianapolis *Freeman* before coming to Chicago, was another Washington satellite. In 1903, Washington toyed with the idea of

[27] *Appeal*, February 3, 1900; August Meier, "Negro Racial Thought in the Age of Booker T. Washington," unpublished doctoral dissertation, Columbia University, 1957, pp. 474–75; for the *Appeal*'s activities in Chicago see the issues of January 28 and February 25, 1888, January 4, 1890, and March 22, 1912. Established as the *Western Appeal*, the paper changed its name to the *Appeal* after the first few years.

[28] *Appeal*, July 3, 1897.

[29] *Ibid.*, January 12, 1901; Meier, "Negro Racial Thought," pp. 474–75.

[30] *Appeal*, June 13, 1903.

financing a pro-Tuskegee newspaper in Chicago, and Sweeney sought the editorship. But Washington evidently mistrusted Sweeney and the project never materialized.[31] The next year, however, Sweeney obtained control of the *Conservator* and for a few months converted that normally anti-Tuskegee paper into a Washington organ.[32] In 1905, he launched his own newspaper, the *Chicago Leader*, which, despite an attractive format and a range of features unusual for a Negro paper of its day, folded after two years of publication.[33]

During the same month in 1905 that the ill-fated *Leader* commenced publication, another small Negro weekly made its debut. Calling itself the *Chicago Defender*, this little four-page sheet was destined to revolutionize Negro journalism. The *Defender* was the brain child of Robert S. Abbott, whose career was a model of Negro business achievement and self-advancement. Abbott was born on St. Simon's Island, off the coast of Georgia, and learned the printing trade at Hampton Institute. He came to Chicago in 1897, studied at Kent College of Law, and, after an unsuccessful attempt to earn a living as an attorney, went into the job printing business. He launched the *Defender* in 1905 with a total capital of twenty-five cents and an initial press run of three hundred copies.[34]

Abbott never firmly aligned himself with either school of racial thought. The *Defender* was always friendly to Washington personally, and in 1908, S. Laing Williams told Washington that Abbott was safely in the Tuskegee camp.[35] Abbott clearly disliked the "talented tenth" theory of W. E. B. Du Bois and often attacked Du Bois's haughty, aristocratic mien.[36] Moreover he was a firm

[31] Meier, "Negro Racial Thought," pp. 605–6; August Meier, "Booker T. Washington and the Negro Press," *Journal of Negro History* (Washington), 38 (January, 1953): 75.

[32] For evidence of the *Conservator*'s position under Sweeney, see Booker T. Washington to S. Laing Williams, July 9, 1904, and Williams to Washington, July 14, 1904, Washington Papers.

[33] *Appeal*, May 27, 1905; S. Laing Williams to Booker T. Washington, January 30, 1908, Washington Papers.

[34] Roi Ottley, *The Lonely Warrior: The Life and Times of Robert S. Abbott* (Chicago: Henry Regnery & Company, 1955), pp. 17–99.

[35] S. Laing Williams to Booker T. Washington, January 30, 1908, Washington Papers; see also Ottley, *The Lonely Warrior*, pp. 124–27.

[36] See for example, *Defender*, March 7, 1914.

believer in race pride and race solidarity: on one occasion, he attacked the NAACP for its predominantly white leadership.[37] Yet Abbott's *Defender* was the most militant Negro newspaper in Chicago and its pleas for racial justice and equal rights were as radical as those of the most avowedly anti-Tuskegee organ. "Why Fight for Flag Whose Folds Do Not Protect?" the *Defender* asked rhetorically on the eve of World War I.[38] And during one of Chicago's many housing incidents, the *Defender* advised a Negro family whose home had been besieged by whites to arm themselves and "be prepared to fight and fight to kill."[39]

Perhaps the severest critic of Booker T. Washington in Chicago was Julius F. Taylor, the free-swinging editor of the *Broad Ax*. A maverick who totally defies categorization, Taylor came to Chicago in 1899, moving his four-year-old newspaper with him from Salt Lake City. Taylor was a western Democrat and strong supporter of William Jennings Bryan, and he expounded a doctrine of economic radicalism that was unusual among the Negroes of his day.[40] Taylor's other specialty was "preacher-baiting." An avowed non-believer, he sharply criticized the leading Negro ministers in the city and attacked clergymen who used their pulpits as political forums.[41] Taylor was never an influential figure in Chicago, as his views were too heretical and his methods of character assassination too unsavory. But his brand of personal polemics kept Chicago Negro leaders in a perpetual state of apoplexy. Taylor customarily branded anyone he disliked as a drunk, adulterer, or thief.[42]

Next to the preachers, Booker T. Washington and his Chicago followers occupied the prime position in Taylor's demonology. An ardent Democrat, Taylor resented Washington's involvement in Republican politics. He regularly referred to Washington as "the greatest white man's 'Nigger' in the world," and "the Great Beggar

[37] *Ibid.*, March 1, 1913.   [38] *Ibid.*, March 14, 1914.

[39] *Ibid.*, February 11, 1911.

[40] See for example, *Broad Ax*, April 7, 1906, or any issue in 1899.

[41] For example, Taylor's attacks on Archibald J. Carey, *Broad Ax*, September 13, 1902, September 12, 1903.

[42] For an amusing account of Carey's reaction to Taylor's attack, see Joseph Logsdon, "Reverend A. J. Carey and the Negro in Chicago Politics," unpublished master's thesis, University of Chicago, 1961, pp. 27–29.

of Tuskegee."[43] After 1910, however, he adopted a friendlier tone toward Washington and began to print news releases from Tuskegee and the national self-help organizations. Taylor explained his change of heart by arguing that Washington had moderated his political partisanship and was devoting himself more exclusively to educational matters.[44] But possibly Washington exerted pressure through one of his Chicago friends to halt the unfavorable publicity Taylor had been giving him.[45] In any case, the *Broad Ax* lost its verve and, although published until 1931, declined steadily after World War I.

Both the old elite and the new middle-class leaders responded to external pressures: the rising tide of white hostility and the segregation and discrimination it produced. Their responses reflected both ideological beliefs and personal interests. The older leaders, who retained an uncompromising commitment to integration, had the most to lose in a segregated society. Their business, professional, political, and social circles had included whites and they wanted to maintain their associations with White Chicago. The new leaders, who accepted the philosophy of self-help and racial solidarity, on the other hand, stood to benefit from separate Negro development. Their economic and political endeavors depended upon the support of a cohesive, concentrated Negro community. To suggest a link between ideology and interest does not imply that these men were cynics. But their positions on racial matters were conditioned by their circumstances, and their ideas in turn influenced the subsequent course of community development.

[43] *Broad Ax,* May 16, October 3, 1903, July 4, 1908, July 17, 1909, April 23, 1910.

[44] See for example, Taylor's coverage of the 1912 Negro Business League convention, *Broad Ax,* August 24, August 31, 1912.

[45] Helen Buckler suggests that Dan Williams was "lining up the *Broad Ax*" for Washington before his break with Tuskegee in 1907, but there is no evidence of a change in Taylor's editorial policy until after 1910. *Doctor Dan,* p. 234. Saunders Redding maintains that Fannie Barrier Williams won Taylor over to the Tuskegee camp when she was wooing Washington on her husband's behalf. But Williams got his job in 1908, so again the dates do not coincide. *The Lonesome Road* (Garden City, N.Y.: Anchor Books, 1958), pp. 168, 202. Meier describes Washington's methods of securing newspaper support ("Booker T. Washington and the Negro Press," pp. 67–90) but makes no mention of the *Broad Ax.*

The rhetoric of Chicago's Negro leadership in the early twentieth century frequently seemed to reflect the national debate between Booker T. Washington and W. E. B. Du Bois. And the lines were frequently drawn on the basis of this ideological feud. Yet, it would be misleading to suppose that developments in Chicago were simply national developments in microcosm. The new leaders emerged in Chicago in response to local conditions and problems. The self-help ideology has periodically gained ascendancy in times of mounting white hostility; Booker T. Washington did not invent it, he merely gave it vogue. So too in Chicago, the adherents of self-help and racial unity replaced the proponents of militant protest as the city's color line hardened and the prospects for integration grew dimmer. Washington's dominance of Negro affairs forced many Chicago Negro leaders to devote much of their time and energy to support or oppose the Tuskegee leadership. But their prime concern was the future of the Negro community in Chicago.

The ideological conflict produced only sporadic attempts to establish racial action organizations. These organizational efforts usually resulted in ad hoc committees, formed to handle a particular grievance, but rarely lasting more than a few months. In 1906, for instance, Negroes throughout the country were infuriated by the incident at Brownsville, Texas. A group of armed men "shot up" the town, and white residents quickly blamed Negro soldiers who were stationed at a local post. Some of the soldiers apparently had been involved, but none would confess and no positive identification could be made. Nevertheless, President Theodore Roosevelt approved an order to discharge all of the soldiers without honor, including many with long and distinguished military records.[46] In Chicago, a white group seriously aggravated the situation by inviting Senator Ben Tillman to the city to lecture on the affair. A committee of Negro leaders, headed by Archibald J. Carey, held an indignation meeting at Bethel Church where Carey "preached a highly sensational sermon . . . to an overflowing audience; . . . every

[46] Emma Lou Thornbrough, "The Brownsville Episode and the Negro Vote," *Mississippi Valley Historical Review* (Cedar Rapids, Iowa), 44 (December, 1957): 470.

point of attack against the president was cheered to the echo."[47] The committee then called on Mayor Dunne urging him to prevent Tillman from speaking in Chicago. The mayor was unable to halt the Senator's appearance, but he refused to preside over the meeting.[48]

In 1903, several integrationist leaders attempted to establish a protest association on a more permanent level. The Equal Opportunity League was formed as a reaction to "a seeming desire on the part of a certain class of citizens to separate the Afro-American pupils in the public schools from the whites." Although the legal segregation of the schools was not imminent, the organizers of the league—Edward Morris, Charles Bentley, James Madden, Ferdinand Barnett, Edward Wilson, and John G. Jones—"deemed it necessary to call a meeting and, by registering a strong protest, forestall any move in that direction by the school board."[49] The establishment of the organization coincided with a statewide meeting in Springfield to organize the Equal Rights and Protective League of Illinois. Anti-Tuskegee men dominated both the Chicago delegation to the state meeting and the local league. At Springfield, they attempted to write into the platform a clause critical of Washington but were met with opposition from downstate delegates.[50] At home, they sponsored an address by W. E. B. Du Bois and functioned for over a year as the voice of militant protest in Chicago.[51] But the group's leaders were unable to sustain interest, and within two years the League was dead.

In 1905, two members of the Equal Opportunity League, Charles Bentley and James Madden, attended the first Niagara conference in Ontario. Upon their return, they established an Illinois branch of the Niagara movement, which attempted to carry on the work of the ill-fated League. Again, their first major task was to respond to a threat of school segregation. In 1906,

[47] S. Laing Williams to Booker T. Washington, November 26, 1906, Washington Papers.

[48] *Broad Ax*, November 24, December 1, 1906.

[49] *Appeal*, October 24, 1903; see also *Broad Ax*, December 19, 1903, January 29, 1905.

[50] *Appeal*, October 17, 1903.

[51] *Broad Ax*, December 19, 1903, January 29, 1905.

the group played a key role in securing the appointment of a
Negro to the New Chicago Charter Commission, which, according to reports, was considering a clause in the charter permitting
segregated schools. Members of the branch also protested when
Thomas Dixon's play, *The Clansman*, opened in Chicago; with
the help of Jane Addams, they induced the city's drama critics
to ignore the production. With the decline of the Niagara movement nationally after 1908, however, the Illinois branch atrophied and died.[52]

The Tuskegee group considered such protest activities futile.
S. Laing Williams, writing to Booker T. Washington at the time
of the Brownsville affair, said that he had been invited to par-
ticipate in the protest but had refused because "I do not believe in indignation meetings and do not feel like criticizing
the president unless he does something wholly wrong and in the
spirit of race hatred."[53] Washington replied:

> I very much fear that these frequent meetings held by these
> agitators is hurting us tremendously in the North. . . . If
> our people would have a meeting once in a while for the
> purpose of starting a bank, insurance company or building
> a railroad or opening a coal mine it would be far different,
> but practically every time the white man hears from the
> Negro in an organized capacity it is in connection with a
> meeting of condemnation or protest.[54]

The new middle-class leaders attempted to organize along the
lines Washington suggested. In 1901, the National Negro Business League held its second annual convention in Chicago and
provided an impetus for local leaders to form a Chicago branch
of the League. Theodore Jones spearheaded the drive and
gathered around him a group of businessmen including Lloyd
Wheeler and Oscar De Priest.[55] The League operated sporadically

[52] Elliott M. Rudwick, "The Niagara Movement," *Journal of Negro History,*
42 (July, 1957): 187.

[53] S. Laing Williams to Booker T. Washington, November 26, 1906, Washington Papers.

[54] Booker T. Washington to S. Laing Williams, December 3, 1906, Washington Papers.

[55] *Appeal,* April 27, August 24, 1901.

for several years as a semiofficial mouthpiece for Booker T. Washington, sponsoring the principal's visit to Chicago in 1904.[56] But it never made a real impact on the city's Negro community. S. Laing Williams was forced to admit in 1909 that "most of the more prosperous men here are indifferent and fail to co-operate."[57] When the national organization met in Chicago for the second time, in 1912, the local branch was almost moribund. The League's lack of a concrete program for business cooperation was probably the major cause of its failure.

By the end of the prewar era, the most important racial defense organization in the city was the Chicago branch of the National Association for the Advancement of Colored People. The NAACP was founded in New York in 1909 by a group of white progressives, headed by Mary White Ovington and William English Walling, and it soon attracted many of the Negro militants who had been allied with the Niagara movement. Within a year after its establishment, the NAACP sponsored a meeting in Chicago, which featured as speakers such prominent whites as Jane Addams and Rabbi Emil Hirsch as well as several local Negro leaders. Early in 1911, the national office sent an organizer to Chicago and by the end of the year a local branch had been established, which served as host to the Association's third annual conference in 1912.[58]

The NAACP differed from previous racial action organizations in Chicago. Primarily a legal and legislative action association dedicated to equal rights and integration, the group was avowedly interracial and in its early years was dominated by white progressives. Just five of the twelve members of the organizing committee were Negroes and the first president was Judge Edward O. Brown, a white man. Of the men and women who played leading roles during the first few years, only two,

[56] *Broad Ax*, April 9, 1904; S. Laing Williams to Booker T. Washington, March 28, 1904, Washington Papers.

[57] S. Laing Williams to Booker T. Washington, July 12, 1909, Washington Papers.

[58] Minutes of the Executive Committee, National Association for the Advancement of Colored People (National Office, NAACP, New York, N.Y.), November 29, 1910, May 2, November 14, 1911, January 4, 1912; *Defender*, January 20, 1912.

Charles Bentley and George Hall, were Negroes.[59] White leadership in the NAACP ran counter to the growing emphasis on
self-help and racial solidarity and led to criticism of the organization by Negroes. "It is strange indeed," declared the *Broad
Ax*, "that an association or combination, which is supposed to
be gotten up in the interests of the Colored People should be
absolutely controlled in every particular by those belonging to
an opposite race."[60] The *Defender* concurred: "The Society for
the Advancement of Colored People to accomplish much good
must enroll more citizens who are close to the needs and troubles
of colored people in being colored themselves."[61]

During its first years, the Chicago NAACP worked to defeat
several discriminatory bills before the state legislature—most of
which had been introduced by downstate legislators. Boxer Jack
Johnson's marriage to a white woman led to a rash of proposals
for legislation barring interracial marriage, and one southern
Illinois representative even introduced a Jim Crow streetcar bill.
A railroad employees' bill, introduced by progressives and supported by the Brotherhood of Railway Trainmen, would have required railroads to replace Negro porters, who often doubled
as flagmen, with full-time white flagmen who belonged to the
Brotherhood. None of the bills passed, although it is unlikely
that the NAACP played a critical role in their defeat. The
intermarriage and streetcar bills were doomed from the start,
and the railroad companies played the major role in blocking
the full crew bill.[62] The NAACP also sought to broaden the state
civil rights law and, in 1915, led the effort to ban the showing
of *The Birth of a Nation* in Chicago.[63]

[59] *Defender*, January 20, 1912; *Crisis*, 6 (May, 1913): 38–39; *Crisis*, 7
(February, 1914): 249.

[60] *Broad Ax*, February 1, 1913.   [61] *Defender*, March 1, 1913.

[62] *Crisis*, 6 (May, 1913): 38–39; *Crisis*, 6 (June, 1913): 71; *Crisis*, 6 (July,
1913): 144; Minutes of the Executive Committee, NAACP, March 11, 1913,
January 5, 1914.

[63] *Crisis*, 8 (July, 1914): 141–42; *Crisis*, 10 (June, 1915): 85–86, 88; Julius
Rosenwald to William C. Graves, April 6, 1915; Graves to Rosenwald, April
9, 1915; Graves to Rosenwald, April 16, 1915; Graves to Rosenwald, April 20,
1915; Rosenwald to Mayor William H. Thompson, May 15, 1915; Emmett J.
Scott to Graves, June 11, 1915, Julius Rosenwald Papers (University of
Chicago Library), cited hereafter as Rosenwald Papers.

Despite some early successes, the Chicago NAACP was faltering by 1915. It still claimed over three hundred members, but, like many branches throughout the country, it suffered from inadequate leadership and an inability to sustain the interest of its members. Julius Rosenwald had pledged 25 per cent of the annual budget, but the pledge was not claimed after 1914, and the branch did not even present a report at the 1915 national conference.[64]

Given the ideological debate over Negro goals, the rise of a new leadership class, and the growing size of the Chicago Negro community, it seems strange that the racial action organizations had such limited success. Several conditions in the community, however, crippled their efforts. First, despite the growing Negro population of Chicago, the leadership class remained small. The men and women discussed in this and the preceding chapter, while not the only Negro leaders in Chicago, constituted a remarkably high percentage of those who could be counted upon in organizational work. Their names appear repeatedly in the accounts of community affairs. Since the Negro masses had little interest in these activities, not enough people were willing to work for racial action groups. Secondly, not only were Negro organizations small, but they also lacked qualified leaders. Professional Negro leaders had not yet appeared in Chicago; all of the organizations depended entirely upon volunteers. Even the NAACP, which had a larger budget than the all-Negro organizations, was unable to hire an executive secretary until 1920. Finally, many Negro leaders in Chicago, particularly the new middle-class leaders, were more interested in the development of community institutions, businesses, and political organizations than in racial advancement associations. For this reason, the main threads of Chicago Negro history in the prewar years can be seen most clearly, not in the activities of racial organizations, but in the development of institutional life on the South Side.

[64] William C. Graves to Julius Rosenwald, January 26, 1920, Rosenwald Papers. Minutes of the Executive Committee, NAACP, January 12, 1915; National Association for the Advancement of Colored People, *Annual Report, 1915*, pp. 17–18, 31.

CHAPTER 5

THE INSTITUTIONAL GHETTO

The rise of the new middle-class leadership was closely inter-related with the development of Chicago's black ghetto. White hostility and population growth combined to create the physical ghetto on the South Side. The response of Negro leadership, on the other hand, created the institutional ghetto. Between 1900 and 1915, Chicago's Negro leaders built a complex of community organizations, institutions, and enterprises that made the South Side not simply an area of Negro concentration but a city within a city. Chicago's tightening color bar encouraged the development of a new economic and political leadership with its primary loyalty to a segregated Negro community. By meeting discrimination with self-help rather than militant protest, this leadership converted the dream of an integrated city into the vision of a "black metropolis."

The oldest and most stable Negro institution in Chicago was the church. The first Negro church in the city, Quinn Chapel A.M.E., was founded in 1847, just fourteen years after Chicago was incorporated. By the end of the century, Chicago had over a dozen Negro churches, and between 1900 and 1915 doubled this number. The majority of these churches were affiliated with the two largest Negro denominations—African Methodist Episcopal and Baptist—and were controlled and supported exclusively by Negroes from the beginning. New churches opened as the community grew and as perpetual dissension within the established congregations resulted in schisms. Most of the Baptist churches were offshoots of Olivet, the oldest and largest Negro Baptist church in the city, while the A.M.E. churches were generally founded by dissident parishioners from Quinn Chapel and Bethel Church.[1]

[1] The most complete source of information on the history of individual churches is the material on churches in "The Negro in Illinois," a file of

The large Baptist and A.M.E. churches generally drew upon the middle class for leadership and financial support.[2] Although by no means abandoning all elements of traditional emotionalism, they appealed to middle-class respectability by conducting decorous, dignified services. The Rev. Elijah Fisher, for example, who served at Olivet Baptist Church from 1903 until 1915, "believed in enthusiastic religion but did not countenance a church in demoniac pandemonium."[3] The large churches were also expanding their secular programs to resemble those of middle-class white urban churches. They no longer concerned themselves solely with matters of the spirit. By 1905, Olivet boasted a complete roster of girls' clubs, boys' clubs, athletic activities, and a literary society, and three years later it sponsored a program for the relief of the unemployed.[4] As early as 1902, Quinn Chapel operated a kindergarten, reading room and library, savings bank, and employment bureau.[5] The Sunday evening forum, pioneered by Reverdy Ransom at Bethel Church, became a familiar feature of many of the more solidly established Chicago

---

reports and interviews compiled by the Illinois Writers Project of the Works Progress Administration (George Cleveland Hall Branch of the Chicago Public Library), cited hereafter as Illinois Writers Project Files. Most of these data are based on interviews with ministers and lay leaders, but the files also include some souvenir booklets and anniversary programs that contain historical sketches of particular churches. Some of this material has been synthesized in St. Clair Drake, "Churches and Voluntary Associations in the Chicago Negro Community," Report of Official Project 465-54-3-386, Works Progress Administration, mimeographed (Chicago, 1940), pp. 29–164. For a discussion of nineteenth century churches and their ministers, see *Chicago Tribune,* November 19, 1893.

[2] Richard R. Wright, Jr., "The Industrial Condition of Negroes In Chicago," unpublished B. D. thesis, University of Chicago Divinity School, 1901, pp. 14–15.

[3] Miles Mark Fisher, *The Master's Slave: Elijah John Fisher, a Biography* (Philadelphia: Judson Press, 1922), pp. 87–88.

[4] Miles Mark Fisher, "History of Olivet Baptist Church of Chicago," unpublished master's thesis, University of Chicago, 1922, pp. 70–71; see also Olivet Baptist Church, Souvenir Booklet, 1926, and Greetings of Olivet Baptist Church, 72nd Anniversary, 1922, in Illinois Writers Project Files.

[5] *Chicago Inter-Ocean,* July 21, 1902; see also items on the history of Quinn Chapel in *Appeal* (St. Paul), November 22, 1890, and July 23, 1898; and the souvenir programs, Quinn Chapel A.M.E. Church, 1847–1947, Centennial Celebration, June 20–27, 1947, and 110th Anniversary, 1957.

churches.[6] Hence, these churches maintained their preeminence by offering a worship service that appealed to a broad, middle stratum of the Negro community, and by expanding their social, intellectual, and athletic activities.

Yet the large, established churches were not able to attract all segments of the increasingly stratified Negro community. On the one hand, many sophisticated upper- and middle-class Negroes were no longer content with traditional Negro religion and sought other forms of religious expression. Julius F. Taylor expressed in exaggerated form the discontent that a growing minority felt about the churches. He wrote in one of his typical anticlerical tirades:

> If we possessed the power, we would abolish or do away with Negro churches and establish in their stead ethical culture societies. . . . How long! Oh how long! will the Negro continue to erect costly and expensive temples unto the Gods, while his children are growing up in rags and tatters and in ignorance, and while poverty and squalor surrounds him on every hand.[7]

The old line churches had even greater difficulty in holding the lowest stratum of Negro society—the poor and the ignorant and, especially, the recent migrants from the South. A survey of 398 persons in a lower-class precinct in 1901 showed that well over one-half had no church affiliations and a disproportionate number of those who belonged were women.[8] Many poor Negroes could not afford church membership, while others were alienated by the predominantly middle-class outlook of the large churches. Although such churches as Quinn Chapel, Bethel, and Olivet continued to dominate Chicago Negro religious life down to 1915, they faced competition from churches appealing to special segments of the population.

During the late nineteenth century, some educated and relatively affluent Negroes gravitated to churches affiliated with the

[6] Reverdy Ransom, *The Pilgrimage of Harriet Ransom's Son* (Nashville, Tenn.: Sunday School Union [1950?]), pp. 82–83; *Appeal,* May 11, 1901; R. E. Moore, *History of Bethel A.M.E. Church* (Chicago: privately printed, 1915).

[7] *Broad Ax* (Chicago), January 25, 1902.

[8] Wright, "The Industrial Condition of Negroes in Chicago," pp. 14–15.

major white denominations—Presbyterian, Episcopalian, Methodist, Episcopal, Congregational, and Roman Catholic—which offered more sophisticated worship services than the traditional Negro churches. By 1900, all of these denominations had attempted to organize among Chicago's Negroes and all except the Congregationalists had been successful. Grace Presbyterian, St. Thomas Episcopal, and St. Mark's Methodist churches boasted among their membership many of the most prominent Negroes in Chicago. Emanuel Congregational Church, founded in the 1880's, was unable to maintain itself, but Lincoln Memorial Congregational Church, established in 1909, became a permanent part of the religious life of the South Side. Unlike the A.M.E. and Baptist churches, these congregations began with white support. St. Mark's grew out of white Methodist missionary efforts. St. Thomas was the offshoot of a white Episcopal church and received white aid even though the bishop thought that the schism would "needlessly establish a color line where none in fact existed."[9] Grace was established by Negro Presbyterians from Tennessee and Kentucky, but was supported in part by white Presbyterians for a decade. Lincoln Memorial received substantial assistance from the Chicago Congregational Missionary and Extension Society.[10]

St. Monica's Roman Catholic Church was a special type of white-affiliated Negro congregation. Like St. Thomas Episcopal Church, it was founded by Negro members of a white church who asked for their own parish "where they might retain and build up their faith which was beginning to be greatly hampered by the growing prejudice in the white church."[11] In 1889, Father Augustus Tolton, the first Negro priest to serve in the United States, came to Chicago to lead the Negro members of

[9] George R. Arthur, "St. Thomas Protestant Episcopal Church," church pamphlet, [no date].

[10] Histories of Grace, St. Thomas, St. Mark's, and Lincoln Memorial Churches in Illinois Writers Project Files; program of 66th Anniversary Tea, St. Thomas Church, 1878–1944, June 18, 1944; 40th Anniversary of Lincoln Memorial Congregational Church, 1909–1949, December 11–14, 1949; Drake, "Churches and Voluntary Associations," pp. 51–107; on St. Thomas, in addition to Arthur, cited above, see *Chicago Conservator*, November 18, 1882; and *Chicago Defender*, January 15, 1916.

[11] History of St. Monica's in Illinois Writers Project Files.

predominantly white St. Mary's Church. Three years later, the Negroes broke away and established their own church, St. Monica's. When Father Tolton died in 1897, St. Monica's reverted to the status of a mission and did not again have a full-time priest until 1910. The Catholic Church attracted some Negroes who sought a more dignified form of worship, but most of St. Monica's members were migrants from Catholic sections of the South, notably Louisiana. Unlike some Protestants, white Catholics in Chicago, most of whom were recent immigrants with adjustment problems of their own, made no significant effort to proselytize among Negroes.[12]

Another unusual church that made a special appeal to Negroes dissatisfied with traditional forms of religious life was the Institutional Church and Social Settlement, founded in 1900 by Reverdy Ransom. Institutional, under Ransom and his successor, Archibald Carey, developed a full program of social services that went well beyond the welfare activities of Quinn Chapel, Olivet, and Bethel. Ransom called Institutional "the first social settlement in the world" for the race and said that it was "not a church in the ordinary sense . . . [but] a Hull House or Chicago Commons founded by Negroes for the help of people of that race."[13] Some hostile Negro ministers told their congregations that Institutional was not a church at all and forbade them to take communion there.[14] Institutional operated a day nursery, a kindergarten, a mothers' club, an employment bureau, a print shop, and a fully equipped gymnasium; it offered a complete slate of club activities and classes in sewing, cooking, and music; its Forum featured lectures by leading white and Negro figures; and its facilities were always available for concerts, meetings, and other civic functions. The church attempted to draw from both segments of the community that were alienated from the old-line congregations. The wide range of social activities was

12 Illinois Writers Project Files; *Chicago Record-Herald*, April 7, 1910; *Appeal*, July 17, 1897 (obituary of Tolton); Marvin Schafer, "The Catholic Church in Chicago," unpublished doctoral dissertation, University of Chicago, 1929, pp. 43, 58–59; John T. Gillard, *The Catholic Church and the American Negro* (Baltimore, Md.: St. Joseph's Society Press, 1929), pp. 48, 85; interview with Dr. Arthur G. Falls, prominent Negro Catholic layman, March 19, 1963.

13 *Inter-Ocean*, July 29, 1900.

14 Ransom, *The Pilgrimage of Harriet Ransom's Son*, pp. 111–12.

designed to attract lower-class Negroes without church affilia-
tion and sophisticated Negroes who found Institutional's emphasis on a social gospel more appealing than the traditional
preoccupation with sin and salvation. For a time, under Ransom and Carey, the church thrived and seemed to provide a
meaningful answer to those who were critical of or indifferent
to the Negro church. But it was unable to survive the World
War I era. As secular agencies began to assume the social functions of Institutional, the church declined and eventually died.[15]

Another solution to the problem of attracting the unchurched—
one more portentous for the future—was the emergence of the
Holiness and Spiritualist churches. These little storefront congregations with their uninhibited worship and informal atmos-
phere were not yet the potent force that they were to become
during the migration era. But several were established in the first
decade of the twentieth century.[16] The Holy Nazarene Taber-
nacle Apostolic Church, for instance, was founded in 1908 by
Mattie L. Thornton. It secured its own building in 1909, held
camp meetings each summer, and even made an unsuccessful
attempt to establish a branch in New York.[17] By 1915, a Spiritualist congregation, the Church of Redemption of Souls, was
operating on State Street.[18]

The Negro churches of Chicago had from the beginning of
their history exemplified the self-help philosophy. Since the mid-
nineteenth century, Negroes had reacted against the hostility of
most white churches by organizing separate congregations where
they could manage their own affairs. The Negro churches, then,
were already self-sufficient by the end of the century and underwent no sudden or unprecedented changes between 1890 and
1915. But certain trends were apparent. The churches were
broadening their programs to include a wide range of social
activities. The large churches, dominated by the middle class,
were still the most important religious institutions in the community, but they now faced competition from new churches,

[15] Illinois Writers Project Files; *Inter-Ocean*, July 29, 1900; Ransom, *The
Pilgrimage of Harriet Ransom's Son*, pp. 93–135; Helen Buckler, *Doctor Dan*
(Boston: Houghton, Mifflin & Company, 1954), pp. 223–25.

[16] Drake, "Churches and Voluntary Associations," pp. 122, 148.

[17] *Defender*, May 17, July 12, 1913.

[18] *Ibid.*, August 28, 1915.

designed to meet the special needs of those at the upper and lower reaches of the social and economic spectrum. The migrations of the World War I period would rapidly accelerate these trends and profoundly change the religious life of the South Side.

Secular institutions in the Negro community were of more recent origin than the churches. Provident Hospital, established in 1891, was Chicago's first Negro civic institution. By the eve of World War I, the Chicago Negro community had perhaps a dozen social service institutions. Some of these were ephemeral while others became permanent fixtures of community life. Most were exclusively Negro institutions, operated by Negroes and intended for the use of the Negro community, although some received assistance from white philanthropists. Although the churches probably remained more important to the bulk of Chicago's Negroes, the secular institutions had become the major civic interest of Negro leaders by 1915.

Provident Hospital was the first and most ambitious Negro civic undertaking in Chicago and its history reveals in microcosm the major trends of community life on the South Side. Daniel Hale Williams, its proud and able founder, was continually rankled by the difficulties Negroes faced in the medical profession. Negro physicians found it almost impossible to secure internships and staff appointments at white hospitals, Negro women were unable to secure nurses' training courses, and Negro patients could not get private hospital rooms. But Williams, with his wide contacts among white medical men and his generally integrationist inclinations, did not want to establish a segregated Negro hospital. Such a project would separate Negroes from the mainstream of the medical profession and give white groups an additional reason for excluding Negroes from white hospitals and training schools.

In 1891, Williams called together a group of Negro community leaders and several of his white medical colleagues for the purpose of organizing the first interracial hospital in the United States. He reasoned that Negroes could operate a hospital just as European ethnic groups and religious denominations had sponsored hospitals in Chicago. Unlike any other hospital in the city, Provident would receive Negroes on an equal basis and provide opportunities for Negro doctors and nurses. But it would not be a hospital for Negroes alone. It would assemble an interracial staff drawn from the best medical talent in the city and admit patients of all races. Provident was to be a model, not of a Negro community institution, but of a venture in interracial cooperation.[19]

Although the Provident undertaking met with opposition from a few hard-line assimilationists, such as John G. Jones,[20] it had the support of most community leaders. It operated with an advisory board of prominent white Chicagoans—particularly medical men—a predominantly Negro board of trustees, and a large membership organization. Three months after incorporation, Provident opened with twelve beds in a small, poorly equipped flat building on South Dearborn Street. But it offered first-rate medical care: Williams' prestige drew to the hospital's staff such outstanding medical names as Frank Billings, Christian Fenger, and Ralph N. Isham, and the nursing school compared favorably with any in the city. Although Provident solicited and received financial contributions from the Negro community, its major support in the early years came from wealthy white Chicagoans, such as Philip Armour, H. H. Kohlsaat, and Florence Pullman. In 1896, the white philanthropists paid for a new sixty-five–bed hospital building further south on Dearborn Street. Kohlsaat bought the land, Armour erected the building, and George Pullman and Marshall Field purchased land for a new nursing school.[21] With the support of its white friends and a growing Negro community to serve, Provident Hospital prospered. By the end of the prewar period, it was on firm financial footing: entirely free of debt, it had an endowment of $50,000 and a plant valued at $125,000, handled a large number of charity cases, and trained twenty-five nurses a year.[22]

[19] The most complete account of the founding of Provident is in Buckler, *Doctor Dan,* pp. 66–84. But see also *Appeal,* April 18 and July 11, 1891; and Robert McMurdy to William C. Graves, December 30, 1912, Julius Rosenwald Papers (University of Chicago Library), cited hereafter as Rosenwald Papers.

[20] *Appeal,* March 21, April 11, April 18, 1891; and see chap. 3.

[21] Buckler, *Doctor Dan,* pp. 73–78, 82–84; Robert McMurdy to William C. Graves, May 24, 1913, Rosenwald Papers.

[22] Robert McMurdy to William C. Graves, December 30, 1912, Rosenwald Papers; Junius B. Wood, *The Negro in Chicago* (Chicago: *Chicago Daily News,* 1916), pp. 17–18.

The thriving hospital of 1915, however, bore little resemblance to Dan Williams' original conception of a truly interracial hospital. Increasing racial tension and Negro race pride had profoundly influenced Provident's development. The doctors and nurses who came out of Provident's internship program and training school could not, despite their qualifications, find positions at white hospitals. Some left Chicago to help found Negro hospitals elsewhere, but many stayed on at Provident. By 1916, all of the nurses except the supervisor and almost all of the staff physicians were Negroes.[23] Moreover, as Provident became a major focus of the civic and philanthropic life of the South Side, Negroes naturally came to regard it as their hospital. Despite the initial help of white philanthropists, Negro contributors provided an ever larger portion of Provident's operational expenses and 90 per cent of its endowment.[24] As a result, many Negroes expected the hospital to provide positions for Negroes as a matter of duty, and Williams found it increasingly difficult to exclude from the staff Negroes whom he considered inadequately trained. The hospital continued to serve a sizable number of white patients, but while 65 per cent of the patients in the early years were white, that figure had dropped to less than 40 per cent by 1912.[25]

These changes were accentuated by the bitter feud between Williams and George Cleveland Hall.[26] The Williams-Hall dispute was partly personal, partly ideological. Hall was jealous of Williams' professional prestige as well as his entree into white social circles. But beyond this, Hall's conception of Provident differed from Williams'. Hall's primary loyalties lay within the Negro community and he participated in a wide range of community activities. He naturally came to regard Provident as part of the community structure, as the medical adjunct of the Negro Business League. Finally gaining control of the hospital board of trustees in 1912, Hall forced through a resolution requiring staff doctors to bring all of their cases to Provident. This was clearly aimed at Williams, who alone among Chicago Negro doctors had a sizable white practice and was admitted to white

[23] Wood, *The Negro in Chicago*, pp. 17–18.

[24] Robert McMurdy to William C. Graves, December 30, 1912, Rosenwald Papers.

[25] *Ibid.*   [26] See chap. 4.

hospitals. Williams resigned from the staff of the hospital he had founded and, embittered by his experience, spent the remainder of his life divorced from the Negro community. With Williams' resignation, the white doctors who had been drawn to Provident by its founder's reputation also left. By World War I, Provident was for all practical purposes a Negro institution.[27]

The Wabash Avenue Young Men's Christian Association was another important focus of community pride. Although still a young institution in 1915, its conception even antedated Provident. In 1889, several community leaders proposed the establishment of "a separate and distinct organization known as the Colored Young Men's Christian Association," but the suggestion aroused immediate opposition from the still dominant integrationists. The weekly *Appeal* declared itself "unalterably opposed to any scheme that draws about it the color line" and reminded its readers that "there is on Madison Street one of the finest Young Men's Christian Association organizations in the country to which all young men are cordially invited regardless of race or color."[28] A protest meeting was held at Olivet Church and, within a month, the proposal was forgotten.[29]

By the early twentieth century, however, the situation had changed. Negroes were no longer "cordially invited" to use the downtown YMCA; in fact, as Ida Barnett pointed out, neither the YMCA, YWCA, Salvation Army, or Mills Hotels admitted Negroes.[30] Moreover many Negro community leaders believed that to serve the youth of the black belt, the YMCA must have an establishment located on the South Side. In 1910, a group of Negro leaders held a rally to raise funds for a YMCA. The voices that had protested in 1889 were now almost mute; no less an integrationist than Ferdinand Barnett led the campaign.[31] Only Edward E. Wilson attacked the project as "the latest concrete example of jim-crowism."[32] Most Negroes heartily ap-

[27] Buckler, *Doctor Dan,* pp. 251–58, 261–62; *Broad Ax,* May 11, 1912.

[28] *Appeal,* November 30, 1889.

[29] *Ibid.,* December 7, December 21, 1889.

[30] *Record-Herald,* January 26, 1912.

[31] *Ibid.,* April 17, 1910.

[32] *Broad Ax,* December 31, 1910; and see chap. 3.

proved the idea. As with Provident Hospital, white philanthropists made the project possible. At the end of 1910, Julius Rosenwald of Sears Roebuck and N. W. Harris, a prominent banker, each pledged $25,000 for a YMCA if the Negro community contributed an additional $50,000.[33]

The fund-raising campaign that followed was conceived by both whites and Negroes as an experiment in Negro self-help. "The best help is self-help," the *Record-Herald* editorialized. "Such effort leads to increased self-respect and also to increased respect on the part of the community in general."[34] Within three weeks, over $65,000 was raised—well over the necessary quota—and additional gifts from Cyrus McCormick and the central YMCA organization brought the total sum to the needed $190,000.[35] In 1913, the Wabash Avenue YMCA opened as "the largest and finest Association building for colored men in the United States."[36] Rosenwald was so pleased that he extended his offer of $25,000 to any Negro community in the United States that could raise the additional sum needed for a YMCA, and the Chicago organization became a prototype for many similar projects throughout the country.

The Colored Women's Club movement provided another example of Negro self-help in the face of mounting discrimination. The women's clubs gained nationwide support during the 1890's, and Chicago, the home of two of the movement's leading spokesmen—Fannie Barrier Williams and Ida Wells-Barnett—was in the vanguard. Even before the organization of the National Association of Colored Women in 1896, Chicago had its Ida Wells Club, dedicated to "civic and social betterment."[37] By the turn of the century, the city had over a half-dozen wom-

[33] Julius Rosenwald to YMCA of Chicago, December 30, 1910, Rosenwald Papers; *Record-Herald*, January 2, 1911.

[34] *Record-Herald*, January 19, 1911.

[35] *Ibid.*, January 3, January 7, January 15, January 16, January 17, 1911; *Inter-Ocean*, January 5, 1911.

[36] Channing H. Tobias, "The Colored Y.M.C.A.," *Crisis* (New York), 9 (November, 1914): 33.

[37] Alfreda Barnett Duster, untitled and unpublished manuscript on the life of Ida Wells-Barnett, in the possession of Mrs. Duster, Chicago, Illinois, chap. 7, pp. 3–4; Elizabeth Lindsay Davis, *The Story of the Illinois Federation of Colored Women's Clubs* ([Chicago?]: [n. p.], [1922?]), pp. 26–28.

en's clubs, which had banded together to form the Colored Women's Conference of Chicago. The clubs operated kindergartens, mothers' clubs, sewing schools, day nurseries, employment bureaus, parent-teacher associations, and a penny savings bank.[38]

The women's clubs sponsored several welfare institutions in Chicago. The first of these, the Phyllis Wheatley Home for Girls, opened in 1896. It provided living accommodations, social facilities, and an employment bureau for single Negro girls who migrated to Chicago and found themselves excluded from the YWCA and similar white organizations. The home also operated a club program and classes in domestic arts for non-resident girls.[39] In 1898, another group of women opened a Home for Aged and Infirm Colored People. Within a year, the home had thirteen occupants and a permanent board of trustees. All of the leading women's clubs contributed to its upkeep.[40]

The women's clubs—and individual Negro women—also worked to maintain facilities for dependent Negro children, who were not welcome at state institutions. Indeed, the state made contributions to private Negro orphanages in order to keep Negro children out of the public homes.[41] Nevertheless, the Negro institutions suffered from lack of funds and generally provided substandard facilities. Although the Amanda Smith School in suburban Harvey, established and operated by an elderly Negro evangelist, was found to be inadequate by state inspectors in 1905, officials allowed it to remain open because it "was the only institution of importance in the state for the care of colored children."[42] Ten years later, at the instigation of

[38] Fannie Barrier Williams, "The Club Movement among Colored Women in America," *A New Negro for a New Century*, ed. J. E. MacBrady (Chicago: American Publishing House, [1900?]), p. 417.

[39] Davis, *The Story of the Illinois Federation*, pp. 95–96; *Broad Ax*, February 16, March 2, 1901; Illinois Writers Project Files.

[40] Davis, *The Story of the Illinois Federation*, pp. 99–101; *Broad Ax*, November 4, 1899.

[41] Louise De Koven Bowen, *The Colored Population of Chicago* (Chicago: Juvenile Protective Association, 1913), [n. p.].

[42] State of Illinois, Board of Administration, Department Visitation of Children, "Report on Amanda Smith Industrial School for Girls," by Charles Virdin, state agent, June 18, 1915, copy in Rosenwald Papers.

state authorities, a group of Negro and white club women accepted positions on the board of trustees and undertook a program of renovation and reorganization.[43] Negroes also maintained three or four other children's homes during the prewar years, but few of these lasted more than a couple of years. Only one Negro orphanage, the Illinois Technical School for Colored Girls, operated by a Roman Catholic order, was under white auspices.[44]

Most Negro institutions were patterned after similar institutions in the white community, and the social settlement movement provided an obvious model for Negro leaders. Ever since Jane Addams converted an old mansion on Halsted Street into a settlement house for Italian and Slavic immigrants on the Near West Side, the idea of social settlements had stirred the imagination of reform-minded Chicagoans. The opening of Hull House in 1889 was followed in quick sucession by the establishment of the Northwestern University Settlement in 1891, the Maxwell Street Settlement in 1893, and a year later, Mary McDowell's University of Chicago Settlement in "Packingtown" and Graham Taylor's Chicago Commons.[45] Miss Addams and her Hull House associates, especially Sophonisba Breckinridge and Edith Abbott, and Miss McDowell took an active interest in the problems of Negro migrants in Chicago, but their settlements were too far from the center of the Negro population to have any real impact. By 1900, both white social workers and Negro community leaders saw the need for a settlement house in the black belt.

Although Negro churches had taken the lead in providing social settlement facilities for Chicago Negroes, the first full-fledged settlement house in the Negro community was founded by a white woman, Celia Parker Woolley, in 1905. Mrs. Woolley was a Unitarian minister of New England antecedents, and her project reflected neoabolitionist sentiments as well as the cur-

[43] *Ibid.*   [44] Bowen, *The Colored Population of Chicago.*

[45] On social settlements in Chicago, see Jane Addams, *Twenty Years at Hull House* (New York: New American Library, 1961); Louise C. Wade, *Graham Taylor: Pioneer for Social Justice* (Chicago: University of Chicago Press, 1964); Graham Taylor, *Chicago Commons Through Forty Years* (Chicago: Chicago Commons Association, 1936); Howard E. Wilson, *Mary McDowell, Neighbor* (Chicago: University of Chicago Press, 1928); and Bessie Louise Pierce, *A History of Chicago* (New York: Alfred A. Knopf, 1957), 3: 465–66.

rent vogue for settlement work. The solution of the Negro problem, she told a Unitarian conference in 1904, depended on establishing "centers in Chicago and other large cities on the plan
of social settlements."[46] Not only would a settlement on the
South Side provide needed social facilities and classes for recently arrived Negroes, it would also be a "center in which white
and colored persons could meet and get to know each other better."[47] To implement her goals, Mrs. Woolley called together a
group of Negro leaders, including Ferdinand and Ida Barnett,
George Hall and S. Laing Williams, and bought a building on
Wabash Avenue—then the dividing line between Negro and
white neighborhoods. Early in 1905, the Frederick Douglass Center, dedicated to promoting "a just and amicable relation between the white and colored people," opened its doors.[48]

Celia Woolley and her husband moved into the Douglass Center and quickly enlisted a number of Negro volunteers to assist
them. The Frederick Douglass Center Women's Club conducted
classes for children; other volunteers aided in running the gymnasium, library, and Sunday Forum.[49] The settlement attempted
to maintain an interracial character and, to some extent, succeeded. "You will find at the Center," wrote S. Laing Williams
in 1908, "generally a genial company of men and women of both
races."[50] Mrs. Woolley and the board of trustees appealed to
both white philanthropists and the Negro community for financial support. Julius Rosenwald was a regular contributor, and
Mrs. George Hall organized an annual charity ball to raise money
for the center.[51]

[46] *Record-Herald*, May 19, 1904.

[47] Quoted by Duster, manuscript on the life of Ida Wells-Barnett, chap. 9,
p. 28.

[48] *Record-Herald*, December 13, 1904; *Inter-Ocean*, December 15, 1904;
Celia Parker Woolley to Julius Rosenwald, May 20, 1912, Rosenwald Papers;
Duster, manuscript on the life of Ida Wells-Barnett, chap. 9, pp. 28–30.

[49] Davis, *Story of the Illinois Federation*, pp. 29–30; Duster, manuscript on
the life of Ida Wells-Barnett, chap. 9, pp. 29–30; weekly notices of activities
in *Broad Ax*, 1905–12.

[50] S. Laing Williams to James A. Thompson, October 3, 1908, Booker T.
Washington Papers (Library of Congress, Washington, D.C.).

[51] Celia Parker Woolley to Julius Rosenwald, May 20, 1912, and Woolley
to Rosenwald, June 3, 1913, Rosenwald Papers; *Broad Ax*, May 13, May 20,
1905.

But Mrs. Woolley's desire to make the center both a social settlement and an experiment in interracial amity resulted in some confusion of purpose. The poor Negroes who most needed the facilities of a settlement house had little interest in Mrs. Woolley's interracial teas and forums. Moreover the Center was located in a middle-class, interracial neighborhood on the edge of the black belt—some distance from the Negro slums. The caustic Julius Taylor charged that the Center was not "of the slightest benefit to the great mass of the Afro-Americans" and was "fast drifting into a mutual admiration society more than anything else."[52] And as a white woman, Mrs. Woolley occasionally offended Negroes who were wont to question her motives. Taylor, for instance, attacked her for addressing Negroes as "you people," and charged that she was reluctant to appoint Negroes to positions of responsibility in the Center.[53]

In 1907, twenty Negroes met to establish a new settlement house on the West Side "limited to the Colored men alone."[54] Their institution opened in 1008 to serve the Negro Community on West Lake and Washington Streets. This neighborhood had lagged behind the South Side in institutional development. The Wendell Phillips Settlement, as it was known after 1911, was staffed exclusively by Negro social workers, undoubtedly in an attempt to avoid the difficulties experienced at the Frederick Douglass Center, but it had an interracial board of directors and sought white financial support. After 1912, 25 per cent of the budget was guaranteed by Julius Rosenwald. Despite frequent administrative and financial difficulties, the settlement remained in operation well into the 1920's and provided the only program of recreational, social, and educational activities open to Negroes on the West Side.[55]

Negroes also made two unsuccessful attempts to organize so-

[52] *Broad Ax*, June 23, 1906.

[53] *Ibid.*, June 30, July 7, 1906.   [54] *Tribune*, August 14, 1907.

[55] Esther W. S. Brophy to Julius Rosenwald, May 15, 1912; Sophonisba Breckinridge to Graham Taylor, October 11, 1912; Rosenwald to Breckinridge, February 26, 1913; Breckinridge to Rosenwald, May 31, 1913; William Graves to Rosenwald, June 21, 1913; Graves to Rosenwald, July 10, 1913; Graves to A. K. Maynard, February 11, 1914—Rosenwald Papers. See also note on Wendell Phillips Settlement by B. H. Haynes, Head Worker, copy in Rosenwald Papers; and *Crisis*, 7 (April, 1914): 269.

cial settlements on the South Side. Richard R. Wright, Jr., one of the first Negro graduates of the University of Chicago Divinity School and later a leading A.M.E. bishop and businessman in Philadelphia, founded a small mission in the heart of the black belt in 1905. Wright's Trinity Mission served the poor Negroes in the slum district just north of Twenty-second Street where no community institutions existed. The mission provided a bath house, employment bureau, correspondence service, and assistance to the sick. But Wright soon left Chicago and the mission disappeared.[56]

In 1910, Ida Wells-Barnett made another attempt "to reach a helping hand to the young men and women farthest down on the ladder of life."[57] The Negro Fellowship League, located on State Street, provided lodging, recreation facilities, and a reading room for recently arrived migrants from the South. Mrs. Victor Lawson, wife of the publisher of the *Chicago Daily News*, anonymously assumed all expenses for three years, including the salary of an executive director. But in 1912, Mrs. Lawson died and a year later her husband, feeling that the League should now be self-supporting, withdrew assistance. Mrs. Barnett was unable to secure sufficient support from Negroes and the League was forced first to move to smaller quarters and finally to disband altogether.[58]

Despite the flurry of civic activity, the South Side's social agencies were inadequate to meet the needs of the growing Negro community. In particular, as a city investigator reported in 1915, "a large district—the heart of the [second] ward—scarcely feels their influence";[59] the slum district in the northern end of the black belt still had few social agencies. Nevertheless, the interest in these institutions among Negro leaders reflected the growing belief that Negroes should themselves organize and manage community services in the black belt. Most of the institutions depended upon white financial support and a few used

[56] *Inter-Ocean*, August 8, 1905; on Wright, see Richard Bardolph, *The Negro Vanguard* (New York: Vintage Books, 1961), pp. 143, 154.

[57] Duster, manuscript on the life of Ida Wells-Barnett, chap. 9, p. 1.

[58] *Ibid.*, chap. 9, pp. 1-3, 11, 20-21; *Broad Ax*, May 7, 1910; Bowen, *The Colored Population of Chicago*.

[59] City of Chicago, Department of Public Welfare, *Preliminary Report of Bureau of Social Surveys, 1915*, p. 5.

white personnel. But by 1915, Negro leaders had responded to discrimination in white institutions by establishing a wide range of Negro-operated community services. These activities had become a major focus of Negro civic life.

After 1900, the new institutions began to replace the older social and fraternal organizations as the center of communal activities. The lodges and fraternal orders in particular, which had flourished since the pre-Civil War era, began to decline in importance in the early twentieth century. Next to the churches, lodges had the longest history of any voluntary associations in Chicago. The Good Samaritans, a national Negro order, had a Chicago lodge as early as 1859, and by the 1880's over forty lodges—many with women's auxiliaries—were operating in the still small Negro community. Most important were the Prince Hall Masons, who, on the national level, traced their history back to the 1780's when a group of Boston Negroes, denied recognition by white Masons, received a charter from the Grand Lodge of England. The Illinois Grand Lodge organized in 1867, and by 1885, there were fifteen Masonic lodges in Chicago.[60] Perhaps next in importance were the Odd Fellows who had six chapters in the city in the 1880's.[61] The lodges included among their members many community leaders in the late nineteenth century: John Jones, Ferdinand Barnett, and Theodore Jones were all prominent Masons, while Edward Morris was one of the national leaders of the Odd Fellows. The politicians, in particular, found the lodges useful bases for political support: Ed Wright was an Odd Fellow and Robert R. Jackson, who belonged to almost all of the fraternal orders, had a special interest in the Knights of Pythias.[62] Lodge social affairs were events of

[60] Drake, "Churches and Voluntary Associations," pp. 45, 64, 71, 75–77; I. C. Harris, *Colored Men's Professional and Business Directory of Chicago* (Chicago: I. C. Harris, 1885), p. 16; *Conservator*, December 23, 1882; *The Most Worshipful Prince Hall Grand Lodge, Illinois and Jurisdiction, 1867–1940*, pamphlet published by Grand Lodge [1940?].

[61] Harris, *Colored Men's Professional and Business Directory*, p. 16.

[62] Harold Gosnell, *Negro Politicians: The Rise of Negro Politics in Chicago* (Chicago: University of Chicago Press, 1935), pp. 110–11; *Broad Ax*, December 27, 1902; M. S. Stuart, *An Economic Detour: A History of Insurance in the Lives of American Negroes* (New York: Wendell Malliet & Company, 1940), pp. 11–13; Proceedings of the 23rd Annual Communication of the Most Worshipful Grand Lodge Ancient, Free and Accepted Masons of the State of Illinois and Jurisdiction, Chicago, 1889, pp. 25–36.

community-wide interest; over two thousand of the "best colored people" attended the Knights Templar Ball in 1900.[63] The lodges also served a benevolent function, providing benefits for sickness or death in a period when few Negroes carried insurance.[64]

But by the first decade of the twentieth century, the lodges were waning. Geared primarily for small, relatively homogeneous communities, the lodges found it difficult to compete for membership and prestige in a city with a wide variety of other institutions and activities and an increasingly differentiated social structure. The lodges found it difficult to maintain their benefit programs in the face of competition from commercial insurance companies.[65] Moreover the social service institutions replaced the lodges as centers of civic activities, and social clubs appealing to particular strata in the community assumed their position as the focus of Negro social life.

By 1900, the social clubs had begun to reflect the growing delineation of class lines in the Negro community. The Ladies' Whist Club, for instance, which included in its membership Mesdames Edward Morris, Julius Avendorph, Edward Wilson, and Dan Williams, pointedly excluded Mrs. George Hall, while Dr. Hall was unable to gain admittance to the Chicago branch of Sigma Pi Phi, the most exclusive national Negro men's club.[66] The class consciousness of the old elite was further reflected by the organization in 1902 of the Chicago Old Settlers' Club, "to keep the old settlers in touch with each other, and to cherish and keep fresh those memories of early colored life in Chicago."[67] Closely related to the upper-class social clubs were the literary societies. The Prudence Crandall Club, organized in 1887 for "mutual improvement," included among its members the venerable Mrs. John Jones, widow of Chicago's pioneer Negro leader, Charles Bentley, James Madden, Ferdinand Barnett,

[63] *Chicago World,* January 27, 1900.

[64] Stuart, *An Economic Detour,* pp. 11–13.

[65] In 1906, for instance, the Masons had a prolonged debate over the future of their sick benefit programs. See Proceedings of the 40th Annual Communication . . . Bloomington, Illinois, 1906.

[66] *Appeal,* January 12, 1901; Buckler, *Doctor Dan,* pp. 228, 254.

[67] John H. Taitt, *The Souvenir of Negro Progress: Chicago, 1779–1925* (Chicago: DeSaible Association, 1925), [n. p.].

and Lloyd Wheeler.[68] A special type of social club that grew up before Chicago's biracial system had begun to harden was the Manasseh Society, an organization of Negro men with white wives. In 1892, the society boasted over five hundred members. Still active in 1912, it declined as interracial social contacts decreased.[69]

Members of the new middle class, refused admittance to the most exclusive of the old clubs, began to form social organizations of their own. The Appomattox Club was founded in 1900 by Ed Wright as a rendezvous for the professional politicians, but it soon became a favorite of business and professional men as well and a center of Negro social life in general. Visiting dignitaries were invariably entertained in the club's comfortable quarters on Wabash Avenue, and the group's periodic balls and receptions were described in detail in the Negro press. By the 1920's, a Negro editor could state that "every man in Chicago who holds any kind of responsible position or occupies a big place politically, belongs to the Appomattox Club."[70] In 1911, the Post Office employees, an important segment of the new Negro middle class, formed another prominent social organization—the Phalanx Forum. Founded for social, civic, and benevolent purposes, the Phalanx sponsored social affairs and safeguarded the interests of its members. The organization maintained close ties with the Appomattox Club and with the Republican political organization.[71]

The development of secular institutions and organizations illustrated the major currents of prewar Negro community life. The changes in attitude toward such establishments as Provident Hospital and the YMCA reflected the trend toward sepa-

[68] *Appeal,* January 7, 1888.

[69] *Appeal,* February 27, 1892; *Defender,* January 27, 1912; St. Clair Drake and Horace Cayton, *Black Metropolis* (New York: Harcourt, Brace & Company, 1945), pp. 54, 145–46. Drake and Cayton erroneously date the founding of the Manasseh Society as the early twentieth century; it was a thriving organization by the early 1890's.

[70] *Chicago Whip,* July 6, 1929; see also *Defender,* June 26, 1920; and Gosnell, *Negro Politicians,* pp. 111, 138.

[71] Gosnell, *Negro Politicians,* pp. 313, 317; Henry W. McGee, "The Negro in the Chicago Post Office," unpublished master's thesis, University of Chicago, 1961, pp. 16–17; and see chap. 2.

ratism. The development of a wide range of social clubs catering to specific groupings in the community was a manifestation of increasing social differentiation. The growth of characteristically metropolitan institutions, such as social settlements and a YMCA, to challenge the traditional roles of the church and the lodge, indicated that the Chicago Negro community was developing an urban pattern of behavior. It could no longer rely upon the institutions that had dominated the civic life of rural and small town Negro communities. It now confronted urban problems that demanded urban solutions.

CHAPTER 6

BUSINESS AND POLITICS—THE QUEST FOR
SELF-SUFFICIENCY

The doctrine of self-help, although prominent in the development of Negro social service institutions, was above all a business philosophy. Its leading exponents were businessmen and it constantly emphasized the importance of Negro business enterprises in increasing the affluence and self-respect of the Negro community. As a result, the development of Negro businesses in Chicago in the prewar years created community-wide interest and continually concerned the Chicago Negro leadership.

Before 1890, the most successful Negro businesses in Chicago depended primarily upon white patronage. Three prosperous catering firms—the French Company, C. H. Smiley, and D. H. Weir—the John Jones Clothes Cleaning and Repairing Establishment, operated after Jones's death by Lloyd Wheeler, and several Negro-owned barber shops and express companies served a white clientele.[1] Most of these businesses were the outgrowths of the personal and domestic service trades in which Negroes were concentrated. Since they involved service that Negroes had traditionally performed, whites were willing to patronize them. But by the turn of the century, most of these concerns were on the decline. European immigrants were driving Negroes out of the barbering, catering, and tailoring trades. By 1908, Theodore Jones's express company and Lloyd Wheeler's cleaning and tailoring shop had gone out of business.[2]

The businesses that emerged in the early twentieth century

[1] I. C. Harris, *Colored Men's Professional and Business Directory of Chicago* (Chicago: I. C. Harris, 1885); Richard R. Wright, Jr., "The Industrial Condition of Negroes in Chicago," unpublished B. D. thesis, University of Chicago Divinity School, 1901, pp. 16–18, 19.

[2] Helen Buckler, *Doctor Dan* (Boston: Houghton, Mifflin & Company, 1954), p. 256; *Broad Ax* (Chicago), October 17, 1908.

were oriented to the Negro market. But among these enterprises, too, service establishments predominated. Of one hundred and four Negro businesses enumerated in a 1901 survey of the Third Ward, there were fifteen barber shops, fifteen restaurants and hotels, twenty-two wood and coal companies, eight saloons, and six bootblacks.[3] Twelve years later, a survey of one hundred and eight Negro businesses on State Street showed a similar concentration of service trade enterprises—barber shops, beauty salons, saloons, restaurants, and pool rooms.[4] First, Negroes had had experience in the service trades that they did not have in retailing and manufacturing. Secondly, it usually required a smaller outlay of capital to open a service shop than it did to establish a store or factory, and few Negro businessmen had either the ready cash or the credit necessary to stock goods or invest in expensive equipment. The enterprises surveyed in 1901 had an average capital investment of less than $600.[5] Finally, a Negro businessman who opened a clothing or a hardware store in the black belt faced competition from well-established, well-financed white merchants. A Negro barber, saloonkeeper, or restaurateur, on the other hand, found relatively little competition, as whites were reluctant to provide services of this sort for Negroes.

A few businessmen attempted ventures on a larger scale. Probably the most successful of these were the real estate dealers. As middle-class Negroes sought to escape the slums by moving into previously white neighborhoods, real estate agents saw an opportunity to make neat profits by buying property and obtaining leases on flats in transitional areas on the edge of the black belt. In spite of white competition, at least ten Negroes were carrying on successful real estate businesses on the South Side by 1907.[6] Jesse Binga, the most prominent of them, employed a number of assistants, and his "Binga Block" at Forty-

<hr>

[3] Wright, "The Industrial Condition of Negroes in Chicago," pp. 16–18.

[4] Louise De Koven Bowen, *The Colored Population of Chicago* (Chicago: Juvenile Protective Association, 1913, [n. p.]). The major difference between the two surveys is the decline of wood and coal companies between the first and the second. But this may be because the 1913 survey was taken on State Street—a busy thoroughfare unsuited to businesses of this type.

[5] Wright, "The Industrial Condition of Negroes in Chicago," p. 18.

[6] *Broad Ax,* November 23, 1907; Monroe Work, "Negro Real Estate Holders of Chicago," unpublished master's thesis, University of Chicago, 1903, pp. 28–29.

seventh and State Streets was billed as "the longest tenement row in Chicago." Binga used the money he made in real estate to launch his celebrated Binga Bank in 1908; it was the first Negro-owned financial institution in Chicago.[7]

Two Negro businessmen tried to break into the retailing and manufacturing trades; one failed, the other succeeded. Sandy Trice opened a small haberdashery as a sideline while working as a porter for the Illinois Central Railroad. The store did well enough to enable him to leave the railroad in 1905 and devote full time to his business. Trice put in a complete line of men's, women's, and children's clothing and incorporated the store, bringing into the management such prominent South Side figures as Archibald Carey and Richard R. Wright, Jr. Proudly hailed as "the best stocked and managed store ever operated by a colored man in the history of Chicago," the Trice company prospered for a few years, but found it increasingly difficult to compete with white stores in the black belt and failed in 1909.[8]

Far more successful was the Overton Hygienic Manufacturing Company, which moved to Chicago in 1911. Anthony Overton, a lawyer and former municipal court judge, had established his business in Kansas City in 1898 to manufacture baking supplies. After a few years of moderate success, Overton added a cosmetics line and soon discovered that far greater opportunities awaited him in face powder than in baking powder. The special cosmetic needs of Negro women had been almost ignored by white firms, and Negro businessmen were just beginning to tap this unexploited market. Madame C. J. Walker had developed the first successful hair-straightening preparation in 1905, and by the eve of World War I, she was a millionaire with a large factory in Indianapolis and a luxurious home in Harlem. Overton's High Brown Face Powder met with similar, if less spectacular, success. In 1915, Overton's firm was capitalized at $268,000, had thirty-two employees, and manufactured sixty-two different items.[9]

[7] Inez Cantey, "Jesse Binga," *Crisis* (New York), 34 (December, 1927): 329, 350, 352; *Chicago Defender*, January 13, 1912.

[8] *Appeal* (St. Paul), September 9, 1905, June 23, 1906; *Chicago Whip*, July 17, 1920.

[9] "Some Chicagoans of Note," *Crisis*, 10 (September, 1915): 242; John McKinley, "Anthony Overton: A Man Who Planned for Success," *Reflexus* (Chicago), I (April, 1925): 14–15, 56; Anthony Overton's unpublished

Negro journalism was not yet big business in the prewar years and the average Negro newspaper in Chicago was a one-man operation. The *Conservator*, the city's first Negro weekly, probably never had a circulation of more than one thousand. Julius Taylor's *Broad Ax* often made extravagant circulation claims, but its advertising columns were always slim and it never employed anyone other than Taylor himself. Sheadrick B. Turner moved his *Illinois Idea* to Chicago from Springfield just before the turn of the century and published it until after World War I; like Taylor, he used his paper as a personal organ and it eventually helped him win a seat in the state legislature, but the journal never enjoyed more than modest economic success. There was also a host of ephemeral personal newspapers, none of them lasting more than a few years: Allison Sweeney's *Chicago Leader* was printed from 1905 until 1907; William Neighbors, a real estate dealer, published the *Illinois Chronicle* from 1912 until 1915; B. F. Harris' *Chicago World* survived for only a few weeks in 1900. The Adams brothers were more successful with their *Appeal*, but it was never really a Chicago newspaper.[10]

Negro journalism became big business with the rise of Robert Abbott's *Chicago Defender*. Already the most successful Negro paper in Chicago by 1915, the *Defender* was soon to become one of the largest Negro-owned businesses in the country. For the first years of publication, however, Abbott, like his competitors, struggled along with no help, small circulation, drab format, and little advertising. The *Defender* began to change after 1910, when Abbott hired J. Hockley Smiley as his assistant. The

memoirs in the possession of Olive Diggs, Chicago, Illinois. On Madame Walker, see Richard Bardolph, *The Negro Vanguard* (New York: Vintage Books, 1961), p. 257, and Roi Ottley, *New World A-Coming* (Boston: Houghton, Mifflin & Company, 1943), pp. 171–73.

[10] For a general history of Chicago Negro newspapers, see Ralph N. Davis, "Negro Newspapers in Chicago," unpublished master's thesis, University of Chicago, 1939. Of the newspapers mentioned in the above paragraph, only the *Broad Ax* and the *Appeal* have complete files still available; scattered issues of the *Conservator* and the *World* are extant. Historical sketches of most of these newspapers can be found in "The Negro in Illinois," a file of reports and interviews compiled by the Illinois Writers Project of the Works Progress Administration (George Cleveland Hall Branch of the Chicago Public Library), cited hereafter as Illinois Writers Project Files.

hard-drinking foppish Smiley made up in imagination what he lacked in newspaper experience. He borrowed freely from William Randolph Hearst's journalistic techniques and converted the *Defender* from another boiler-plate sheet into the first modern Negro newspaper. During Smiley's five-year tenure, the *Defender* featured banner headlines, often printed in red, sensational treatment of the news, and a firm and passionate commitment to the rights of the rank and file of its readership—the Negro masses. At his most flamboyant, Smiley would not hesitate to invent stories. "From his vivid imagination," reported a colleague, "came lynchings, rapes, assaults, mayhems and sundry 'crimes' against innocent Negroes in the hinterlands of the South, often in towns not to be found on any maps extant."[11] By the time of Smiley's death in 1915, the *Defender*, now audaciously proclaiming itself the "World's Greatest Weekly," was a hard-hitting, flamboyant organ of racial protest well on its way to becoming the first Negro newspaper in history with a mass circulation.[12]

Such individual Negro business ventures as Binga's real estate and banking operations, Trice's store, Overton's factory, and Abbott's newspaper had strong ties with the Negro business philosophy. They all consciously tried to secure Negro customers by emphasizing the importance of their enterprises to the cause of race advancement. In the cases of Overton and Abbott, the businesses were geared to special Negro needs.

Cooperative business enterprises were even more directly the outgrowth of the ideology of self-help and racial solidarity. These ventures, like Negro social service institutions, resulted from white discrimination. Although organized on a profit basis, they not only adopted the rhetoric of race advancement through self-help, but their leaders were genuinely motivated by a desire to provide services and facilities that were otherwise unavailable to Negroes.

Negro leaders throughout the country saw great promise for cooperative ventures in the insurance field. Not only did white

[11] Quoted in Roi Ottley, *The Lonely Warrior: The Life and Times of Robert S. Abbott* (Chicago: Henry Regnery & Company, 1955), p. 107.

[12] Ottley, *The Lonely Warrior*, pp. 85–99, 105–14. The files of the *Defender* are extant and nearly complete beginning in 1909. For Abbott's racial philosophy, see chap. 4.

insurance companies refuse to hire Negro agents, but they generally exacted higher premiums from Negroes and often sold Negroes only industrial policies. In response to these conditions, Negroes founded insurance companies in several southern cities before World War I. Usually the outgrowths of mutual benefit or church relief societies, they enjoyed considerable success. There was, however, no comparable development in Chicago in this period. The fraternal orders did not evolve into commercial insurance companies and not until after the wartime migration did Chicago Negroes succeed in establishing a firm to rival the thriving insurance operations in Atlanta and Durham.[13]

Chicago Negroes made several unsuccessful efforts to start insurance companies. In the late 1890's, a group of community leaders attempted to organize the United Brotherhood Fraternal Insurance Company, but their efforts failed when an officer absconded with the funds.[14] In 1913, another group, including Robert S. Abbott, met to lay plans for the Progressive National Life Insurance Company; again, the company failed to materialize.[15] More important for the future was the white-owned Royal Life Insurance Company organized in 1912. Royal was the first insurance company to hire Negroes in executive and clerical capacities. It opened a district office on the South Side completely staffed by Negroes. Virtually all of the Negro life insurance companies organized in Chicago after World War I were founded by former Royal employees.[16]

Negroes were completely excluded from white-owned commercial amusements—skating rinks, dance halls, and amusement parks. As performers, they were banned from America's most successful professional sport—baseball. A Chicago baseball official, Cap Anson of the White Stockings, had persuaded his colleagues to adopt a firm policy of Negro exclusion in the late

[13] M. S. Stuart, *An Economic Detour: A History of Insurance in the Lives of American Negroes* (New York: Wendell Malliet & Company, 1940), pp. 35–36.

[14] *Broad Ax*, December 8, 1900; Buckler, *Doctor Dan*, p. 178.

[15] *Broad Ax*, May 17, 1913.

[16] J. E. Mitchem, "Life Insurance," *Scott's Blue Book* (Chicago: [n. p.], 1937), pp. 45–46; interview with Edward S. Gillespie, vice-president, Supreme Life Insurance Company, March 21, 1963.

1880's.[17] Throughout the prewar years, Chicago Negro leaders made repeated attempts to counter this discrimination by organizing Negro baseball clubs and other recreational enterprises. Robert R. Jackson and Beauregard F. Moseley promoted the first successful baseball team on the South Side—the Leland Giants. The Leland Giants Baseball and Amusement Association raised funds for an "all Negro-owned" baseball park at Sixty-ninth and Halsted Streets, operated a dance hall and roller skating rink—the Chateau de la Plaisance—and attempted to establish an amusement park and summer hotel for Negroes.[18]

In 1910, Moseley called together a group of Negro baseball officials from throughout the Midwest and the South to organize a National Negro Baseball League.[19] Moseley's statement of purposes was a clear exposition of the doctrine of self-help. Negroes, he pointed out, "are already forced out of the game from a national standpoint" and were finding it increasingly difficult to play with white semiprofessional teams on the local level. This "presages the day when there will be [no opportunities for Negro baseball players], except the Negro comes to his own rescue by organizing and patronizing the game successfully, which would of itself force recognition from minor white Leagues to play us and share in the receipts." So, Moseley exhorted, "let those who would serve the Race and assist it in holding its back up . . . organize an effort to secure . . . the best club of ball players possible."[20] Moseley's appeal met with enthusiasm but no financial support, and the venture never advanced beyond the planning stage.

Chicago fielded two baseball teams in 1911, one more than it could support, and within a year the Leland Giants had failed and only the newly organized American Giants were playing a regular schedule.[21] "The baseball situation," reported the *Broad Ax* in 1912, "is quite forlorn and hopeless," a condition brought

[17] Hy Turkin and S. C. Thompson, *The Official Encyclopedia of Baseball* (New York: A. S. Barnes, 1951), p. 555.

[18] *Broad Ax*, November 2, 1907, May 9, 1908, May 21, 1910. Notices of activities at the Chateau de la Plaisance appeared weekly in the *Broad Ax* from 1907 through 1910.

[19] *Broad Ax*, December 31, 1910.   [20] *Ibid.*, January 21, 1911.

[21] *Ibid.*, December 31, 1910, May 18, 1912.

about by "a lack of the Negroes themselves to organize" and by an excessive desire "to compete for patronage and prowess." Not only had the League failed to materialize, but the only remaining team in Chicago played in a white-owned park, "paying the money to John M. Schorling that should be received by the Race to whom the patrons of the game belong."[22] As with the insurance business, the dream of a Negro baseball league was not to be realized until after the war.

The only cooperative business ventures to achieve a measure of success were the cemetery associations. Encountering discriminatory prices and even exclusion in white cemeteries, Negroes opened two cemeteries of their own in the Chicago area. Mount Glenwood Cemetery, dedicated in 1908, advertised itself as the only Chicago cemetery with a non-discriminatory clause in its charter.[23] Lincoln Cemetery, founded three years later, was operated by a cooperative organization that drew support from the fraternal lodges.[24]

Several other cooperative business ventures had short lives in prewar Chicago. The Black Diamond Development Company, a firm that owned land in the natural gas fields of Kansas, thrived for several years, selling stock to the public; its officers included Archibald Carey and S. Laing Williams.[25] In 1910, a group of real estate men banded together to organize the Northern Asset Realization Company "to do mortgage banking business and a general brokerage business in real estate."[26] But Negro cooperative businesses usually encountered the same problems faced by individual Negro businesses. They floundered as a result of inexperience, inadequate capital, and the difficulty in securing credit from white financial institutions.

Before the 1890's there was no separate Negro political organization in Chicago. Negroes participated in the activities of the Republican organization and, to a far lesser extent, the Democratic organization, and occasionally received rewards for their

[22] *Ibid.*, May 18, 1912.

[23] *Chicago Record-Herald*, September 7, 1908; *Broad Ax*, August 26, 1911.

[24] Illinois Writers Project Files.

[25] *Broad Ax*, October 27, 1906, January 26, July 27, 1907.

[26] *Ibid.*, May 21, 1910.

services. The Republicans reserved a few political offices for Negro nominees. After 1882, a Negro was regularly nominated for the state legislature and, less frequently, for the County Board of Commissioners; under the Illinois voting system, the nominees were usually assured of election.[27] At times, political leaders bid for Negro support by appointing a Negro to a minor city or county post or by appearing at a Negro ceremonial function.[28] But for the most part, Negroes received only political crumbs. Without a political organization rooted in their own community, Negro politicians lacked the leverage to demand more.

The inadequacy of the traditional Negro approach to politics was graphically demonstrated in 1906 when Ferdinand Barnett ran as a Republican candidate for the municipal court. Like most of the Negro candidates who had preceded him, Barnett was not a professional politician, but a race leader and civic reformer who regarded politics as one of several avenues to Negro advancement. He received the Republican nomination not because he was able to wield political power of his own, but as a reward for services to the party. He ran for a citywide office and could win only with substantial white support.

Barnett's candidacy aroused vigorous white opposition, and every daily newspaper but one urged that he be defeated.[29] "The bench," wrote a white correspondent to the *Chicago Chronicle,* "is a position of absolute authority and white people will never willingly submit to receiving the law from a negro."[30] According to the hostile *Examiner,* the Republican leadership "had no idea when they nominated Barnett that his election would create the unfavorable comment on themselves that it had."[31] The election appeared to be a Republican sweep with Barnett, although the least successful Republican judicial candidate, apparently elected by some five hundred votes over his nearest Democratic rival. But the Democrats demanded a recount and the election board

[27] Harold Gosnell, *Negro Politicians: The Rise of Negro Politics in Chicago* (Chicago: University of Chicago Press, 1935), pp. 65–67, 81–83.

[28] *Ibid.,* pp. 198–99; Claudius Johnson, *Carter Harrison I* (Chicago: University of Chicago Press, 1928), p. 196.

[29] *Broad Ax,* November 17, 1906.

[30] *Chicago Chronicle,* November 8, 1906.

[31] *Chicago Examiner,* November 12, 1906.

declared, amid charges of fraud, that Barnett had lost by three hundred votes.[32]

Negro leaders, stunned by Barnett's defeat, learned an important lesson. They saw that it was almost impossible to elect a Negro to an important citywide office. Although a Negro might slip by the white electorate when running for a minor post, his candidacy for a major office was certain to arouse enough hostility to defeat him. Barnett ran almost 20,000 votes behind any other Republican candidate for the bench. "No colored candidate," mused S. Laing Williams, "could have been treated much worse in the South."[33] As the converse of this proposition, Negro leaders learned that they could make new political gains by concentrating not on citywide positions but on ward offices where a well-organized Negro electorate could assure success. A few Negroes even suggested an independent party in which Negroes would "get together, quit both the democratic and republican parties and work for their own interests."[34] Although this plan never gained wide support, Negro politicians became increasingly aware of the importance of an independent, professional Negro organization within the Republican party that could mobilize the growing Negro electorate.

Between 1906 and 1915, a core of professional politicians—Ed Wright, Oscar De Priest, Robert R. Jackson, and their lieutenants —laid the groundwork for a political organization that was to become a major force in Chicago politics after World War I. They labored under favorable conditions. The Negro community was growing rapidly enough to provide an adequate base of political support. It was geographically concentrated in two South Side wards, enabling the politicians to gain the maximum benefit from those votes that they could mobilize. And the political balance of power in Chicago—both between the parties and between warring factions within the Republican party—was precarious enough to give the leaders of any sizable voting bloc considerable leverage.[35]

[32] Record-Herald, November 8, November 19, November 23, 1906; Gosnell, Negro Politicians, p. 85.

[33] S. Laing Williams to Booker T. Washington, November 16, 1906, Booker T. Washington Papers (Library of Congress, Washington, D.C.).

[34] Chicago Daily News, November 10, 1906.

[35] For a discussion of Chicago politics in the early twentieth century, see Charles E. Merriam, Chicago: A More Intimate View of Urban Politics (New

The Illinois Republican party in the early twentieth century suffered from a serious factional split. Senator William Lorimer, the "blond boss" of the West Side of Chicago, headed one faction. A ruthless machine politician, Lorimer pursued a tough brand of personal politics and assiduously cultivated minority group support. Continually attacked by reform groups and by the press, he was unseated by the United States Senate in 1912 on bribery charges. The leadership of his faction then passed on to two other tough Chicago politicians—Fred Lundin and Lundin's protégé, William Hale Thompson. The other faction of the party was headed by Charles S. Deneen, who served as a reform governor from 1905 until 1913 and had the backing of the "respectable" elements within the Republican party.[36]

A few reform-minded Negroes, such as Ferdinand and Ida Barnett, supported Deneen,[37] but the professional Negro politicians allied themselves with Lorimer and his successors, Lundin and Thompson. There were several reasons for this. First, and probably most important, while the Deneenites controlled the State House, Lorimer's followers ran the party in Chicago and had power over city patronage.[38] Secondly, the Negro politicians never really trusted the middle-class reformers and "pseudo-aristocrats" who gathered around Deneen. Many of the causes the Deneenites espoused aroused little enthusiasm among Negroes. The political reforms of which progressives were so fond, for instance, appeared to many Negroes as schemes to deprive them of political privilege. Negroes could elicit favors from party bosses, but what could they expect from a preponderantly white electorate under a system of direct primaries, initiative, referendum, and recall?[39] And such economic and moral reforms as the

York: Macmillan Company, 1929); Lloyd Wendt and Herman Kogan, *Big Bill Thompson* (Indianapolis: Bobbs-Merrill & Company, 1953); and Lloyd Wendt and Herman Kogan, *Lords of the Levee* (Indianapolis: Bobbs-Merrill & Company, 1943).

[36] Merriam, *Chicago*, pp. 178–221; Gosnell, *Negro Politicians*, pp. 37–39; Wendt and Kogan, *Big Bill Thompson, passim*.

[37] *Defender*, April 6, 1912.   [38] Gosnell, *Negro Politicians*, pp. 37–38.

[39] See for example *Defender*, September 7, 1912; and George W. Ellis, "The Negro in the Chicago Primary," *Independent* (New York), 72 (April 25, 1912): 890–91. For A. J. Carey's decision to join the Lorimer faction, see Joseph Logsdon, "Reverend A. J. Carey and the Negro in Chicago Politics," unpublished master's thesis, University of Chicago, 1961, pp. 40–44.

abolition of the segregated vice district and the full crew railroad employment bill contained obvious perils to Negro interests.[40]

Working with the Lorimer Republicans, but exercising enough independence to retain political leverage, Negro politicians made substantial gains between 1906 and 1915. By taking advantage of traditional Negro loyalties to the Republican party, Wright and his colleagues attempted to establish control over the Negro voters of the Second and Third Wards. A well-organized bloc of Republican voters was of prime importance to the Lorimerites. Not only did they need this support in general elections, but they particularly needed it in primary battles against the Deneenites, when the strongly Republican black belt constituted a significant proportion of the electorate.

The goals of the Negro politicians were imperfectly realized in the prewar years because two powerful white politicians stood in their way. Congressman Martin Madden and Second Ward Alderman George Harding, both allies of Lorimer and Thompson, remained the strongest figures on the South Side, and Wright and De Priest frequently ran afoul of them. Moreover personal jealousies within the Negro organization retarded development. But by 1915, the Wright-De Priest combination had amassed enough power to elect a Negro alderman, secure significant appointive offices, and force every politician in Chicago to take cognizance of the Negro vote.[41]

The major goal of the Negro politicians was to elect a Negro alderman. By 1910, the Second Ward was 25 per cent Negro and five years later Negroes were probably in a majority.[42] Negroes believed that they were entitled to at least one of the two aldermen who represented the ward. Ed Wright, running as one of four candidates for the Republican aldermanic nomination in 1910, hoped that with solid Negro support and a few white votes he could win. He made an impassioned plea for racial solidarity. "For the sake of the race of which you are a part," he exhorted, ". . . arouse from your slumber and realize that on your shoulder rests a responsibility as a man."[43] "We must have a colored alderman," the *Defender* editorialized, "not because others are not friendly, but because we should be represented just the same

[40] See chaps. 1 and 4.

[41] Gosnell, *Negro Politicians,* pp. 74–75, 154–57, 168–70, 190.

[42] *Ibid.,* p. 74, and see Table 3.   [43] *Defender,* January 29, 1910.

as the Irish, Jews and Italians."[44] But the regular Republican ward organization, headed by George Harding, supported a white candidate and Wright finished third with just 18 per cent of the vote.[45]

Two years later, Wright tried again. "The Poles, the Jews and all the other nationalities are insisting on adequate representation in public affairs," he said. "The colored Republicans comprise fully one half of the Republican voters of the 2nd ward and are entitled to one alderman."[46] But again Wright faced the opposition of the regular organization and when Oscar De Priest, hoping to win future favors from the white bosses, refused to support him, his defeat was foreordained.[47] In 1914, Wright did not make the race himself, but supported William R. Cowan, a prominent Negro real estate dealer, for the Republican aldermanic nomination. Cowan lost, but amassed an impressive 45 per cent of the vote, and an independent Negro candidate, running in the general election, received 21 per cent of the vote.[48]

The Madden-Harding Republican organization in the Second Ward now realized that they must meet Negro demands or face defeat. Negro pressure for representation was increasing, and in 1914, when the white leadership refused to endorse Cowan, Wright made a strong bid to capture control of the organization. Madden insisted that it was his duty to support the incumbent white alderman, but he promised to support a Negro candidate when the time was right.[49] That time came just a year later. George Harding was elected to the State Senate and did not run for reelection to the City Council. In the Republican primary, three Negroes opposed five white candidates. The strongest of the Negroes was Oscar De Priest, who had been quietly winning support for years and now boasted the endorsements of thirty-eight precinct captains, and a host of ministers, women's clubs, professional associations, and independent workers. Moreover

[44] *Ibid.*, February 5, 1910.

[45] *Broad Ax*, March 26, April 9, 1910.   [46] *Defender*, February 3, 1912.

[47] *Ibid.*, March 9, 1912; Gosnell, *Negro Politicians*, p. 170.

[48] *Defender*, February 21, February 28, 1914; *Broad Ax*, February 14, February 21, February 28, 1914; Gosnell, *Negro Politicians*, p. 74.

[49] *Broad Ax*, February 14, 1914.

De Priest had remained loyal to the regular organization over the years. With the support of Madden and Harding, he won handily.[50]

The Negro politicians also succeeded in increasing Negro representation in the state legislature. In 1914, with large Negro electorates in two Senatorial districts, both Robert R. Jackson and Sheadrick B. Turner were sent to Springfield.[51] Negro electoral successes were accompanied by an increasing number of Negroes in major appointive offices. At least one Negro had served regularly in the city law office since 1891. But with the election of Mayor Thompson in 1915, both Ed Wright and L. B. Anderson were appointed assistant corporation counsels and Archibald Carey was named an investigator in the law department.[52] Even before Thompson's election, Carey had been appointed to the motion picture censorship board, enabling him to act as watchdog against films containing racial insults.[53] Governor Dunne, a Democrat, named both Carey and Robert Jackson to the state commission in charge of the 1915 Emancipation Exposition.[54]

The growing importance of the Negro electorate was also reflected in the increasing sensitivity of white politicians to Negro feelings. As early as 1900, a state legislator with a sizable Negro constituency walked out of a Springfield hotel when it refused to accommodate the Fisk Jubilee Singers.[55] The Second Ward aldermen attempted to look out for Negro rights in the City Council and Congressman Madden championed the Negro cause in the House of Representatives.[56] One of Mayor Thompson's first official acts after his election was to ban the showing of the racist

[50] *Defender*, January 2, January 16, February 6, February 27, 1915; *Broad Ax*, November 28, 1914; Gosnell, *Negro Politicians*, pp. 170–71.

[51] Gosnell, *Negro Politicians*, pp. 67, 375; *Defender*, November 14, 1914.

[52] *Defender*, July 17, August 7, 1915; Gosnell, *Negro Politicians*, pp. 198–99.

[53] *Defender*, March 7, March 14, 1914; Logsdon, "Reverend A. J. Carey," p. 23.

[54] *Broad Ax*, July 26, September 13, 1913; Logsdon, "Reverend A. J. Carey," pp. 24–25.

[55] *Chicago World*, January 27, 1900.

[56] City of Chicago, *Journal of the Proceedings of the City Council, 1914–15*, p. 88; Gosnell, *Negro Politicians*, p. 78.

film, *The Birth of a Nation,* in Chicago.[57] But most of these acts were largely ceremonial; there was still much to be done before Negroes could demand a more meaningful type of political recognition.

Although the history of Negro politics in the late nineteenth and early twentieth century was chiefly the history of Negro Republicanism, a few Negroes broke with tradition to support the Democratic party. When the Cook County Colored Democratic Club opened headquarters in 1888, one old Negro wept "to think that colored men should be Democrats."[58] Yet, Carter Harrison I, who served as mayor throughout most of the 1880's, and his son, Carter Harrison II, who succeeded him in the 1890's, attracted considerable Negro support. Despite their southern origin, the Harrisons actively sought Negro votes and appointed a few Negroes to municipal jobs.[59]

The Democrats, however, failed to hold their gains. Ignoring the pleas of their Negro supporters, they never nominated a Negro for even a minor elective office. Moreover, as migration from the South swelled the population of the black belt, it brought with it voters who regarded the Democrats as the natural enemies of the Negro people and whose previous experiences committed them to the Republican party. Julius Taylor continued to support the Democrats and, in 1903, the usually Republican *Conservator* supported Carter Harrison II for reelection as mayor. But the Negro Democratic organization split into two rival groups—the Cook County Democratic League and the Thomas Jefferson Club—and, with the tide running strongly against them, became ineffectual forces in Chicago politics.[60]

The course of Negro political life in Chicago between 1890 and 1915 paralleled the development of the Negro business and institutional structure. White discrimination, Negro race consciousness and mounting Negro ambition resulted in significant changes. Negroes no longer worked to achieve minor political favor by supporting the white organization and seeking

[57] *Chicago Tribune,* April 26, 1915.   [58] *Appeal,* August 28, 1888.

[59] Johnson, *Carter Harrison I,* p. 196.

[60] *Broad Ax,* August 12, 1899, May 26, 1900, April 6, April 20, May 18, 1901, September 9, 1902; *Appeal,* April 4, 1903.

white electoral support. Instead, Negro politicians, like Negro businessmen and civic leaders, sought self-sufficiency: they attempted to build a separate Negro organization dependent upon Negro support. Once again, the philosophy of self-help and racial solidarity provided Negroes with an alternative to an increasingly subordinate role within the white structure.

As the prewar era drew to a close, the Chicago Negro community was becoming an increasingly self-contained enclave within the city. Isolated from the mainstream of Chicago life, it had begun to pursue an independent course of development. Its leaders talked less of an integrated city, more of a self-sufficient Negro metropolis on the South Side. It remained to be seen whether such a goal was economically, politically, and socially possible.

PART II

THE MIGRATION YEARS, 1915–20

CHAPTER 7

FROM THE SOUTH TO THE SOUTH SIDE

The World War I era is usually viewed as the major turning point in the history of Negroes in the North. Between 1915 and 1920, the great migration destroyed the notion that the Negro problem would remain a southern problem and that northerners could simply allow southern whites to handle "their Negroes" as they saw fit. The migration of Negroes from the rural South to the urban North became, after 1915, a mass movement. The gradual prewar influx from the border states gave way to a sudden, large-scale migration of poorly educated, unskilled Negroes from the most backward areas of the Deep South. While the earlier movement had been little noted outside of the Negro community, the new migration was charted and graphed, analyzed and evaluated, deplored and defended in the newspapers, on public platforms, and in legislative committees. It became one of the major social issues of the day. In the summer of 1917 and again in the summer of 1919, the northern Negro problem moved from the forums to the streets. A series of race riots in a score of northern and border cities gave violent notice that urban white northerners could no longer ignore the Negroes who lived in their midst.

Chicago was a focal point of the great migration and of the racial violence that came in its wake. The growing stockyards, steel mills, and foundries of Chicago, deprived of immigrant labor by the outbreak of war in Europe, provided new and unprecedented industrial opportunities for southern Negroes. As the terminus of the Illinois Central Railroad, Chicago was the most accessible northern city for Negroes in Mississippi, Louisiana, and Arkansas. Moreover many southern Negroes who had barely heard of Cleveland or Detroit knew of Chicago: they read about it in the most popular Negro newspaper in the country—the flamboyant and racially militant *Defender;* they addressed their mail to it when they ordered goods from the great national mail-order

houses—Sears Roebuck and Montgomery Ward; and they heard
tales of it from the Pullman porters and dining-car waiters who
worked the rails throughout the South. So, between 1916 and
1919, they came—some 50,000 of them—to crowd into the burgeoning black belt, to make new demands upon the institutional
structure of the South Side, and to arouse the hostility of the
Negro community's white neighbors. For three years, journalists,
ministers, Negro and white civic leaders pointed with mounting
concern to the inadequacy of Negro housing and the increasingly
frequent outbreaks of racial violence as the black belt expanded.
But neither the political nor the economic leaders of Chicago
could be stirred into action. The climax was inevitable: for four
tragic days in the summer of 1919, Chicago experienced one of
the worst race riots in American history. Race relations had become Chicago's most serious municipal problem.

The events of 1916–19 made white Chicagoans far more aware
of the city's Negro community, but did not basically alter the
pattern of Negro life in Chicago. The ghetto was already well-
formed by the eve of World War I; the migration and the riot
merely strengthened both the external and internal forces that
had created it. The new wave of white hostility and racial friction made separate community life seem ever more necessary. At
the same time, the enlarged black belt required expanded services,
facilities, and institutions to meet the needs of the recent migrants. Thus the events of the war years contributed to the pattern of white discrimination and Negro self-help that had been
developing since the 1890's. The period between 1915 and 1920
was more a time of continuity than of change. The black enclave
that had formed during the prewar years was strengthened by
population growth and racial conflict and emerged in 1920 a
fully-developed Negro ghetto.

A variety of circumstances combined to produce the World
War I Negro migration. Many Negroes chose to leave the rural
South for the same reasons that induced thousands of white farmers to move to the city: diminishing returns in agriculture, the
ebbing of opportunity on the farm compared with the city, and
discontent with rural life and institutions. But other circumstances
peculiar to the situation of the southern Negro contributed to
the exodus. The system of share tenancy and crop liens often

prevented Negro farmers from making a profit, and unscrupulous planters and merchants systematically exploited the ignorant tenants. Despite increasing industrialization, economic opportunity in the South did not keep pace with the growth of population, and the Negro, excluded from the new industries, did not share in the opportunities that developed. The caste system had begun to harden in the 1880's: Jim Crow legislation, inferior schools, legal injustice, and lynchings were ever present factors in southern Negro life. Both economic and social conditions, therefore, contributed to what Gunnar Myrdal has called "accumulated migration potentialities."[1]

Although southern Negroes had ample reason to emigrate before World War I, relatively few did. The ties of home and family exercised a natural restraining influence. But, more important, Negroes had few opportunities outside the South before 1915. Northern industry found an ample labor supply in the hundreds of thousands of European immigrants who annually made their way across the Atlantic, and except during strikes, industrialists adhered to a rigid color line in their hiring practices. Throughout the North, a pattern similar to that found in Chicago prevailed: only in domestic employment and in the service trades could Negroes find positions.[2]

During World War I, however, the North became more attractive and the South more intolerable; new conditions transformed migration potentialities into a mass exodus. With the outbreak of the European war, immigration fell from an all-time high of 1,218,480 in 1914 to 326,700 in 1915; in 1918, only 110,018 immigrants entered the country.[3] At the same time, the war precipitated an expansion of American industry necessitating a larger labor supply. Employers were forced to turn to the home labor

[1] Gunnar Myrdal, *An American Dilemma* (New York: Harper & Brothers, 1944), p. 193; see also Thomas J. Woofter, Jr., *Negro Migration* (New York: W. D. Gray, 1920), pp. 14–15; and Louise V. Kennedy, *The Negro Peasant Turns Cityward* (New York: Columbia University Press, 1930), pp. 42–52.

[2] See chap. 2.

[3] U.S. Bureau of Immigration, *Annual Report of the Commissioner-General of Immigration, 1922*, p. 108. It has often been maintained that the labor supply was further diminished by the emigration of European aliens returning to their native lands to fight in the war. Official reports, however, show a steady decrease in the number of emigrant aliens departing each year from 1914 to 1917. *Annual Report, 1922*, pp. 106–7.

market in order to fill vacancies, and the color bar quickly fell.[4]

Just as opportunities were opening in the North, cotton culture experienced a crisis that uprooted thousands of Negroes in the black belts of the South. The Mexican boll weevil had crossed the Rio Grande in 1892. Steadily spreading its destruction north and eastward, it had, by 1915, ruined thousands of acres of crops in the cotton-producing areas of Mississippi and Alabama and had just begun to ravage southwestern Georgia. The weevil did not destroy southern agriculture, but it made necessary a major reorganization: planters reduced their cotton acreage, altered their methods of planting and cultivating cotton, and put greater emphasis on food crops and livestock. Mixed farming required fewer laborers, and Negro croppers and laborers were, in any case, untrained for the new agriculture. As a result, landowners reduced the number of tenants and workers on their land, forcing many of them to seek work elsewhere.[5]

The plight of the southern tenant and farm worker was further aggravated by the low price of cotton in 1913 and 1914 and by a series of disastrous floods in 1915 and 1916. In many cases, the floods provided a climax to the chain of misfortunes that had beset planters and tenants alike for years. A case recorded by a Labor Department investigator illustrates the operation of the various disruptive factors in southern agriculture and its final result—emigration:

> A prominent citizen of Selma [Alabama] owns 7000 acres of land in Dallas County. Before the boll weevil reached the state he was accustomed to plant the whole of this in cotton, and ran 2500 plows annually. For the past three or four successive years he has realized no profits, but has constantly suffered a loss on the capital invested. When the floods of July, 1916, virtually wiped out the crops of his tenants, he decided that as a matter of sound business he could not afford to make additional outlay in the advancement of provi-

[4] Charles Wesley, *Negro Labor in the United States, 1850–1925* (New York: Vanguard Press, 1927), pp. 290–91; Kennedy, *The Negro Peasant Turns Cityward*, pp. 42–44.

[5] U.S. Department of Labor, *Negro Migration in 1916–17* (Washington: Government Printing Office, 1919), pp. 17–18, 58–60, 78–79; Emmett J. Scott, *Negro Migration During the War* (New York: Oxford University Press, 1920), pp. 13–15.

sions to them, the result being that the great majority were obliged to move elsewhere.[6]

Northern fever swept through the South in 1915 and 1916 much as America fever had infected much of Europe throughout the nineteenth century. First, southern Negroes heard only vague rumors of a better life in the North. Soon, however, they were confronted with concrete alternatives to their present plight. Labor agents, sent south first by the railroads and later by the steel companies, met Negroes on street corners, at churches, in barber shops, and in pool rooms. They offered free transportation plus the prospect of high wages to any laborer who agreed to migrate.[7]

Once it had begun, the migration generated its own momentum. Although southern whites, fearful of losing their work force, passed a series of stringent ordinances that effectively crippled the agents, this did not halt the migration.[8] The arrival of each migrant in the North created a new contact with potential migrants, and personal communication made the agents superfluous. "I am well and thankful to say I am doing well," wrote a Negro woman, recently arrived in Chicago, to a friend in the South. "I work in Swifts packing Co., in the sausage department. . . . We get $1.50 a day. . . . Tell your husband work is plentiful here and he wont have to loaf if he want to work."[9] A man in East Chicago wrote to a friend in Alabama:

Now it is true that the (col.) men are making good. Never pay less than $3.00 per day for (10) hours—this is not prom-

[6] U.S. Department of Labor, *Negro Migration in 1916–17*, p. 71.

[7] The role of the labor agents has often been exaggerated, due to widely publicized southern attempts to proscribe their activities. But they were undoubtedly important in the initial stages of the migration. See Scott, *Negro Migration During the War*, pp. 36, 55; Charles S. Johnson, "The New Negro in a New World," *The New Negro*, ed. Alain Locke (New York: Albert & Charles Boni, 1925), pp. 280–81; U.S. Department of Labor, *Negro Migration in 1916–17*, pp. 66, 85; and *Chicago Defender*, August 19, 1916.

[8] *Defender*, August 12, 1916; *Crisis* (New York), 13 (January, 1917): 123; Scott, *Negro Migration During the War*, pp. 36–37, 73–74; U.S. Department of Labor, *Negro Migration in 1916–17*, pp. 62–63.

[9] "Letters of Negro Migrants of 1916–18," collected under the direction of Emmett J. Scott, *Journal of Negro History* (Washington), 4 (October, 1919): 457.

ise. I do not see how they pay such wages the way they work labors. they do not hurry or drive you. . . . I wish many time that you could see our People up here as they are entirely in a different light.[10]

Personal letters brought news of the excitement of city life, of decent treatment by whites, and of high wages. They provided assurance that the North was not just a chimera, and they must have influenced thousands of Negroes who might otherwise have indefinitely postponed their decision. When a letter from a departed member of the family contained money, it offered even more concrete evidence of success in the North. And occasionally a migrant returned home in person, flushed with prosperity, and took back with him friends and relatives who aspired to similar affluence.[11]

Along with the letters from the North came "The World's Greatest Weekly"—Robert Abbott's lively, hard-hitting *Chicago Defender*. The *Defender* publicized and encouraged the migration and, in the process, became the leading Negro journal in the country. The migration appealed to both sides of Abbott's racial ideology—to his belief in Negro protest and his commitment to racial solidarity and self-help.[12] On the one hand, by leaving the South, Negroes were effectively protesting against oppression and injustice; on the other hand, by coming to the North, they were swelling the urban black belts and strengthening Negro economic, political, and institutional life.

In encouraging the migration, the *Defender* played upon every emotion. It portrayed stark contrasts between northern freedom and southern tyranny. The North, the *Defender* asserted, offered not only economic opportunity but a chance for human dignity:

> Every black man for the sake of his wife and daughter should leave even at a financial sacrifice every spot in the south where his worth is not appreciated enough to give him the standing of a man and a citizen in the community. We know full well that this would almost mean a depopulation of that section and if it were possible we would glory in its accomplishment.[13]

[10] *Ibid.*, 4: 464.

[11] Scott, *Negro Migration During the War*, p. 36; *New York Times,* October 7, 1917.

[12] See chap. 6. [13] *Defender,* October 7, 1916.

Every act of violence in the South hammered home the lesson. After a particularly brutal lynching in Memphis, the *Defender* asked: "Do you wonder at the thousands leaving the land where every foot of ground marks a tragedy, leaving the graves of their fathers and all that is dear, to seek their fortunes in the North?"[14] When southern whites told Negroes that they would freeze to death in the North, the *Defender* compiled a list of Negroes who had frozen to death in the South, and asked: "If you can freeze to death in the north and be free, why freeze to death in the south and be a slave?"[15]

In the spring of 1917, the *Defender* set a date—May 15—for the "Great Northern Drive."[16] It supplemented its polemic with photographs, cartoons, and even poems: "Some are coming on the passenger,/ Some are coming on the freight,/ Others will be found walking,/ For none have time to wait."[17] Even more persuasive were the notices of job opportunities in the North. "More positions open than men for them," read a *Defender* headline. In northern Illinois and southern Wisconsin, "there is a dire shortage of molders" and "employers will give men a chance to learn the trade at $2.25 a day."[18] These items were substantiated by advertisements for help in the *Defender*'s classified columns.[19]

The *Defender* was widely read in the South. Its local news columns indicated that its largest readership outside of Chicago was in Kentucky, Tennessee, and the Gulf States. Prospective migrants deluged the *Defender*'s office with praises for the paper's message and requests for job information. "Permitt me to inform you," wrote a correspondent from Texas, "that I have had the pleasure of reading the Defender for the first time in my life and I never dreamed that there was such a race paper published and I must say that its *some* paper."[20] White southerners attempted to control the distribution of the *Defender* as they had curbed the labor agents. A daily newspaper in Athens, Georgia, called the Chicago weekly "the greatest disturbing element that has yet entered Georgia," and elsewhere in the South city authori-

---

14 *Ibid.*, May 28, 1917.

15 *Ibid.*, February 24, 1917.   17 *Ibid.*, May 28, 1917.

16 *Ibid.*, March 24, 1917.   18 *Ibid.*, April 30, 1917.

19 For a selection of such advertisements, see Scott, *Negro Migration During the War*, pp. 17–18.

20 "Letters of Negro Migrants," 4: 327.

ties seized copies of the newspaper.[21] But they could not effectively halt the *Defender*'s circulation nor minimize its influence.
Emmett Scott summed up the paper's impact on southern Negroes: "In it they could read the things they wanted to hear most,
expressed in a manner in which they would not dare express it.
It voiced the unexpressed thoughts of many and made accusations
for which they themselves would have been severely handled."[22]

The offer of an agent, an encouraging letter from a friend in
the North, or the appeal of the militant Negro press, coming
after years of smoldering discontent, sparked the final decision
to migrate. Through these media, tenant farmers and sharecrop-
pers, displaced by agricultural reorganization or disastrous floods,
or merely weary of their marginal economic status and the pro-
scriptions of the southern caste system, learned of the opportunities that awaited them in Chicago, Detroit, and Cleveland. Each
southern Negro who chose to migrate made a highly personal
decision, but he was frequently influenced by the power of mass
suggestion. Wherever Negroes gathered, particularly in the country towns of the South, the North became the principal topic of
conversation. Jeremiah Taylor of Bobo, Mississippi, for instance,
was resigned to his farm until one day his son came back from
town with the report that folks were leaving "like Judgment day."
Taylor went to town, skeptical, and came back determined to
move north.[23] As friends departed, many persons went along just
because "it seemed like everybody was heading that way." A
woman in Macon wrote to her friend in Chicago: "May you dont
no how much I mis you. . . . it is lonesome her it fills my heart
with sadiness to write to my friends that gone. . . . May now is
the time to leave here. . . . if I stay here I will go crazy."[24]

The early migrants had only vague notions of what they might
expect at their destinations, and they often headed north with
visions of fantastic wages and unbounded liberty.[25] Moreover as
the image of the North filtered south through the promises of
agents, the glowing letters of friends, and the appeal of the Negro

[21] *Defender*, September 15, 1917.

[22] Scott, *Negro Migration During the War*, p. 30.

[23] Johnson, "The New Negro in a New World," p. 280.

[24] "Letters of Negro Migrants," 4: 454–55.

[25] Scott, *Negro Migration During the War*, pp. 28–29.

press, it took on a mythical quality that gave to the migration an almost religious significance. The rhetoric of the migration was highly charged with biblical imagery: the Flight out of Egypt; Bound for the Promised Land; Going into Canaan; Beulah Land. A party of migrants on their way from Mississippi to Chicago held solemn ceremonies when their train crossed the Ohio River; they stopped their watches, knelt down to pray, and sang the gospel hymn, "I Done Come Out of the Land of Egypt With the Good News."[26]

The lure of the Promised Land was particularly compelling for the younger generation. Their fathers had been reared in the immediate aftermath of slavery, when the plantation tradition was still strong and Negroes were loyal to those "Southern gentlemen of the old school" who took a paternalistic interest in them. But the sons came into friendly contact with whites less frequently and found it difficult to live with whites on the terms accepted by their fathers. A Negro preacher in Mississippi told a Labor Department investigator:

> My father was born and brought up as a slave. He never knew anything else until after I was born. He was taught his place and was content to keep it. But when he brought me up he let some of the old customs slip by. But I know there are certain things that I must do and I do them, and it doesn't worry me; yet in bringing up my own son, I let some more of the old customs slip by. He has been through the eighth grade; he reads easily. For a year I have been keeping him from going to Chicago; but he tells me this is his last crop; that in the fall he's going. He says, "When a young white man talks rough to me, I can't talk rough to him. You can stand that; I can't. I have some education, and inside I has the feelings of a white man. I'm going."[27]

The emotions engendered by the exodus were closely linked to a growing Negro race consciousness. Despite the wide variety of individual motives, the migration developed a certain coherence; it grew out of the Negro people's common historical experiences and common grievances. Prior to 1915, southern Negroes had no means of expressing their discontent because no alternative was open to them. But with the broadening of oppor-

[26] *Ibid.*, pp. 44–45.

[27] U.S. Department of Labor, *Negro Migration in 1916–17*, p. 33.

tunities in the North, they were able to act positively and independently to improve their status. As Ray Stannard Baker observed, Negroes were "acting for themselves, self consciously . . . they are moving of their own accord."[28] A Labor Department investigator reported that "the Negroes just quietly moved away without taking their recognized leaders into their confidence any more than they do the white people about them."[29] Here then was a self-conscious, independent racial movement. The migrants saw themselves not merely as men in search of better jobs, but also as Negroes seeking a greater degree of freedom. The initial impetus was primarily economic, but as the movement took form, as the vision of Canaan put into sharper focus the tyranny of Egypt, the exodus became, in E. Franklin Frazier's words, "one of the most crucial mass movements in the history of the Negro in the United States."[30]

The volume, direction, and impact of the 1916–19 migration differed markedly from earlier migration patterns. Before the war, Negro migration had been gradual, had included both westward and northward movements, had usually involved short distances, and had attracted relatively little attention. Ever since emancipation, the Negro population had shifted within the South—from the antebellum black belts to the newer agricultural areas of the upper piedmont and the Southwest and to the new cities—Birmingham, Miami, Houston.[31] Many Negroes had migrated from the Upper South to such border cities as St. Louis, Baltimore, and Washington, and a slow but steady stream of migrants had flowed into the small Negro colonies of New York, Philadelphia, and Chicago.[32] During World War I, on the other hand, large numbers of Negroes moved so suddenly as to cause wide-

[28] Ray Stannard Baker, "The Negro Goes North," *World's Work* (New York), 34 (July, 1917): 319.

[29] U.S. Department of Labor, *Negro Migration in 1916–17*, p. 95.

[30] E. Franklin Frazier, *The Negro in the United States,* rev. ed. (New York: Macmillan Company, 1957), p. 527.

[31] Lionel C. Florant, "Negro Migration, 1860–1940," unpublished manuscript prepared for the Carnegie Corporation of New York, 1942 (Schomburg Collection, New York Public Library), pp. 30–37; Woofter, *Negro Migration,* p. 117.

[32] Florant, "Negro Migration, 1860–1940," pp. 40, 43; and see chap. 1.

spread notice and alarm. The direction of the new migration was almost exclusively from south to north—the earlier westward migration was no longer prominent—and a large proportion of the new population shift was of a long distance nature.

The largest influx of Negroes between 1916 and 1919 occurred in the key northern industrial states—Pennsylvania, Illinois, Ohio, New York, and Michigan, in that order—while the southern black belt states—Mississippi, Georgia, South Carolina, Alabama, and Louisiana—experienced the greatest Negro emigration.[33] Although Negroes continued to move from the Lower South to the Upper

[33] Simon Kuznets, *et al.*, *Population Redistribution and Economic Growth, United States, 1870–1950* (Philadelphia: American Philosophical Society, 1957), 1: 107–231. It is impossible to obtain data from raw census reports because the census, before 1940, asked no questions directly relevant to population mobility. Kuznets and his associates, however, use the census material on population growth for the various states and, by employing life survival ratios, eliminate from these figures that proportion of the change that would have resulted from natural growth. They are then able to estimate the net intercensal gains and losses, by state, attributable to internal migration.

All statistical data relevant to the World War I migration are based on the intercensal period, 1910–20. We must generally accept, without quantitative evidence, the consensus of opinion that the bulk of the migration during this decade occurred between 1916 and 1919. This would, of course, coincide with the period of greatest demand for unskilled labor in northern industry; but possibly, contemporary observers, swayed by the enormous publicity that accompanied the exodus during the peak years, exaggerated the size of the World War I migration. Elliott M. Rudwick, for instance, suggests that this was the case in East St. Louis. His own estimates of Negro migration, based on school enrollment and military draft figures, are considerably lower than contemporary estimates. (*Race Riot at East St. Louis* [Carbondale: Southern Illinois University Press, 1964].) Furthermore, census data are often unreliable for the South and are notoriously so in regard to Negroes. The 1920 census, considered generally substandard, has been criticized in particular for errors in enumerating the Negro population. (LaVerne Beales, "Negro Enumeration of 1920," *Scientific American* [New York], 14 [April, 1922]: 352–60; Kelly Miller, "Enumeration Errors in Negro Population," *Scientific American*, 14 [February, 1922]: 168; and V. D. Johnston, "Negro Migration and the Census of 1920," *Opportunity* [New York], 1 [June, 1923]: 235–38.) Even assuming the accuracy of census figures, we can learn nothing of intrastate migration, stages, and steps in the migration process, nor the activities of those who migrated and returned within the same intercensal period. Analysis can be based only on data showing population changes in the various cities, states, and regions, and on data indicating the state of birth of those living outside of their native states.

South and from the Upper South to the North, a large portion of the World War I migrants went directly from the Gulf and South Atlantic states to the North. Generally, they followed meridians of longitude: Negroes from the Carolinas and Georgia moved to New York and Philadelphia; Negroes from Alabama, Mississippi, and Louisiana followed the Illinois Central and the Gulf, Mobile, and Ohio railroads to Chicago, Detroit, and Cleveland.[34] The migrants concentrated heavily in the largest northern industrial cities. Of the ten Northern cities with more than 25,000 Negroes in 1920, all but two—Pittsburgh and Kansas City—registered gains of over 50 per cent in the decade, 1910-20. In Detroit, the Negro population increased 611 per cent, in Cleveland 308 per cent, in Chicago 148 per cent, and in Philadelphia and Indianapolis 59 per cent.[35]

Chicago was one of the principal destinations of the World War I migrants. Its location at the head of two major southern railroads, its industrial opportunities, and the fame of its Negro community attracted many of the Negroes who were seeking new homes in the North. By the early spring of 1916, Chicago employers began to fear a labor shortage. In March, the government employment service had over a thousand openings that it was unable to fill.[36] Chicago's business leaders lagged behind their eastern counterparts in sending labor agents into the South, but during the summer of 1916 Chicago became aware of an increasing influx of southern migrants.[37] With American entry into the war early in 1917, the labor shortage became critical, and the major packing houses, steel mills, and foundries adopted a policy of actively encouraging migration to Chicago. "A new problem, demanding early solution, is facing Chicago," announced the *Tribune* in March, 1917. "It pertains to the sudden and unprecedented influx of southern Negro laborers."[38]

The migration to Chicago continued unabated until the business recession of 1919-20, and it brought an undetermined num-

[34] Kuznets, *et al.*, *Population Redistribution and Economic Growth*, 1: 299-348. Here Kuznets and his associates analyze data on state of birth in order to trace the course of internal migration.

[35] U.S. Bureau of the Census, *Fourteenth Census, 1920*, 2: 48.

[36] *Chicago Tribune*, March 5, 1916.

[37] *Ibid.*, July 25, 1916.   [38] *Ibid.*, March 15, 1917.

ber of southern Negroes into the city. Contemporary observers often exaggerated the size of the influx. A *Tribune* reporter estimated that 40,000 Negroes entered the city between January, 1916, and March, 1917, and a year later, a Methodist minister claimed that between 75,000 and 100,000 had come to Chicago since the beginning of 1917.[39] Undoubtedly many migrants that entered the city subsequently moved on to Detroit, Milwaukee, or Cleveland. In any case, the 1920 census placed Chicago's Negro population at 109,458, an increase of 65,355 since 1910.[40] Otis and Beverly Duncan estimate that 94 per cent of this increase, or approximately 61,000, was the result of migration.[41] Part of the inmigration occurred before 1916, so probably no more than 50,000 Negro migrants settled in Chicago during the period, 1916–20.[42]

As in the prewar years, most of the migrants to Chicago came from outside the state. They continued to come from the border states and the Upper South, but for the first time large numbers of Negroes poured into the city from the Deep South—particularly Mississippi, Alabama, Georgia, and Louisiana. Over 60 per cent of the Negro population increase in Illinois between 1910 and 1920 was registered among Negroes born in the Lower South and, for the first time, Illinois had more Negroes from the Lower South than from the Upper South and border states.[43]

[39] *Ibid.*, March 15, 1917, April 4, 1918.   [40] See Table 1.

[41] Otis D. Duncan and Beverly Duncan, *The Negro Population of Chicago: A Study of Residential Succession* (Chicago: University of Chicago Press, 1957), p. 34. To derive this estimate, the Duncans use life survival ratios. For an explanation of their technique, see pp. 306–8 of their book.

[42] This, of course, assumes the accuracy of the 1920 census, perhaps a questionable assumption.

[43] Quantitative data on state of birth are unavailable for the Chicago Negro population, but Table 9 shows the state of birth of Illinois Negroes in 1910 and in 1920. The intercensal increase in the number of Negroes born in the various states gives a rough approximation of the volume of migration from these states. Tennessee remained a major source of Illinois' Negro migrants, but it was eclipsed by Mississippi and Alabama, while Georgia and Louisiana registered gains that far outstripped Kentucky and Missouri. As noted in chapter 1, the pattern of distribution for Illinois is not necessarily identical with the pattern for Chicago Negroes. But any observations on the increased migration from the Deep South into Illinois would undoubtedly be even more true for Chicago. First, a comparison between Tables 8 and 9 shows that

The trend toward Negro concentration within the city received new impetus from the migration. By 1920, 35 per cent of Chicago's Negroes lived in census tracts that were over 75 per cent Negro. Only 7.4 per cent lived in neighborhoods less than 5 per cent Negro—a sharp reduction from 32.7 per cent in 1910. Half of the Negro population now lived in predominantly Negro census tracts, and 90 per cent lived in tracts that were at least 10 per cent Negro. In short, the majority of Chicago's Negroes now lived in

TABLE 8

NATIVITY OF NEGROES
CHICAGO, 1910–20

AREA OF BIRTH	1910		1920		INCREASE		
	Number	Per Cent	Number	Per Cent	Number	Per Cent of Total	Per Cent Increase 1910–20
Born in Illinois...	8,519	19.3	16,274	14.9	7,755	11.9	88.4
Born in other states.........	34,017	77.1a	91,095	83.2b	57,078	87.3	167.8
Foreign born.....	664	1.5	1,020	0.9	356	0.5	53.6
Others..........	903	2.0	1,069	1.0	166	0.3	18.4
Total..........	44,103	100.0	109,458	100.0	63,355	100.0	148.2

SOURCES: U.S. Bureau of the Census, *Negro Population in the United States*, 1790–1915, p. 74; U.S. Bureau of the Census, *Fourteenth Census*, 1920, vol. 2, *Population*, 661.

a Compare to 15.8 per cent whites born in other states.

b Compare to 15.5 per cent whites born in other states.

black enclaves; the "scattered" portion of the Negro population had almost disappeared.[44]

The pattern of Negro settlement in Chicago continued to follow the outlines established before the turn of the century. Instead of expanding the boundaries of the Negro districts, the migration converted the old South Side black belt from a mixed neighborhood into an exclusively Negro area. There was remarkably little

a smaller percentage of the Chicago population was born in Illinois than was true for the state as a whole. Second, it is probable that migration from the nearby border states—Missouri, Kentucky, Tennessee—was greater in southern and western Illinois than in Chicago.

[44] See Tables 4, 10, and 11.

TABLE 9

STATE OF BIRTH OF ILLINOIS NEGROES
1910–20

AREA OF BIRTH	1910		1920		INCREASE		
	Number	Per Cent	Number	Per Cent	Number	Per Cent of Total	Per Cent Increase 1910–20
Illinois............	35,917	33.2	44,130	24.4	8,213	11.3	22.9
Middle West (except Illinois)[a]							
Ohio..............	2,766		3,516		750		
Indiana............	2,731		3,738		1,007		
Iowa..............	797		1,122		325		
Michigan..........	750		1,014		264		
Kansas............	728		1,379		651		
Wisconsin.........	285		385		100		
Minnesota.........	120		209		89		
Nebraska..........	105		242		137		
North Dakota......	12		14		2		
South Dakota......	5		19		14		
Region..........	8,299	7.7	11,638	6.4	3,339	4.6	40.2
Northeast							
Pennsylvania.......	765		1,094		329		
New York.........	524		695		171		
Massachusetts......	140		249		109		
New Jersey........	82		200		118		
Connecticut........	45		74		29		
Rhode Island......	24		47		23		
Maine.............	20		21		1		
New Hampshire....	5		6		1		
Vermont...........	5		17		12		
Region..........	1,610	1.5	2,403	1.3	708	1.1	40.2
Upper South and Border							
Tennessee..........	15,303		23,995		8,692		
Kentucky..........	13,314		16,470		3,156		
Missouri..........	9,732		11,704		1,972		
Virginia...........	3,326		3,586		260		
North Carolina.....	1,175		1,763		588		
Maryland..........	643		677		34		
District of Columbia	268		399		131		
West Virginia......	229		296		67		
Oklahoma..........	126		597		471		
Delaware..........	24		32		8		
Region..........	44,140	40.8	59,519	32.9	15,379	21.1	34.8

SOURCES: U.S. Bureau of the Census, *Negro Population in the United States*, 1790–1915, pp. 75–79
U.S. Bureau of the Census, *Fourteenth Census*, 1920, vol. 2, *Population*, pp. 636–40.

[a] Middle West totals (including Illinois): 1910—44,216 and 40.9 per cent; 1920—55,768 and 30.8 per cent; 1910–20 increase, 11,522 (15.8 per cent of total) and 26.1 per cent.

TABLE 9—*Continued*

AREA OF BIRTH	1910		1920		INCREASE		
	Number	Per Cent	Number	Per Cent	Number	Per Cent of Total	Per Cent Increase 1910–20
Lower South							
Mississippi.........	4,612		19,485		14,873		
Alabama...........	3,208		13,668		10,460		
Georgia...........	2,874		10,185		7,311		
Louisiana..........	1,609		8,078		6,469		
Arkansas..........	1,354		3,091		1,737		
South Carolina.....	1,217		2,636		1,419		
Texas.............	789		2,692		1,903		
Florida...........	243		1,020		777		
Region..........	15,906	14.7	60,855	33.6	44,949	61.6	282.6
West							
Colorado..........	89		182		93		
California.........	77		207		130		
Washington........	32		80		48		
New Mexico.......	18		39		21		
Montana..........	13		33		20		
Idaho.............	8		31		23		
Arizona...........	8		31		23		
Oregon...........	6		15		9		
Nevada...........	6		4		−2		
Wyoming..........	4		18		14		
Utah..............	8		18		10		
Region..........	269	0.2	658	0.4	389	0.5	144.6
Not specified and born abroad......	1,980	1.8	1,826	1.0	−154	−0.2	−7.8
Total Negro......	109,049	......	182,274	......	73,225	....	67.1

Summary

	Number	Per Cent	Number	Per Cent	Number	Per Cent of Total	Per Cent Increase 1910–20
Born in Illinois.....	35,917	33.2	44,130	24.4	8,213	11.3	22.9
Born outside Illinois.	70,224	64.9	135,073	74.6	64,849	88.9	92.3
Total Negro......	109,049	......	182,274	......	73,225	....	67.1

TABLE 10

DISTRIBUTION OF NEGROES
BY CENSUS TRACTS
CHICAGO, 1910–20

PER CENT NEGRO	NUMBER OF CENSUS TRACTS	
	1910	1920
None..........	94	135
Under 1.........	249	264
1– 2...........	26	26
2– 5...........	33	23
5–10...........	11	5
10–20...........	6	12
20–30...........	5	6
30–50...........	3	12
Over 50.........	4	16

NOTE: see Map 3, "Census Tracts of Chicago, 1910," and Map 4, "Census Tracts of Chicago, 1920."

TABLE 11

TEN CENSUS TRACTS WITH HIGHEST
NEGRO PERCENTAGE
CHICAGO, 1910–20

1910		1920	
Tract Number	Per Cent Negro	Tract Number	Per Cent Negro
295	61.0	341	86.6
336	58.0	338	84.8
292	54.9	339	84.5
288	53.5	344	83.8
373	47.3	343	82.8
296	42.2	337	81.6
264	32.7	342	78.3
278	29.9	432	77.2
333	25.1	382	76.3
330	21.8	388	75.6

SOURCES: unpublished census data for 1910, and Burgess and Newcomb, *Census Data for the City of Chicago*, 1920.

change in the area of Negro settlement despite the 148 per cent population increase.[45] To be sure, a few new Negro neighborhoods emerged: sizable Negro colonies appeared for the first time near the steel mills of South Chicago, in the middle-class community of Roseland on the far South Side, and in the ethnically mixed Near North Side. But, for the most part, the population increase was reflected less in the expansion of the black belt than in a sharp rise in the density of Negro settlement within the black enclaves. In 1910, only four census tracts were predominantly Negro; by 1920, there were sixteen. In 1910, no census tract was more than 61 per cent Negro; in 1920, ten were over 75 per cent Negro and they ranged upward to almost 87 per cent. A predominantly black enclave now stretched from Thirty-first Street south to Fifty-fifth; only a few blocks wide at its southern end, it broadened north of Thirty-ninth Street extending almost to Lake Michigan. The West Side area of Negro settlement was still racially mixed, but the Negro population had grown there too; three West Side census tracts were now over 30 per cent Negro.

The quantitative data confirm contemporary observations: an unprecedented influx of Negro migrants from the Deep South swelled Chicago's black belt and converted it into a solidly Negro community that cut through the heart of the South Side. The migration brought to fruition the varied strains of prewar Chicago Negro history. Within the Negro community, self-help activities proliferated: businesses, welfare institutions, and political organizations expanded to serve a larger and more concentrated black belt. At the same time, the protest aspects of the migration —so clearly articulated in the pages of Abbott's *Defender*—created a feeling of racial consciousness that eventually led both to black nationalism and to a new type of Negro militancy. The effect of the migration on the attitudes of the white community was even more critical. The sporadic racial violence of the prewar years reached crisis proportions: the situation deteriorated so rapidly that, by the beginning of 1919, civic leaders—both Negro and white—realized that the city was on the brink of full-scale racial war. In short, if the migration did not mark a sharp break with the past, it accelerated the trends that had been apparent before the war and prepared the way for the flowering of Chicago's "black metropolis" during the 1920's.

[45] See Maps 3 and 4.

CHAPTER 8

THE STRUGGLE FOR HOMES AND JOBS

Chicago was strange and forbidding to the Negro migrant who had lived all of his life on a Mississippi plantation or in a small Alabama town. Men in worn, outmoded suits carrying battered luggage, and women clutching ragged, barefooted children crowded into the Illinois Central station on Twelfth Street looking hopefully for a familiar face. Park Row—the little drive running from Michigan Avenue to the station—was solidly packed with people. There the migrants mingled with local Negroes who came down every Sunday to meet a friend or a relative or just to see who had arrived. If there was no one to meet them, the newcomers seldom knew where to go. They might ask a Red Cap to direct them to the home of a friend—unaware that without an address the porter could be of little help in a city as large as Chicago. Or they might employ one of the professional guides who, for a fee, would help them find lodging. Some of the guides were honest, others were little more than confidence men. Travelers Aid and the railroad police tried to help the migrants and prevent exploitation; but for the newcomer without friends or relatives, the first few days were often a terrifying experience.[1]

Somehow or other, most of the migrants made their way to the South Side black belt. There they found the constricted, increasingly self-contained Negro community that had developed in the prewar years. Housing was scarce, but not impossible to find. Although there was no new construction during the war, many of the old wooden houses west of State Street stood empty, vacated by Negroes who had moved into the more desirable homes to the east.[2] The old core of the black belt, between State and Went-

[1] The description of the migrants' arrival is based on an interview with Chester Wilkins, who worked for many years as a Red Cap and, eventually, Chief Usher at the Illinois Central Station, Chicago, March 28, 1963.

[2] Chicago Commission on Race Relations, *The Negro in Chicago: A Study of Race Relations and a Race Riot* (Chicago: University of Chicago Press,

worth, for many years a festering slum, deteriorated further during the migration years. Two-story frame houses, devoid of paint, stood close together in drab, dingy rows, surrounded by litters of garbage and ashes. Ordinary conveniences were often nonexistent: toilets were broken or leaked; electricity was rare; heating and hot water facilities failed to function.[3] A 1911 study of several blocks along Federal Street had shown that almost 25 per cent of the houses were in bad repair, about 50 per cent in fair repair, and another 25 per cent in good repair.[4] In a study of a comparable area in 1923, an investigator found that over 41 per cent of the residential buildings were in bad repair, 40 per cent in fair repair and only about 14 per cent in good repair.[5] Landlords had nothing to gain by improving these old houses; they merely allowed them to decay and collected whatever rent they could from Negroes who were unable to find—or to afford—better housing.

The more affluent of the migrants, who had sold their property in the South and come to Chicago with ready funds, sought homes in the more desirable neighborhood east of State Street. There the quality of housing varied widely. On the broad avenues—Wabash, Michigan, South Park, Grand Boulevard—stood homes that a generation before had been the finest in the city. Though somewhat faded now, many were still comfortable, well-equipped, and commodious. On the side streets and the lesser avenues, rows of connected flat buildings, usually of stone or brick, provided less attractive, although often adequate, accommodations.[6]

1922), pp. 93, 186; Junius B. Wood, *The Negro in Chicago* (Chicago: *Chicago Daily News*, 1916), *passim*.

[3] Chicago Commission on Race Relations, *The Negro in Chicago*, pp. 152–53, 191–92; Alice Q. Rood, "Social Conditions Among the Negroes on Federal Street Between Forty-fifth and Fifty-third Streets," unpublished master's thesis, University of Chicago, 1924, pp. 15–16, 41–45.

[4] Alzada P. Comstock, "Chicago Housing Conditions: VI: The Problem of the Negro," *American Journal of Sociology* (Chicago), 18 (September, 1912): 241–57.

[5] Rood, "Social Conditions Among the Negroes," p. 25. Rood and Comstock each surveyed segments of Federal Street that were, at the time of their studies, the heart of the Negro slum. Rood used Comstock's schedule cards and attempted to apply the same criteria in evaluating the adequacy of the houses.

[6] Chicago Commission on Race Relations, *The Negro in Chicago*, pp. 187–91.

But the neighborhood had declined since Negroes first entered it around 1900. Many of the old homes had begun to deteriorate and frequently were in need of repair or lacked necessary sanitary facilities.[7] The homes east of State were still far better than the rickety shacks on Wentworth and Federal; but they were no longer the choice property that they had once been.

Despite the low quality of most black belt housing, overcrowding was not yet a major problem during the migration period. To the contrary, families often found that all available housing was too large for their needs. Even the ramshackle houses in the Federal Street slum were relatively roomy. Most of the apartments there occupied an entire floor and usually housed no more than one person per room.[8] On the basis of a 1917 study, the Race Relations Commission concluded that "Negroes have more space in their living quarters than do other Chicago people housed in similar grades of dwellings."[9]

The large size of the apartments often forced families to fill vacant rooms with lodgers in order to raise money for the rent. In the 1911 study of living conditions on Federal Street, 31 per cent of the persons queried had been lodgers; 35 per cent of the postwar sampling were lodgers.[10] Lodging became a regular way of life in the black belt; "the people are rushing here by the thousands," wrote a Chicago woman to a friend in the South, "and I know if you come and rent a big house you can get all the roomers you want."[11] Many families, however, took lodgers for other than financial reasons. The survey of the Race Relations Commission indicated that "lodgers were often found in families where the income from that source did not appear to be needed."[12] During the migration, many of the older settlers took in relatives and friends, newly arrived from the South, until the

[7] *Ibid.*, pp. 188, 192.

[8] Rood, "Social Conditions Among the Negroes," pp. 27–28.

[9] Chicago Commission on Race Relations, *The Negro in Chicago*, p. 157.

[10] Comstock, "Chicago Housing Conditions," 18: 244–45; Chicago Commission on Race Relations, *The Negro in Chicago*, p. 158. These two surveys are not directly comparable. But it is probable that the high proportion of lodgers was maintained throughout the migration era.

[11] "Letters of Negro Migrants of 1916–18," collected under the direction of Emmett J. Scott, *Journal of Negro History* (Washington), 4 (October, 1919): 457.

[12] Chicago Commission on Race Relations, *The Negro in Chicago*, p. 164.

newcomers could find permanent quarters of their own. There were few hotels and guest houses in the black belt, and migrants frequently depended upon their old friends for temporary housing.[13]

To meet the need for smaller apartments, some landlords began to divide up large houses into little "kitchenette" units—usually two or three rooms with cooking facilities. An owner of a spacious house east of State could increase his income substantially by renting "kitchenettes" to six or seven families rather than leasing flats to two families. In the 1920's and 1930's, when overcrowded conditions became prevalent on the South Side, the kitchenette arrangement was viewed as an evil. But at its inception it represented an advance; it allowed small families to secure housing without renting more space than they needed.[14]

The migrants did not often come into direct competition with whites for housing. Few of them could afford apartments or homes in the predominantly white districts east of the black belt, and they had no reason to seek homes among the hostile Irish and Poles in the overcrowded neighborhood west of Wentworth Avenue. But the influx of the migrants precipitated a crisis in housing by pushing the older settlers across the boundaries of the Negro ghetto. Middle- and upper-class Negroes were no longer able to find satisfactory homes on the avenues just east of State Street. Wabash and Indiana Avenues had begun to deteriorate by 1910, and with the migration, Prairie, Calumet, and even stately South Park Avenue, though still racially mixed, were becoming predominantly working-class neighborhoods. So, as Negro families had tried to escape the slum fifteen years before by moving east of State Street, many now moved beyond Cottage Grove Avenue into Kenwood and Hyde Park and south of Fifty-fifth Street into Woodlawn. The hostility they met went far beyond the sporadic resistance of the prewar years and led directly to the racial violence that terrorized Chicago in 1919.[15]

13 *Ibid.*, p. 165.

14 Interview with Grace Garnett, Negro landlady, transcript in "The Negro in Illinois," a file of reports and interviews compiled by the Illinois Writers Project of the Works Progress Administration (George Cleveland Hall Branch of the Chicago Public Library), cited hereafter as Illinois Writers Project Files.

15 The housing conflict and the violence it engendered are fully treated in chapter 11.

The job market for Negroes, unlike the housing market, vastly expanded during the migration years. This expansion had been a major factor in bringing the migrants to Chicago in the first place. The migrants of the prewar years had taken jobs as janitors, porters, and personal servants. The World War I migrants were hired as laborers at Swift, Armour, Pullman, and International Harvester, in jobs previously restricted to white workers.

The shift in the occupational position of Negroes in Chicago during the migration decade was striking. In 1910, over 51 per cent of the male Negro labor force was engaged in domestic and personal service trades; this figure dropped to 28 per cent in 1920. The proportion of Negroes engaged in manufacturing, on the other hand, more than doubled, and the proportion occupied in trade tripled. Factory work, rather than domestic and personal service, was the most important source of employment for Negroes by 1920. Negroes barely held their own in the various domestic services despite the sharp population increase. In manufacturing, on the other hand, the percentage of Negroes among unskilled laborers increased fivefold and the percentage among semiskilled workers tenfold. Negroes now constituted 4 per cent of the labor force in manufacturing—close to the percentage their numbers would warrant.

The change among women was less dramatic. A smaller proportion of Negro women were in domestic trades and a larger proportion were in manufacturing, but domestic service continued to be the largest source of employment. Almost 64 per cent of the Negro women were engaged in this type of work—over 90 per cent as household servants and almost 14 per cent as laundresses. Yet for the first time, a sizeable minority of Negro women worked in factories. In 1910, almost all of the Negro women classified under the manufacturing trades were dressmakers, seamstresses, and milliners working in their own homes. But in 1920, over three thousand Negro women—15 per cent of the female Negro labor force—were unskilled and semiskilled factory operatives. Negro women also broke into commercial laundry work during this decade: in 1910 they had constituted only 4 per cent of the labor force in commercial laundries; by 1920, this figure had climbed to 36 per cent.[16]

Despite this important shift in the employment pattern, Ne-

[16] See Tables 7 and 12.

TABLE 12

Males and Females over Ten Engaged in Selected Occupations
Chicago, 1920

Selected Occupations	Total Number of Jobs	Number of Jobs Held by Negroes	Percentage of Total Jobs Held by Negroes	Percentage of Negro Labor Force in Particular Occupations
		Males		
Manufacturing				
45 specified trades[a].......	239,145	4,445	1.9	9.9
Semi-skilled, unspecified...	89,433	2,944	3.3	6.5
Iron and Steel Industries..	22,240	422	1.9	0.9
Packing Houses[b]..........	6,325	1,490	23.6	3.3
Laborers, unspecified......	79,171	8,837	11.2	19.6
Building and general....	18,259	1,835	10.0	4.1
Iron and Steel Industries	24,931	3,355	13.4	7.4
Packing Houses[b]........	6,781	1,242	18.3	2.8
Other..................	3,825	81	2.1	0.2
Occupational total......	411,574	16,307	4.0	36.1
Transportation				
Chauffeurs.............	17,077	928	5.4	2.1
Teamsters..............	14,501	542	3.7	1.2
Laborers[c]...............	18,409	1,303	7.1	2.9
Mail Carriers...........	2,500	183	7.3	0.4
Engineers, firemen, motormen, switchmen.......	17,794	108	0.6	0.2
Conductors.............	7,540	4	....	....
Occupational total......	98,510	3,441	3.5	7.6
Trade				
Store Clerks[d].............	14,189	173	1.2	0.4
Deliverymen.............	8,536	303	3.6	0.7
Laborers—coal yards, lumberyards, warehouses...	4,230	398	9.4	0.9
Laborers, stockyards[b].....	16,517	5,304	32.1	11.8
Laborers and porters in stores.................	6,248	1,210	19.3	2.7
Retail dealers	41,137	528	1.3	1.2
Salesmen in stores[d].......	40,616	126	0.3	0.3
Occupational total......	172,264	8,461	4.9	18.8

Source: U.S. *Fourteenth Census*, 1920, vol. 4, *Population: Occupations*, pp. 1076–79.

[a] Includes officials, foremen, apprentices.

[b] The distinction between packing house and stockyards workers is undoubtedly inexact. See note in *Fourteenth Census*, vol. 4, p. 15.

[c] Includes laborers for express companies, garages, street building firms and railroads.

[d] These classifications undoubtedly overlap.

TABLE 12—*Continued*

Selected Occupations	Total Number of Jobs	Number of Jobs Held by Negroes	Percentage of Total Jobs Held by Negroes	Percentage of Negro Labor Force in Particular Occupations
	Males			
Professional				
Lawyers.................	4,553	95	2.1	0.2
Physicians..............	4,887	195	4.0	0.4
Clergymen..............	2,169	215	9.9	0.5
Teachers...............	1,800	26	1.4	0.1
Actors.................	1,019	57	5.6	0.1
Musicians..............	3,415	254	7.4	0.6
Dentists...............	2,288	68	3.0	0.2
Occupational total	43,528	1,191	2.7	2.0
Public Service				
Laborers...............	3,368	473	14.0	1.0
Guards and Watchmen....	5,372	183	3.4	0.4
Policemen..............	5,938	105	1.8	0.2
Occupational total	22,682	959	4.2	2.1
Domestic and Personal				
Barbers and hairdressers..	5,982	469	7.8	1.0
Elevator operators........	3,181	393	12.4	0.9
Janitors................	9,375	1,822	19.4	4.0
Laundry operatives.......	2,082	350	16.8	0.8
Porters[e]................	6,003	4,679	77.9	10.4
Servants...............	8,040	1,942	22.5	4.3
Waiters................	6,869	2,315	33.7	5.1
Occupational total......	55,798	12,666	22.7	28.1
Clerical				
Bookkeepers, cashiers, accountants, stenographers	23,285	69	0.3	0.2
Office clerks.............	70,367	1,659	2.4	3.7
Messengers..............	7,792	254	3.3	0.6
Occupational total......	111,719	2,026	1.8	4.5
Total employed........	919,819	45,123	4.9	100.0

[e] Not including porters in stores.

TABLE 12—*Continued*

Selected Occupations	Total Number of Jobs	Number of Jobs Held by Negroes	Percentage of Total Jobs Held by Negroes	Percentage of Negro Labor Force in Particular Occupations
	Females			
Manufacturing				
Dressmakers, seamstresses[f]	8,513	1,070	12.6	5.2
Milliners................	4,341	103	2.4	0.5
Semi-skilled, unspecified	50,811	2,542	5.0	12.2
clothing industry.......	16,596	440	2.7	2.1
Laborers, unspecified......	4,653	591	12.7	2.8
Occupational total......	77,427	4,456	5.8	21.5
Trade				
Store clerks[d]............	13,330	518	3.9	2.5
Saleswomen[d]............	13,343	112	0.8	0.5
Occupational total......	34,711	933	2.7	4.5
Professional				
Actresses...............	1,028	65	6.3	0.3
Musicians...............	3,058	134	4.4	0.6
Teachers...............	11,739	138	1.2	0.7
Nurses.................	5,004	116	2.3	0.6
Occupational total......	27,633	705	2.6	3.8
Domestic and Personal				
Barbers and hairdressers..	2,156	729	33.8	3.5
Boardinghouse keepers....	3,677	334	9.1	1.6
Charwomen..............	1,280	123	9.6	0.6
Housekeepers............	4,982	315	6.4	1.5
Laundresses[g]	6,638	2,853	43.0	13.7
Laundry operatives.......	3,907	1,409	36.1	6.8
Servants...............	26,184	6,250	23.9	30.1
Waitresses..............	5,175	678	13.1	3.3
Occupational total......	60,304	13,235	21.9	63.8
Clerical				
Bookkeepers, cashiers, accountants, stenographers	58,995	478	0.8	2.3
Office clerks............	37,968	594	1.6	2.9
Occupational total......	98,818	1,125	1.1	5.4
Total employed........	311,535	20,755	6.7	100.0

[f] Not in factories.

[g] Not in laundries.

groes remained at the bottom of the occupational ladder. Over half of the Negro men engaged in manufacturing were listed as laborers—a classification used for the unskilled.[17] Most of the Negro transportation workers were either laborers or chauffeurs; positions as engineers, motormen, switchmen, and conductors were still completely closed to them.[18] The sharp increase in the number of Negroes engaged in trade was the result of the massive influx of Negro workers into the stockyards, where they generally worked in unskilled jobs.

For Negro women, the job market remained highly constricted. Clerical occupations were still almost closed to Negroes, and the women employed by industrial and commercial firms were almost always unskilled workers—kitchen helpers, chambermaids, ironers in laundries, or common laborers in garment and lampshade factories. Women with high school—and even college—educations still had no real alternative to domestic service.[19] The two large mail order houses, Sears Roebuck and Montgomery Ward, hired Negro women as temporary help, but the downtown stores and the Chicago Telephone Company—major employers of female labor—refused to even experiment with Negro help.[20]

The migration gave birth to a black proletariat in Chicago. Before the war, Negroes had been outside the mainstream of the city's economic life. As domestic workers, porters, and waiters, they had been engaged in peculiarly Negro occupations—out of touch with white workers of similar status, isolated from the labor movement, nearly deprived of any opportunity to advance. It remained to be seen whether the Negro's new occupational position would permanently change this situation and whether Negroes would be able to maintain their foothold in industry. And it was not yet certain whether the Negroes' concentration in unskilled work would remain a permanent feature of Negro economic life or whether it would disappear as Negroes acquired skills.

[17] See the instructions to the census workers on the use of this term in U.S. Bureau of the Census, *Fourteenth Census, 1920*, 4: 30.

[18] In addition to the census reports, see Chicago Commission on Race Relations, *The Negro in Chicago*, pp. 391–92.

[19] Forrester B. Washington, "Reconstruction and the Colored Woman," *Life and Labor* (Chicago), 8 (January, 1919): 4–5.

[20] Chicago Commission on Race Relations, *The Negro in Chicago*, pp. 380–83, 391–92.

The occupational adjustment of the southern migrants was frequently difficult. Most of the newcomers found themselves in work vastly different from their previous occupations. Of 225 migrants interviewed by the Race Relations Commission, only ninety-one utilized previous experience and training after moving to Chicago.[21] The majority had been farmers in the South. Others, who had worked in skilled trades at home, found that they were unable to pursue their vocation in Chicago: northern employers often imposed higher standards of competence and many craft unions maintained rigid color bars. Even professional people frequently took unskilled and personal service jobs: women who had taught in southern Negro schools, for instance, could rarely qualify to teach in Chicago and were often forced into domestic work.[22]

Many migrants from the rural South were unprepared for the long, regular hours required in the mills, factories, and stockyards of Chicago. As farmers, handymen, and personal servants at home, their work schedules had often been informal and flexible. The rigid, six-day week demanded by Chicago industries necessitated a change in the newcomers' way of life. A. L. Jackson of the Wabash Avenue YMCA told of the migrant who had come to him complaining that he had lost his job. Had he gone to work every day? Jackson asked. "Goodness no," the man replied. "I just had to have some days of the week off for pleasure."[23] The superintendent of a company employing a large number of Negroes commented: "The southern Negroes have not yet become reconciled to working six days a week. Down South they are accustomed to taking off Saturdays, and they are quite frequently absent on Saturday."[24] But gradually, the migrants adjusted. "The man who comes here," A. L. Jackson predicted, "will want to keep pace with his brothers in the north in living and recreation and will find it necessary to work every day in order to keep up. His manner of living, the pleasures he affords himself . . . will be added to a changed condition of life."[25]

The migrants were compensated for what they sacrificed in leisure and informality. They earned more money than they ever

21 *Ibid.*, p. 167.   22 *Ibid.*, pp. 166–68.

23 Quoted by Wood, *The Negro in Chicago*, p. 7.

24 Chicago Commission on Race Relations, *The Negro in Chicago*, p. 373.

25 Wood, *The Negro in Chicago*, p. 7.

had before. Wages for unskilled labor in the leading Chicago industries ranged from a minimum of 42.5 cents an hour in the packing houses to 61 cents an hour at Argo Corn Products and International Harvester. The average was nearly 50 cents an hour. In the building trades, an unskilled laborer could earn up to $1.00 an hour. Most companies worked from forty-eight to sixty hours a week, so $25.00 was not an unusual week's wages.[26] For a man who had been earning 75 cents a day as a farm laborer in the South, this was an enormous salary. Women generally averaged from $12.00 to $18.00 a week for factory work in Chicago and could earn that much, plus room and board, in domestic service.[27] Negroes received the same wages as white workers for comparable work, although in a few instances Negroes were assigned to certain kinds of piecework that yielded smaller earnings.[28]

A less tangible but perhaps even more important compensation was the independence that industrial work offered. In the rural South, Negroes were personally dependent upon white landowners in an almost feudal sense. Personal supervision and personal responsibility permeated almost every aspect of life. In prewar Chicago, the service trades, in which Negroes were concentrated, also placed a high premium on personal loyalty and servility; domestic workers, for example, who lived in the homes of their white employers, had little time for their private lives. In the factories and yards, on the other hand, the relationship with the "boss" was formal and impersonal, and supervision was limited to working hours. Between 1918 and 1920, employers had difficulty in finding domestic help even when they offered higher wages than competing factories.[29] "I can save more when I'm in service," admitted a maid who had quit to work in a mail-order house, "but the other things you have to take—no place to entertain your friends but the kitchen, and going in and out the back doors. I hated all that. . . . They almost make you a slave." A migrant who had left domestic work in Georgia for a job in a Chicago box factory was even more vehement: "I'll never work in nobody's kitchen but my own any more. No indeed! That's the one thing that makes

---

[26] *Ibid.*, pp. 7–8; Chicago Urban League, *Annual Report, 1919;* Chicago Commission on Race Relations, *The Negro in Chicago,* pp. 366–67.

[27] Chicago Commission on Race Relations, *The Negro in Chicago,* pp. 367, 370.

[28] *Ibid.*, p. 365.   [29] *Ibid.*, p. 371.

me stick to this job. You do have some time to call your own."[30]

In addition to higher wages and independence, there was hope that the breakthrough in industry would provide opportunity for advancement that Negroes had not previously enjoyed. Negroes, to be sure, were entering at the bottom—in the unskilled occupations—but so had the Poles and Czechs back in the 1880's, and many of them had moved into supervisory and even managerial positions. Yet, there were already indications that the Negroes' ladder of advancement in industry would have slippery rungs. In the stockyards, for instance, Negroes were systematically passed over when new foremen were named; a Negro might be appointed subforeman over an all-Negro gang, but he was never allowed to supervise a mixed group of workers.[31]

Even more portentous was the massive layoff of Negro workers during the recession of 1919–20. In the spring of 1919, the packing houses laid off 15,000 workers—a large proportion of them Negroes. One company spokesman insisted that "no discrimination is being shown in the reducing of our forces." But he admitted that many Negroes were among the first to be released. "It is a case of the survival of the fittest, the best man staying on the job. It is a fact that the southern Negro cannot compete."[32] The Negro women who had entered industry and trade during the war found it particularly difficult to maintain their gains. The mail-order houses hired Negroes to meet a temporary rush, but they never integrated them into their regular work force and released them as soon as business leveled off. One employer told the Department of Labor that he had hired Negro girls "solely on account of the shortage of labor" and "as soon as the situation clears itself no more colored help will be employed."[33] The recession was of short duration and by 1921 jobs were plentiful again. But the experience of 1919–20 indicated that Negro industrial gains were tenuous and depended—far more than white jobs—upon continuing business prosperity.

[30] *Ibid.*, p. 387.

[31] Alma Herbst, *The Negro in the Slaughtering and Meat Packing Industry in Chicago* (New York: Houghton, Mifflin & Company, 1932), pp. xxi–xxiii; Chicago Commission on Race Relations, *The Negro in Chicago*, p. 390.

[32] *Chicago Tribune*, April 12, 1919.

[33] Washington, "Reconstruction and the Colored Woman," 8: 4.

The breakthrough in industry gave Negroes their first major contact with the labor union movement. Before the war, Negro workers had generally encountered unions only in the hostile role of strikebreakers. But they had made a few inroads into the union movement. The stockyards strike of 1904 had persuaded the Butcher Workmen's Union that its only protection against Negro strikebreakers was the organization of Negro workers.[34] Several other unions followed suit: by 1915, the Hod Carriers' Union, the Flat Janitors' Union, and the International Ladies Garment Workers' Union—all organized in major fields of Negro employment—admitted Negroes on a non-discriminatory basis. Another group of unions admitted Negroes, but organized them into separate locals; this included the musicians', painters', and waiters' unions. Finally, such unions as the railroad brotherhoods, the machinists, the sheet metal workers, the electrical workers, the plumbers and the electricians continued to bar Negroes either by constitutional provision, local option, or informal agreement.[35]

The most significant confrontation of Negroes with the union movement in the migration era came in the stockyards where thousands of newly hired Negro workers found themselves in the midst of an aggressive union organization drive. Early in 1916, the Amalgamated Meat Cutters and Butcher Workmen of North America launched a campaign designed to take advantage of the wartime labor shortage and to halt the steady decline the union had suffered since its defeat in 1904. The drive received new impetus in 1917 when the packing companies signed contracts with the federal government to supply a thousand carloads of meat daily. The unions now had assurance that to protect its own interests the government would mediate in any stockyards labor dispute. The Stockyards Labor Council was formed in the summer of 1917; all local unions with jurisdiction over packinghouse workers joined in the Council, which cooperated with—but remained apart from—the Butcher Workmen's Union.[36]

34 See chap. 2.

35 Oscar D. Hutton, "The Negro Worker and the Labor Unions in Chicago," unpublished master's thesis, University of Chicago, 1939, pp. 5–6; Erie W. Hardy, "Relation of the Negro to Trade Unionism," unpublished master's thesis, University of Chicago, 1911, passim; Chicago Commission on Race Relations, The Negro in Chicago, pp. 412–20.

36 Herbst, The Negro in the Slaughtering and Meat Packing Industry in Chicago, pp. 28–30; Sterling Spero and Abram Harris, The Black Worker

Unable to secure a direct agreement with the employers, the Council threatened a strike late in 1917. As expected, the President's Mediation Commission intervened and signed separate agreements with the employers and the union in order to assure the fulfillment of government contracts. Early in 1918, both sides agreed to the appointment of Judge Samuel Alschuler as arbitrator for the industry. For nearly four years, all labor-management disputes were referred to Alschuler. During this period, both the union and the companies attempted to win the support of the unskilled workers in preparation for the day when a direct confrontation could no longer be postponed.[37]

Negro workers provided a special and serious problem for the union organizers. Although the Butcher Workmen had a nondiscriminatory policy, several of the unions within the Stockyards Labor Council barred Negroes.[38] Moreover, the southern Negroes who predominated in the yards were ill-disposed toward unions. They had only the vaguest notion of union purposes and their limited experience with unions convinced them that they were white men's organizations. "Unions ain't no good for a colored man," said one migrant. "I've seen too much of what they don't do for him." Another stockyard worker, who had come from Alabama in 1916, admitted that he didn't understand unions, that he "can't understand why they strike and keep men out of work."[39] By 1917, an estimated twelve thousand Negroes worked in the yards, and the management, aware of Negro antipathy toward the unions, was consciously increasing this number.[40] The union's

(New York: Columbia University Press, 1931), pp. 268–71; Horace Cayton and George Mitchell, *Black Workers and the New Unions* (Chapel Hill: University of North Carolina Press, 1939), pp. 242–43; Chicago Commission on Race Relations, *The Negro in Chicago*, pp. 412–13; Edna L. Clarke, "History of the Controversy Between Labor and Capital in the Slaughtering and Meat Packing Industry of Chicago," unpublished master's thesis, University of Chicago, 1922, pp. 102–6.

[37] Herbst, *The Negro in the Slaughtering and Meat Packing Industry in Chicago*, pp. 37–41; Cayton and Mitchell, *Black Workers and the New Unions*, pp. 246–47.

[38] Cayton and Mitchell, *Black Workers and the New Unions*, p. 242; Spero and Harris, *The Black Worker*, p. 270.

[39] Chicago Commission on Race Relations, *The Negro in Chicago*, p. 424.

[40] Herbst, *The Negro in the Slaughtering and Meat Packing Industry in Chicago*, p. 34; Catherine E. Lewis, "Trade Union Policies in Regard to the

future depended upon a successful organization campaign among the Negro workers.

The Stockyards Labor Council attempted to bring Negro workers into the union and, at the same time, avoid antagonizing Jim Crow locals within the Council. The union hired two Negro organizers, and with their help established Local 651, with headquarters in the heart of the black belt. Local 651 was never a formally segregated organization; admission was open to white workers and, officially at least, Negroes could join other locals. The union argued that Local 651 was established merely for the convenience of Negroes who lived in the black belt. But, clearly, the Local was a conscious attempt to placate anti-Negro elements within the Council: the issue had been referred to Samuel Gompers, who had suggested a separate Negro organization. Moreover, members of Local 651, unlike the members of other locals affiliated with the Labor Council, all received membership cards in the butchers' union, even though they might be mechanics, plumbers, or electricians. The all-white unions, associated with the Council, thus maintained their color lines. This situation was finally modified by providing for interchangeability of membership in all of the Council's locals. But many Negroes continued to view Local 651 as a segregated organization, and the task of breaking down Negro resistance to the union movement remained difficult.[41]

The union and the employers vied for the support of Negro community leaders in their bid to win the loyalty of the Negro workers. Local 651 won the backing of the newly organized Chicago Urban League. T. Arnold Hill, executive director of the League, spoke in favor of the Stockyards Labor Council, but insisted "that if he and his colleagues were expected to advise the colored workers to join the union, they expected the union men themselves to be fair to colored workers."[42] George Cleveland

---

Negro Worker in the Slaughtering and Meatpacking Industry of Chicago," unpublished master's thesis, University of Chicago, 1945, pp. 24–27.

[41] Herbst, *The Negro in the Slaughtering and Meat Packing Industry in Chicago*, pp. 32–35; Cayton and Mitchell, *Black Workers and the New Unions*, pp. 243–44; Chicago Commission on Race Relations, *The Negro in Chicago*, pp. 412–13; Lewis, "Trade Union Policies in Regard to the Negro Worker," pp. 26–27.

[42] *Chicago Whip*, July 19, 1919.

Hall, president of the Urban League, said that the Council's organizational drive provided a good opportunity "for Negroes to show that they are not natural born strikebreakers."[43] The racially militant and economically radical *Chicago Whip*, the city's newest Negro weekly, was even more enthusiastic. It gave wide and sympathetic coverage to union activities and editorially urged Negroes to support the Council's efforts.[44]

The packing companies countered by seeking the support of more conservative Negro leaders and by underwriting "Negro organizations" of their own. The companies won endorsements from the Wabash Avenue YMCA and from the ministers of several leading churches that had received generous financial contributions from the packers. A. L. Jackson, executive director of the YMCA, was allegedly on the companies' payroll, and Armour bought three hundred YMCA memberships for its Negro employees.[45] Not content with working through existing Negro organizations, the companies subsidized a Negro promoter, Richard Parker, who organized an employment agency, a newspaper, and a company labor union. The employment agency recruited Negro workers in the South, aiding management's attempt to use Negro employees as a buffer against the union's organizational drive. Parker warned his recruits that they would lose their jobs if they joined any union other than his—the American Unity Labor Union. This organization, a union in name only, billed itself as "the only colored labor union at the yards." It promised job security and played upon Negro fears that the real union, with its white leadership, would sell out the interests of Negro workers. Responsible Negro leaders attempted to expose Parker as a pawn of the packers, but he nevertheless succeeded in confusing the issue of unionism for many Negro employees.[46]

The packing companies were also able to use the city's mounting racial tensions against the union. In July, 1919, the union

[43] *Chicago Defender*, February 23, 1918.

[44] See, for example, *Whip*, February 27, 1920; and see chap. 10.

[45] *Whip*, August 15, 1919; Spero and Harris, *The Black Worker*, p. 273.

[46] Herbst, *The Negro in the Slaughtering and Meat Packing Industry in Chicago*, pp. 35–36; Chicago Commission on Race Relations, *The Negro in Chicago*, pp. 422–23; Cayton and Mitchell, *Black Workers and the New Unions*, pp. 245–46; Lewis, "Trade Union Policies in Regard to the Negro Worker," pp. 27–28; Spero and Harris, *The Black Worker*, pp. 271–73.

planned a mass meeting and parade in which black and white workers were to march together in a demonstration of solidarity. The packers persuaded the police that the Negroes were armed and that the parade would precipitate a race riot. On the morning of the event, the police tried to induce the union leaders to cancel the parade and, unable to do that, insisted that Negroes and whites march separately.[47] Three weeks later, the long-feared riot finally materialized. Although it had little to do with labor conditions and there was no violence in the yard, the union found it exceedingly difficult to promote racial harmony while whites and Negroes were battling in the streets.

By the end of 1919, the union realized that its drive to organize Negro workers had failed. "To be frank," admitted the secretary of the Stockyards Labor Council, "we have not had the support from the colored workers which we expected. Our method of propaganda may have been weak somewhere; probably we do not understand the colored worker as we do ourselves. . . . Be that as it may, the colored worker has not responded to the call of unionism."[48] At the height of the stockyards organizing drive, probably no more than one-third of the Negro workers belonged to the union.[49] The antiunion tradition among Negroes, the tactics of the companies, and the union's compromising position on the issue of segregated locals contributed to the union's failure to win Negro workers to their cause. When the union finally went out on strike in 1921, the companies again defeated them by using Negro strikebreakers.

Next to the stockyards, Negroes made their most important breakthrough in the steel industry. But here, the union did not even try to win Negro support. The Amalgamated Association of Iron, Steel, and Tin Workers began an industry-wide organizational drive in 1918 that culminated, a year later, in a major steel strike. Although Negroes made up 10 to 12 per cent of the work force in the Chicago steel mills, they played a decidedly minor role in union activities. The Amalgamated had previously been an association of skilled workers; only with the greatest trepidation

---

[47] *Whip,* July 19, 1919; Herbst, *The Negro in the Slaughtering and Meat Packing Industry in Chicago,* pp. 41–43; Spero and Harris, *The Black Worker,* pp. 275–76.

[48] *Whip,* January 24, 1920.

[49] Spero and Harris, *The Black Worker,* p. 271.

did it begin to organize the unskilled, and it gave no thought whatsoever to the special problems of Negroes. Moreover, as in the Stockyards Labor Council, several unions connected with the organizing committee barred Negroes from membership. Negroes could join the Amalgamated, but without a concerted drive to win their support, few did. Although many Negroes walked out with their white co-workers in 1919, they played no part in union activities. Most of them gradually drifted back to work together with many recent Negro migrants hired by the mills as strikebreakers.[50]

In several other trades, the unions attempted to make inroads among Negro workers, but their success was limited. In the ladies garment industry, the employers broke a strike in 1917 by hiring four hundred fifty Negro workers. The International Ladies Garment Workers' Union subsequently organized these employees and, so long as the wartime labor shortage lasted, the industry was forced to meet union demands. But after the war, the employers opened several non-union shops on the South Side employing Negro women at low wages, and despite the union's non-discriminatory policy Negro women continued to act as strikebreakers.[51] When non-discriminatory unions, such as the I.L.G.-W.U., organized Negroes, the employers often refused to hire them. Many employers were willing to hire Negroes only if they could pay them lower wages or use them to break strikes; if they had to meet the union scale, they preferred white workers.[52] But few unions could convince their white members to strike in support of Negro co-workers.

In the railroad trades, the established unions completely barred Negroes from membership, and the only union activity came from Negroes themselves. The Railwayman's International Benevolent

[50] Cayton and Mitchell, *Black Workers and the New Unions*, pp. 76–79; Spero and Harris, *The Black Worker*, pp. 256–61; William Z. Foster, *The Great Steel Strike and Its Lessons* (New York: B. W. Heubsch, 1920), pp. 205–7; Chicago Commission on Race Relations, *The Negro in Chicago*, p. 430; Commission of Inquiry, Interchurch World Movement, *Report on the Steel Strike of 1919* (New York: Harcourt, Brace & Company, 1920), pp. 177–78.

[51] Spero and Harris, *The Black Worker*, pp. 337–39; Chicago Commission on Race Relations, *The Negro in Chicago*, pp. 414–15.

[52] Spero and Harris, *The Black Worker*, p. 338; Chicago Commission on Race Relations, *The Negro in Chicago*, p. 415.

Industrial Association was organized in Chicago in 1915 to protest "against unfair and bad working conditions of the employer and against unfair practices of the American Federation of Labor and the railway brotherhoods."[53] The Association aimed to bring all types of Negro railway workers—porters, firemen, waiters, Red Caps—into a single union. During its first three years, it attracted fewer than a hundred members, but in 1918 it took advantage of government control of the railroads to launch an organizational drive. The Association billed itself as the "one organization strong enough of purpose, active and aggressive enough in leadership to speak at the right place and at the right time for all classes of Negro railway employees."[54] At its peak, the Association claimed 15,000 members throughout the country, but it declined and disappeared soon after 1920.[55]

Negroes also had organizations of their own in the painting, music, and waiting trades. Here, however, they did not establish their own unions but formed all-Negro locals affiliated with predominantly white unions. The musicians' local was a strong autonomous union, chartered in 1902, which had the same wage scale as the white union and access to equally lucrative contracts.[56] The Negro locals in the painters' and waiters' unions, on the other hand, were makeshift organizations designed chiefly to keep Negroes out of the white locals. A waiters' strike in 1920 failed primarily because of Negro strikebreakers.[57]

In 1920, the unions reported a Negro membership of over twelve thousand in Chicago. This constituted 18 per cent of the Negro work force. By comparison, the unions claimed 24 per cent of the white work force.[58] At first glance, this is an impressive figure, given the late entry of Negroes into industry and the special difficulties the unions faced in organizing Negroes. But despite these numerical gains, the unions had not won a dependable

---

[53] Quoted in Chicago Commission on Race Relations, *The Negro in Chicago*, p. 410.

[54] *Defender*, September 21, 1918.

[55] Spero and Harris, *The Black Worker*, pp. 311–12.

[56] "History of Local 208, American Federation of Musicians," in Illinois Writers Project Files (based on interviews).

[57] Chicago Commission on Race Relations, *The Negro in Chicago*, pp. 417–18.

[58] *Ibid.*, pp. 411–12.

and loyal following among Negro workers. They had been unable to win the support of the Negro community or to halt the employment of Negroes as strikebreakers. There are several reasons for their failure. First, despite the efforts of organizations such as the Butcher Workmen and the Ladies Garment Workers, most unions were unable to free themselves from their Jim Crow past and often approached the task of organizing Negro workers with uncertainty and irresolution. Secondly, even the most forthright position on Negro equality could not always overcome many Negroes' long-standing distrust of unions. Moreover, the unions found it impossible to organize many of the recent migrants who could not understand the purpose of union techniques. Finally, the rising racial tension in Chicago during the migration years complicated the task of creating solidarity between white and Negro workers and provided employers with a bludgeon that they used willingly and purposefully.

While the migration simply accelerated prewar developments in housing, it affected basic changes in employment. Before the war, Chicago Negroes had been predominantly personal servants; during the migration era, they became primarily factory workers. Yet, the significance of this shift can be exaggerated. As before, Negroes were concentrated in the least skilled, least desirable jobs; their opportunities for advancement were severely limited; they were subject to periodic layoffs; and they had little hope of obtaining white collar jobs. Negro contacts with the unions had broadened, but black and white workers continued to regard one another with misgivings and distrust. Without doubt, the Negro employment situation had changed; whether it had improved was a moot question.

CHAPTER 9

THE IMPACT OF THE MIGRATION: NEGRO COMMUNITY LIFE

By 1915, most Negro leaders in Chicago were committed to the idea of a separate Negro community with civic institutions, businesses, and political organizations of its own. The debate between the militant integrationists and the advocates of self-help had begun to lose its edge. Some members of the old elite, who held strongly integrationist views, had actively participated in the establishment of a Negro YMCA, Negro social agencies, and co-operative business enterprises. On the other hand, some of the most vigorous exponents of separate development also advocated militant protest against racial discrimination. They saw the need to modify the Tuskegee philosophy when it was transplanted to the North. Many accepted Booker T. Washington's ideas of racial solidarity and self-help but rejected his emphasis on accommodation with the white community. Robert Abbott, for instance, saw no contradiction in applauding Negro civic undertakings and business ventures while at the same time urging a direct attack on racial barriers. By the beginning of World War I, therefore, Chicago's Negro leaders were all Washingtonians and they were all Du Boisians.

Most of the leaders of black Chicago welcomed the migrants and urged the Negro community to aid them in adjusting to urban ways. "The new arrivals rapidly adjust themselves to their changed surroundings," said George Cleveland Hall, now perhaps the most universally esteemed leader on the South Side. But they must be "reached by the proper people and get the right tip." Robert Abbott, who had played a key role in stimulating the migration, described the movement as "merely one group of American citizens moving in their own home country to better their conditions."[1]

[1] *Chicago Daily News*, April 2, 1917.

As the migration progressed, Negro leaders became increasingly aware of the problems presented by the newcomers. The crude, rustic ways of many of the migrants, their inability to maintain accepted standards of cleanliness, and their traditionally sycophantic demeanor in the presence of whites antagonized the old settlers. Not only did the more established Negroes find the newcomers' habits personally offensive but they felt that they diminished the status of all Negroes in the eyes of the white community. The old settlers began to formulate a myth that became an article of faith in later years. Discrimination, they argued, was minimal before the migration and it was the behavior of the newcomers that induced it.[2]

The *Defender,* the first champion of the migration, was also one of the first to criticize the migrants' behavior in Chicago. The paper declared:

> It is evident that some of the people coming to this city have seriously erred in their conduct in public places, much to the humiliation of all respectable classes of our citizens, and by so doing, on account of their ignorance of laws and customs necessary for the maintenance of health, sobriety and morality among the people in general, have given our enemies ground for complaint.

The *Defender* urged the newcomers "to strictly observe the laws, city ordinances and customs" and it submitted a list of twenty-six "don'ts" as a guide for public conduct. The rules ranged from general precepts, such as "don't use liberty as a license to do what you please" to specific admonitions as "don't appear on the street with old dust caps, dirty aprons and ragged clothes."[3] On other occasions, the *Defender* printed blunt advice in bold type: "Keep your mouth shut, please! There is entirely too much loud talking on the street cars among our newcomers."[4] "Go clean up north. . . . In the south a premium was put on filth and uncleanliness. In the north a badge of honor is put on the man or woman who is clean."[5]

The task of helping the migrants adjust to urban life required not haphazard criticisms and admonitions, but concerted educa-

<hr />

[2] See, for example, *Chicago Defender,* April 22, 1939.

[3] *Ibid.,* May 17, 1919.

[4] *Ibid.,* March 24, 1917.   [5] *Ibid.,* August 4, 1917.

tional efforts by civic and welfare organizations. The *Defender* attacked "the glib assumption that matters will eventually adjust themselves"; the situation demanded "positive efforts of constructive social welfare work."[6] At the very onset of the migration, some social workers and church leaders recognized that the migrants would place new demands upon the community. The Cook County Sunday School Association met early in 1917 to discuss "how to handle the . . . newcomers," and the Baptists set up a center for migrants at the Olivet Church.[7] By far the most important organization to respond to the problems of the migration years was the Chicago Urban League. Not a social welfare organization itself, the League attempted to coordinate the efforts of existing agencies, help the newcomers find jobs, gather data on Negro living conditions, and represent Negro interests in the general community.

The Chicago Urban League was a branch of the National League on Urban Conditions among Negroes, which had been founded in New York in 1911. Like the NAACP, the League was an interracial group, reflecting the reform impulse of the progressive era. Unlike the NAACP, it envisaged itself not as a protest organization, but as an extension of the social work movement into the growing urban Negro enclaves. Before World War I, the League operated primarily in New York and in several southern and border cities, where the branches soon atrophied for lack of white cooperation. During World War I, however, the League came into its own by firmly establishing itself in the Northern industrial cities most affected by the migrants.[8]

The president and associate director of the National League came to Chicago late in 1915 to interest local leaders in the establishment of a Chicago Urban League. They called together three groups of people: (1) professional social workers, such as Sophonisba Breckinridge, Edith Abbott, and Celia Parker Woolley; (2) white progressives who had exhibited an interest in the Negro cause—Judge Edward O. Brown, president of the Chicago

[6] *Ibid.*, September 22, 1917.

[7] *Ibid.*, March 24, March 31, 1917.

[8] Arvarh E. Strickland, "The Chicago Urban League, 1915–1956," unpublished doctoral dissertation, University of Illinois, 1962, pp. 9–33; L. Hollingsworth Wood, "The Urban League Movement," *Journal of Negro History* (Washington), 9 (April, 1924): 117–20.

NAACP, Robert Park the eminent University of Chicago sociologist, and Horace Bridges of the Ethical Culture Society; and (3) Negro community leaders, such as George Cleveland Hall, Robert Abbott, A. L. Jackson, and several prominent Negro clubwomen. T. Arnold Hill, an organizer for the national body, agreed to serve as acting secretary of the new Chicago branch. He had originally planned to stay in Chicago for a month; he eventually stayed eight years and became a major figure in the Chicago Negro community.[9]

Hill was primarily responsible for putting the League on an organizational basis. An able, articulate and tactful man, he won friends for the League in the Negro community and among white philanthropists, on whom the League depended for financial support. He made a strong impression on Julius Rosenwald, who described him as a "very conservative, vigorous, educated Negro"— all highly complimentary terms in the philanthropist's lexicon.[10] Rosenwald agreed to underwrite one-third of the League's annual budget, and his secretary, William Graves, became a member of the executive board.[11] Although 75 per cent of the League's membership was Negro, whites accounted for 90 per cent of the financial contributions.[12] After a few months of operation in the YMCA building, the new organization moved to its own office on State Street, and shortly thereafter took over the building of the dying Frederick Douglass Center on Wabash Avenue.[13]

The Chicago Urban League, according to its first president, Robert Park, was designed to do for Negroes what other social

[9] *Defender*, October 30, 1915; Strickland, "The Chicago Urban League," pp. 36–41; "Minutes of the First Meeting of the Executive Board of the Chicago League on Urban Conditions among Negroes, January 10 [1916]," copy in Julius Rosenwald Papers (University of Chicago Library), cited hereafter as Rosenwald Papers; Horace Bridges, "The First Urban League Family: Some Recollections," *Two Decades of Service*, pamphlet (Chicago: Chicago Urban League, 1936), [n. p.].

[10] Julius Rosenwald to E. F. Buffington, September 1, 1922, Rosenwald Papers.

[11] T. Arnold Hill to Julius Rosenwald, January 19, 1917; William Graves to Hill, February 24, 1917; Hill to Graves, April 7, 1917; Graves to Rosenwald, November 23, 1917; Graves to Hill, November 30, 1917—Rosenwald Papers.

[12] William Graves to Julius Rosenwald, November 23, 1917, Rosenwald Papers.

[13] *Defender*, June 21, 1916, March 2, 1917.

agencies were doing for immigrants, to help with "work and wages, health and housing, the difficulties of the adjustment of an essentially rural population to the conditions of a city environment, and to modern life." But Park also realized that racial prejudice made the Negro's problem distinct and engendered in Negroes a counter feeling of racial hostility. The Urban League, he hoped, would convert this racial feeling from "a liability into an asset" by directing "the energies aroused by racial antagonism into constructive channels."[14] To achieve these aims, Park and Hill outlined a concrete program of coordination, investigation, education, and labor relations that the League attempted to follow throughout the migration period.

In trying to coordinate existing welfare programs, the League put its prime emphasis upon efficiency. Arnold Hill and many of the founders of the Urban League were products of the professional social work movement and frowned upon the haphazard manner in which the numerous church, settlement house, and private welfare programs were administered. Hill hoped to bring the various agencies together in order to avoid duplication, delineate areas of interest, and assist the weaker organizations in their work.[15] Inevitably such a program aroused the antagonism of existing agencies that saw the new group as a threat to their own work. Nevertheless, the League achieved notable results. It took over the ailing Wendell Phillips Settlement, cooperated with the wartime agencies in operating a service men's club on the South Side, and acted as a Negro branch of general welfare agencies, such as the Social Service Department of the Cook County Hospital, the United Charities, and the Travelers Aid.[16] According to William Graves, the League brought "cooperation from scores of Negro civic and philanthropic organizations which have been working at cross purposes with much jealousy."[17] The League also operated several civic programs intended specifically for the migrants: Urban League representatives helped the newcomers find housing; League workers spoke at churches on such themes as

[14] Chicago Urban League, *Annual Report, 1917*, p. 3.

[15] "Plan for Work for the Chicago Organization," memorandum from T. Arnold Hill, 1917, copy in Rosenwald Papers.

[16] Strickland, "The Chicago Urban League," pp. 46–48; A. L. Foster, "20 Years of Interracial Good Will," *Two Decades of Service*.

[17] William Graves to Julius Rosenwald, November 23, 1917, Rosenwald Papers.

thrift and hygiene; and a creed of cleanliness distributed by the League outlined simple rules of neatness and decorum.[18] Utilizing Park's theory that racial feeling could be turned into constructive channels, the League organized block clubs and community improvement societies. Through these organizations, Negroes were encouraged to answer the white argument that Negroes depreciate property values by maintaining high standards in their homes and neighborhoods.[19]

Another tenet of the progressive credo that motivated the Urban League was the belief that the compilation of factual data on social problems was the first step toward their solution. The League retained Charles S. Johnson, then a graduate student at the University of Chicago and later a prominent sociologist and educator, to direct its Bureau of Investigation and Records. Johnson investigated Negro migration for the Carnegie Foundation, conducted a study of juvenile delinquency among Negroes, and surveyed Negro housing conditions. He was called into the army in 1918 and his bureau then became moribund, but it was revived in the 1920's with the cooperation of the University of Chicago.[20]

The most important phase of the Urban League's program was its work in the field of labor relations. In this area it received the widest acclaim and at the same time faced its most serious potential problem. The League's Industrial Department operated through the war period as an employment bureau. Migrants were encouraged to register with the Urban League for a job, and employers went to the League's office to obtain Negro labor. In addition to placing the newcomers in the plentiful unskilled jobs, the League also operated training courses for prospective workers and tried to find jobs for them in skilled and clerical work.[21] In

[18] Strickland, "The Chicago Urban League," pp. 48–60; Carl Sandburg, *The Chicago Race Riots, July, 1919* (New York: Harcourt, Brace & Howe, 1919), pp. 35–36.

[19] *Defender,* June 7, 1919.

[20] Strickland, "The Chicago Urban League," pp. 56–58; Chicago Urban League, *Annual Report, 1917,* p. 7; Chicago Urban League, *Annual Report, 1918,* p. 9; *Defender,* June 21, 1916; Foster, "20 Years of Interracial Good Will."

[21] Strickland, "The Chicago Urban League," pp. 63–68; Chicago Urban League, *Annual Report, 1917, passim;* Chicago Urban League, *Annual Report, 1918, passim;* Foster, "20 Years of Interracial Good Will."

1918, the Department of Labor assumed responsibility for the League's employment service, but it left the supervision of the bureau in the hands of the League staff. Federal assistance gave additional impetus to the program, and the League jealously guarded its prerogatives when the Labor Department's newly formed Bureau of Negro Economics threatened to set up a rival employment bureau.[22]

The Urban League's labor program pleased its conservative white benefactors. William Graves told Julius Rosenwald that not only had the League "opened kinds of employment hitherto closed to Colored people," but it had also "been of assistance to many employers whose forces have been reduced by employees volunteering and being drafted for military service."[23] The League identified itself, in most cases, with the interests of the large employers. During the war years, it could do this without contradiction. In labor disputes, the welfare of Negro workers was usually dependent upon the favor of management. When, however, the butchers' union made a real attempt to win Negro support, the League broke with its usual policy and encouraged the union's efforts. The end of the war ushered in a new set of conditions that severely tested the League's policy. Job scarcity and labor unrest made it more difficult to defend vigorously the interests of its Negro clients and at the same time satisfy its white supporters. The dilemma posed by an increasing need for militancy and continued dependence upon white contributions was to plague the Chicago Urban League throughout its history.[24]

Despite this potential difficulty, the Urban League was a notable success in its early years. It brought to the field of community welfare a new kind of professionalism and competence and introduced to Chicago, in T. Arnold Hill, a new kind of Negro leader—the able, well-trained professional. In a period of increasing racial strife, it stressed interracial cooperation and yet recognized ethnocentric attitudes and tried to make constructive use of them. It provided a new focal point for Negro community life, replacing

[22] William Graves to L. Hollingsworth Wood, September 20, 1918; Wood to Graves, September 27, 1918; Graves to Wood, October 2, 1918—Rosenwald Papers.

[23] William Graves to Julius Rosenwald, November 23, 1917, Rosenwald Papers.

[24] Strickland, "The Chicago Urban League," p. 67.

many of the struggling settlement houses, church social programs, and welfare agencies of the prewar years.

Not all of the older civic institutions disappeared. The Urban League absorbed the Frederick Douglass Center and took over the Wendell Phillips Settlement, but Provident Hospital and the Wabash Avenue YMCA—the most important of the prewar institutions—broadened their programs as the migrants poured into Chicago. In 1916 and 1917, Provident conducted a $15,000 fund-raising drive for expansion to meet the new demands. Although it sought help from white benefactors, it solicited Negro support with a special appeal to race pride. Provident, said George Hall, "is the Colored people's hospital. It is an establishment in which, more and more each year, the Colored folks are taking personal pride."[25] The money was raised by the end of 1918.[26]

The YMCA tried to reach the newcomers by establishing industrial baseball teams, glee clubs, and social organizations in the factories, yards, and mills. Through these groups, the Association also conducted forums on thrift and vocational guidance.[27] The directors of the YMCA, A. L. Jackson and George Arthur, were frequently characterized as tools of industrial management. They discouraged Negroes from joining unions, and Arthur admitted that "plant loyalty" was one aim of the Association's industrial program.[28] The YMCA was supplemented by a YWCA, opened by a group of Negro clubwomen in 1915. Independent at first, the group subsequently affiliated with the Chicago YWCA. Its work paralleled that of the men's association. It operated vocational classes, a dormitory, employment bureau, summer camp, library, and recreational program.[29]

Of all aspects of community life, religious activities were most profoundly changed by the migration. Before the war, the large,

[25] *Broad Ax* (Chicago), October 13, 1917; Charles Bentley to Julius Rosenwald, October 16, 1917, Rosenwald Papers.

[26] A. L. Jackson to William Graves, September 17, 1918, Rosenwald Papers.

[27] George Arthur to W. J. Parker, April 10, 1920, Rosenwald Papers.

[28] *Ibid.*; and see chap. 8.

[29] Report on YWCA in "The Negro in Illinois," a file of reports and interviews compiled by the Illinois Writers Project of the Works Progress Administration (George Cleveland Hall Branch of the Chicago Public Library), cited hereafter as Illinois Writers Project Files; *Defender,* May 20, 1922.

middle-class Baptist and Methodist churches had dominated Negro religious life in Chicago. Although they had not completely discarded the emotionalism of traditional Negro religion, these churches had moved toward a more decorous order of worship and a program of broad social concern.[30] The migration, however, brought into the city thousands of Negroes accustomed to the informal, demonstrative, preacher-oriented churches of the rural South. Alienated by the formality of the middle-class churches, many of the newcomers organized small congregations that met in stores and houses and that maintained the old-time shouting religion. Often affiliated with the more exotic fringe sects, Holiness or Spiritualist, these storefront churches became a permanent force in the Chicago Negro community and secured a powerful hold on thousands of working-class Negroes.

The Holiness or Pentecostal churches were the most conspicuous of the new storefront congregations. Although a few churches of this type had existed before the war,[31] they became numerous and prominent only with the migration. By 1920, there were twenty Holiness churches in Chicago, all meeting in storefronts or houses.[32] Most were concentrated west of State Street, among the poorest of the recent migrants. All were small, usually with no more than fifty members, and their organization was highly personal. The preacher, or presiding elder, was commonly an uneducated migrant from the South, who had founded the church while working at another job. He held his congregation together through personal loyalty, and if he died or moved away, the church rarely survived. Doctrinally, the Holiness churches were fundamentalist. Their highly emotional services were marked by rolling, shouting, or "speaking in tongues." Often too the preachers claimed the power to heal. Members of these congregations spent most of their free time in religious activities: some churches held nightly services, and all of them, in addition to Sunday worship, conducted two or three mid-week prayer meetings and periodic revivals and healing campaigns.[33]

[30] See chap. 5.   [31] *Ibid.*

[32] Chicago Commission on Race Relations, *The Negro in Chicago: A Study of Race Relations and a Race Riot* (Chicago: University of Chicago Press, 1922), p. 145.

[33] For a general description of Holiness churches in Chicago, see the report on churches in the Illinois Writers Project Files. On the relationship of the

Elder Lucy Smith was perhaps the most successful of the Holiness preachers; her All Nations Pentecostal Church became a landmark on the South Side in the 1930's. But despite her unusual success, she probably typified in background and motivation those who founded storefront churches during the migration years. A large, heavy-set woman with almost no formal education, Lucy Smith was born on a Georgia plantation in 1875, moved to Atlanta in 1909, and a year later migrated to Chicago. A Baptist by birth, she joined Olivet Church upon her arrival in Chicago. Soon dissatisfied with the formality of the large congregation, she began to attend the smaller Ebenezer Baptist Church, but here too she was unable to find the traditional kind of religion she sought. She then turned to the Stone Church, a predominantly white Pentecostal congregation. The Stone Church provided her with the inspiration she needed to begin her own religious career. "In 1914," she recalled, "I received my baptism and came into the works of the Lord. I continued going to the Stone Church until I received my calling, which is divine healing." Lucy Smith's calling coincided neatly with the arrival of the first wave of World War I migrants, who were receptive to her spiritual message. In 1916, she organized a one-room prayer meeting in her house; ten years later, after numerous moves and changes, she started to erect her own church building. Lucy Smith, according to one observer, was "a simple, ignorant, untrained woman with deep human sympathies, who believed absolutely in her own power to help and heal other people. Calm and serene in that faith, she has drawn together a following from the back streets of Chicago."[34]

Not all of the little storefront churches that sprang up during the migration years were Pentecostal. Many called themselves Baptist, although they often closely resembled the Holiness churches in their uninhibited form of worship.[35] Others were

migration to the development of these churches, see Benjamin E. Mays and Joseph W. Nicholson, *The Negro's Church* (New York: Institute of Social and Religious Research, 1933), pp. 98–99.

[34] Herbert W. Smith, "Three Negro Preachers in Chicago: A Study in Religious Leadership," unpublished master's thesis, University of Chicago Divinity School, 1935, pp. 17–19; report on churches in Illinois Writers Project Files.

[35] Report on churches in Illinois Writers Project Files. In 1920, sixty-seven of the eighty-six Negro Baptist churches in Chicago met in storefronts. Chicago Commission on Race Relations, *The Negro in Chicago*, p. 145.

Spiritualist, a vague term used to identify those religious groups that believed in "communication of the spirit" and that attempted to relay messages to the spirits through mediums. Many Spiritualist churches were merely commercial enterprises that charged fees for readings and advice. But several true Spiritualist churches were organized between 1915 and 1920. These congregations combined the emotional worship service of the Pentecostal and Baptist storefronts with seances and spiritual readings.[36]

A dearth of material makes it difficult to assess the social significance of storefront churches in Chicago. In all probability, they were primarily migrant churches; as the newcomers became acculturated to city ways, they moved to the more established churches, leaving the storefronts to the still more recent arrivals. One observer described the members of Lucy Smith's congregation, for instance, as "new arrivals from the South and those Negroes who have not [been] and probably never will be urbanized."[37] In any case, the emergence of the storefronts was symptomatic of increasing differentiation within the Negro class structure. For the storefronts were decidedly lower-class churches. As some sophisticated upper-class Negroes had broken with the old-line churches to form Episcopalian and Presbyterian congregations, so now the southern-oriented lower class sought religious fulfillment in churches that more closely approximated their values and ideals. While the upper-class churches followed formal, decorous orders of worship and emphasized ethics and social concern, the storefronts allowed the widest range of personal expression and uninhibited emotionalism, and offered a salvation centered religion that ignored and provided an escape from the problems of everyday life.

Despite the rise of the storefronts, the old-line Baptist and Methodist churches grew rapidly during the migration years. Olivet Baptist Church, for example, already the largest Negro church in the city, grew from an estimated membership of four thousand in 1915 to almost nine thousand in 1920. During this period it moved into a new and larger building and vastly expanded its already sizable social and recreational program. Lacey Kirk Williams, who became pastor of the church in 1915, tried to

---

[36] Robert L. Sutherland, "An Analysis of Negro Churches in Chicago," unpublished doctoral dissertation, University of Chicago, 1930, pp. 41–43; report on churches in Illinois Writers Project Files.

[37] Report on churches in Illinois Writers Project Files.

make Olivet a community center. By 1920, a full-time professional staff of sixteen operated a program that included a labor bureau, kindergarten, nursery, and welfare department, in addition to the usual club and athletic activities. For Olivet, as for many other northern churches that tried to provide facilities for the new-comers, this expansion resulted in heavy financial debt. The migrants were unable to contribute an amount commensurate with the new financial burdens they created.[38] Quinn Chapel, the Methodist counterpart of Olivet, did not grow as rapidly. More sedate and formal than Olivet, Quinn Chapel soon gained a repu-tation as a "swank" church, not for the "common herd." The A.M.E. denomination in Chicago claimed a total membership in-crease of about five thousand during the migration years; this figure was matched by Olivet alone.[39]

The Baptist churches, in general, outpaced the Methodist dur-ing this period and secured a preeminent position in Chicago, which they never lost. In 1916, Chicago had thirty-six Baptist churches and twenty-two Methodist. By 1920, the number of Methodist churches had increased to only thirty-four, while there were now eighty-six Baptist churches in the city.[40] Many of the new Baptist congregations were ephemeral little storefronts, but others, although beginning in stores or private homes, grew into large and substantial congregations. Pilgrim, Progressive, Provi-dent, Liberty, and Monumental Baptist Churches, all founded be-tween 1916 and 1919, began as prayer meetings in the homes of migrants recently arrived from the South. Within a decade, all of these congregations had acquired their own buildings and boasted memberships of over five hundred. Primarily migrant churches, they provided a middle ground between the formal, old-line northern congregations and the emotional, uninhibited store-fronts.[41]

[38] Mays and Nicholson, *The Negro's Church,* pp. 178–79; Miles Mark Fisher, "History of Olivet Baptist Church of Chicago," unpublished master's thesis, University of Chicago, 1922, pp. 84–97; *Defender,* September 4, 1920.

[39] Levi J. Coppin, *Unwritten History* (Philadelphia: A. M. E. Book Con-cern, 1919), pp. 341–43.

[40] Junius B. Wood, *The Negro in Chicago* (Chicago: *Chicago Daily News,* 1916), p. 19; Chicago Commission on Race Relations, *The Negro in Chi-cago,* p. 145.

[41] Reports on Pilgrim, Progressive, Provident, Liberty, and Monumental Baptist Churches in Illinois Writers Project Files.

The churches affiliated with white denominations were least affected by the migration. Most of these were upper-class urbanized churches with little to offer the recent arrivals. But there was one exception. St. Monica's Roman Catholic Church had always drawn its membership chiefly from Negroes who had been Catholics in the South; the large migration from Louisiana swelled its ranks between 1915 and 1920. The growth in the Negro Catholic population in Chicago came at a time when anti-Negro sentiment among the white Catholic groups in the city was mounting rapidly. In deference to this feeling, Archbishop Mundelein formulated a policy that resulted in almost complete racial segregation within the Archdiocese of Chicago. In 1917, Mundelein announced that while "until now practically anyone who so desired could affiliate himself with St. Monica's," he now desired "St. Monica's to be reserved entirely for the colored Catholics of Chicago . . . ; all other Catholics of whatever race or color are to be requested not to intrude." The Archbishop said that he took this action so that his "colored children shall not feel uncomfortable in the Catholic Church," and he quickly added that he had "no intention of excluding colored Catholics from any of the other churches in the district."[42] In practice, however, the Archbishop's order provided white parishes with an excuse for excluding Negroes. Many white priests refused to marry or bury Negroes and, in some cases, would not even hear their confessions. Instead they ordered them to go to their own church, which the Archbishop had set aside for them.[43]

[42] George W. Mundelein, *Two Crowded Years* (Chicago: Extension Press, 1918), pp. 291–300.

[43] Interview with Dr. Arthur G. Falls, prominent Negro Catholic layman, March 19, 1963; *Defender,* November 17, 1917.

CHAPTER 10

THE IMPACT OF THE MIGRATION: BUSINESS
AND POLITICS

As the migration gave rise to new civic and religious institutions and encouraged the expansion of existing institutions, it also gave renewed impetus to the drive for Negro business developments. Despite the importance attached to business by the exponents of self-help, Negro businessmen had little to show for their efforts in the prewar years. Jesse Binga, Robert Abbott, and Anthony Overton had made successful beginnings in real estate, banking, manufacturing, and journalism, but many others had failed, and none of the highly touted cooperative business ventures had progressed far beyond the planning stage. The migration vastly expanded the market for Negro business, but it did not remove the barriers that had previously thwarted Negro business achievement: lack of capital, inability to secure credit, and competition from better financed white companies. Although several successful firms began operations during the migration years, Negro business remained more a slogan than an actuality.

The most notable breakthrough in Negro business came in the insurance field. Before the war, the advocates of cooperative business had been unsuccessful in several attempts to organize Negro insurance companies.[1] In the five years following the outbreak of the war, on the other hand, Negroes founded four insurance companies in Chicago. Unlike most of the southern Negro companies, the Chicago firms did not evolve from mutual aid or fraternal societies, but began as corporate financial organizations. Public Life Insurance, established by former employees of the white-owned Royal Insurance Company, the first to hire Negroes, and Pyramid Mutual Casualty were short-lived operations that barely survived the migration era. Underwriters Insurance Com-

[1] See chap. 6.

pany, founded in 1918 by William J. Latham, a recent migrant from Mississippi, and staffed by agents who had worked for the southern-based Negro companies, thrived for a decade before its demise during the depression.[2]

By far the most successful of the new companies was the Liberty Life Insurance Company, destined to become one of the most prosperous Negro business ventures in the country. Liberty was founded in 1919 by Frank L. Gillespie. Born in Arkansas, Gillespie attended Howard University and came to Chicago just after the turn of the century. There he worked successively as a private secretary, a telephone company supervisor, and an agent for Oscar De Priest's real estate firm. Like many of Chicago's Negro insurance men, Gillespie served an apprenticeship at the Royal Insurance Company, which he joined in 1916. Although he soon became Royal's first Negro superintendent, Gillespie found opportunities limited in the white company, and in 1918 laid plans to establish a Negro-controlled firm. He gathered together several prominent Negro businessmen and, a year later, acquired a state charter.[3]

Gillespie used the rhetoric of racial solidarity to sell stock and gain support for his new company. A Liberty advertisement proclaimed:

> At last! At last! the Negroes are going to get together. . . . If we ever expect to get anywhere as a race of people we must first learn to stick together. . . . The day of Negro enterprises of every kind has arrived. . . . The Liberty Life Insurance Company [is] the first old line legal reserve company ever incorporated north of the Mason-Dixon Line that will be owned and controlled by Negroes.[4]

Gillespie maintained that since white companies did not hire Negroes or solicit Negro business, the Negro community should support an enterprise "whereby our people would be able to

[2] J. E. Mitchem, "Life Insurance," *Scott's Blue Book* (Chicago, 1937), pp. 45–46; M. S. Stuart, *An Economic Detour: A History of Insurance in the Lives of American Negroes* (New York: Wendell Malliet & Company, 1940), pp. 321–22.

[3] Stuart, *An Economic Detour*, pp. 72–74, 81–83; interview with Edward E. Gillespie, vice-president, Supreme Life Insurance Company, March 21, 1963; *Chicago Whip*, December 25, 1920.

[4] *Chicago Defender*, September 20, 1919.

secure adequate insurance protection for our families."[5] He sold $100,000 worth of stock in the Negro community, and by late 1920 Liberty was in full operation.[6] One of the few Negro insurance companies to survive the depression, Liberty evolved, through several mergers, into the still-thriving Supreme Life Insurance Company.

Prewar attempts to place Negro baseball on a solid financial footing also came to fruition during the migration period. Excessive competition had destroyed the once-successful Leland Giants, leaving only one team in Chicago—Rube Foster's new and struggling American Giants.[7] Foster, one of baseball's great pitchers, was an exceptionally imaginative and resourceful promoter. His own heroics, his success in finding outstanding Negro players, and his attractive scheduling—which included annual post-season exhibitions with major league teams—soon drew a loyal following. Early in 1920, Foster revived Beauregard Moseley's plan for a Negro baseball league. Meeting in Kansas City with the managers of five other Midwestern teams, he laid the groundwork and became the first president of the National Negro Baseball League. Under Foster's leadership, Negro baseball enjoyed a decade of prosperity: most clubs acquired their own parks, teams traveled by Pullman, and players drew salaries of up to $135 a week. To the great satisfaction of the Negro business advocates, Foster's Giants occasionally outdrew the Cubs or White Sox.[8]

The struggling Negro retailers also sought, through cooperation, to bolster their tenuous position. "Appreciating the need of a greater degree of cooperation among themselves by which they may more effectively control the trade of the members of their race," a number of Negro shopkeepers organized the Colored Commercial Club of Chicago. It was designed to promote the common interests of its members through joint advertising, mutual account adjustment, and cooperation in securing business loans and legal advice.[9] Despite such efforts, however, whites main-

[5] *Ibid.*, January 17, 1920.

[6] *Whip*, December 25, 1920.   [7] See chap. 6.

[8] *Chicago American*, August 24, 1955; Edwin B. Henderson, *The Negro in Sports* (Washington: Associated Publishers, 1939), pp. 146–48, 153.

[9] *Broad Ax* (Chicago), December 22, 1917.

tained their control over most retail businesses on the South Side. A survey of State Street businesses taken in 1918 revealed that little had changed since earlier surveys in 1901 and 1913.[10] Of five hundred stores and shops, 340 were run by whites. Only in the restaurant, hairdressing, real estate, and undertaking businesses were Negroes competing successfully. Whites retained their virtual monopoly of the grocery, clothing, furniture, hardware, and department stores.[11]

Regardless of the repeated call for cooperative effort, the most successful Negro businesses remained the three large individual enterprises launched in the previous era—Jesse Binga's bank, Anthony Overton's Hygienic Manufacturing Company, and Robert Abbott's *Defender*. Binga's real estate interests expanded with the migration and his bank continued to prosper. In 1919, Binga took out a state charter for his bank, which had previously operated as a private bank.[12] Negro leaders hailed the incorporation of the Binga State Bank as a major step in the development of Negro business in Chicago. The *Defender* called the reorganized bank "a house of rock-ribbed foundation, which will relieve the miserable conditions brought about by kindred institutions headed by men lacking experience, credit and substantial backing."[13] For a decade, the Binga Bank stood as a model of Negro business success; its collapse in 1930 ended an era in the history of Negro enterprise. Overton's cosmetic business enjoyed comparable success during the migration years. Overton put up a new factory building to house his concern and launched a magazine—the *Half-Century*—to advertise his products. By 1920, he was preparing to extend his operations into banking and insurance. Overton's Douglas National Bank and Victory Life Insurance Company were to emerge in the mid-1920's as bastions of the South Side's Negro business structure.[14]

But the most spectacular business success of the migration era was the *Chicago Defender*. Abbott's newspaper soared to na-

[10] See chap. 6.   [11] *Broad Ax*, January 19, 1918.

[12] *Defender*, July 10, 1920; Abram L. Harris, *The Negro as Capitalist* (Philadelphia: American Academy of Political and Social Science, 1936), p. 144.

[13] *Defender*, December 13, 1919.

[14] Anthony Overton, unpublished memoirs in the possession of Olive Diggs, Chicago, Illinois.

tional prominence as the result of its migration campaign.[15] Circulation skyrocketed: Emmett Scott estimated a national circulation of 50,000 in 1916, 125,000 by 1918.[16] The *Defender* itself claimed 283,000 during the wartime peak.[17] During these years, the *Defender* became a national newspaper. Abbott sought representatives throughout the country and often employed railroad porters and waiters to distribute the papers in the South. By 1916, the *Defender* circulated in seventy-one towns.[18] As its readership broadened, the paper began to attract national advertisers; by the end of the migration era, its columns carried not only notices for Chicago stores, but advertisements for nationally distributed products. Unlike white newspapers, however, the *Defender* continued to depend primarily upon circulation for its revenue.[19]

The postwar *Defender* published a thirty-two page paper each week and turned out both city and national editions with a combined circulation of about 180,000.[20] After many profitless years, Abbott was now on his way to becoming Chicago's first Negro millionaire. His next goal was to acquire his own printing plant During the 1919 race riot, the white firm that regularly printed the *Defender* refused to print the paper for fear of retaliation from white rioters. Only by rushing the galleys and newsprint to Gary, Indiana—twenty miles away—was Abbott able to turn out a riot edition. This incident convinced Abbott that he must print the paper himself. The next year, he bought a cylinder press and installed it in a large building on Indiana Avenue. Amid elaborate celebration, Abbott opened his new facilities early in 1921. With sixty-eight employees and a plant valued at almost a half million dollars, the *Defender* was by far the largest Negro business in Chicago and one of the largest in the country.[21]

At the peak of the *Defender's* popularity, a new and vigorous

[15] See chap. 6.

[16] Emmett J. Scott, *Negro Migration During the War* (New York: Oxford University Press, 1920), p. 30.

[17] Roi Ottley, *The Lonely Warrior: The Life and Times of Robert S. Abbott* (Chicago: Henry Regnery & Company, 1955), p. 139.

[18] *Ibid.*, pp. 136–37.

[19] *Ibid.*, p. 200. This is characteristic of most Negro newspapers.

[20] *Ibid.*, p. 188.

[21] *Ibid.*, pp. 188–202; *Defender*, May 14, 1921.

competitor made its first appearance. The *Chicago Whip* was founded in 1919 by an energetic young businessman, William C. Linton, and two recent Yale Law School graduates, Joseph D. Bibb and Arthur C. MacNeal. Linton, a southerner by birth and the son of a prominent A.M.E. churchman, had been educated at Morris Brown University in Atlanta and at Syracuse University and had started the newspaper, with almost no capital, shortly after moving to Chicago. Within a few months, he brought in Bibb, whom he had known at Morris Brown where Bibb's father was a dean, and MacNeal, who had come to Chicago just out of law school to accept the executive secretaryship of the local NAACP.[22]

The *Whip* carried Abbott's formula of crime, sex, and race to a new height. Beneath eye-catching headlines, such as "Girl's Head Almost Severed" or "Man Traps Wife, Shoots Her Lover Dead," the *Whip* preached racial militancy and, in its early years, economic radicalism.[23] According to Bibb, the *Whip*'s appeal was to the working-class people west of State Street; the middle class opposed the paper's radical approach.[24] Nevertheless, middle-class business and political leaders provided the *Whip* with financial support. Anthony Overton, Jesse Binga, George Cleveland Hall, Lacey Kirk Williams, Robert R. Jackson, and Oscar De Priest all helped the *Whip* survive its difficult first years.[25] By the end of 1920, the newspaper was solvent, and it never missed an issue until its demise during the depression. But the *Whip* never seriously challenged the *Defender*'s preeminence; it always remained a strictly local paper, and its peak circulation was only about sixteen thousand.[26]

To the businessmen, the migrants represented a vastly expanded Negro market; to the politicians, they represented a greatly enlarged Negro electorate. Like the businessmen, the professional

[22] *Whip*, July 6, 1929; *Chicago Tribune*, October 1, 1955.

[23] A discussion of the *Whip*'s racial and economic ideology appears later in this chapter. For sample headlines, see any issue of the *Whip*, 1919–24.

[24] Interview with Joseph Bibb, March 29, 1963.

[25] *Whip*, July 6, 1929.

[26] Ralph Davis, "Negro Newspapers in Chicago," unpublished master's thesis, University of Chicago, 1939, p. 16.

politicians used this new source of strength to solidify their gains of the previous period. By 1915, Negro politicians had built an organization of their own within the Republican party and amassed substantial strength in the predominantly Negro Second Ward. The ward organization was still in white hands: Congressman Martin Madden was ward committeeman, and George Harding, although no longer an alderman, remained probably the most powerful political figure on the South Side. But the Negro politicians had sent one of their number to the city council, acquired several attractive patronage positions, and forced white politicians to heed Negro wants and aspirations.[27]

No one better understood the importance of the Negro vote than William Hale Thompson, elected mayor of Chicago in 1915. To most Americans and to many Chicagoans, "Big Bill" became a symbol of the infamous Chicago of the 1920's—violent, corrupt, and gangster-ridden. But the majority of Chicago's Negroes never faltered in their loyalty to him, and they helped elect him to three terms as mayor. The Thompson-Negro alliance was partly fortuitous. As heir to the Lorimer faction of the Republican party, Thompson naturally gained the support of many Negro politicians who had been in Lorimer's camp. And as mayor during the migration era, he was able to make an immediate appeal to Negroes who had already been conditioned by their southern experience to support the Republican party. But Thompson and his lieutenants cleverly took advantage of these circumstances by making a concerted effort to win and hold the allegiance of Negro voters.

Thompson assiduously cultivated Negro political leaders and campaigned vigorously on the South Side. "I'll give you people the best opportunities you've ever had if you elect me," he promised a Negro audience in 1915. "I'll give your people jobs, and any of you want to shoot craps go ahead and do it."[28] Thompson kept his promises. He appointed Edward Wright and Archibald Carey to positions in the corporation counsel's office and reserved a generous number of lesser jobs for Negroes. With

[27] See chap. 6.

[28] Lloyd Wendt and Herman Kogan, *Big Bill Thompson* (Indianapolis: Bobbs-Merrill & Company, 1953), pp. 94–96, 103–4, 112–14. See also Harold Gosnell, *Negro Politicians: The Rise of Negro Politics in Chicago* (Chicago: University of Chicago Press, 1935), pp. 38–62.

Thompson's backing, Negroes secured important elective offices—alderman, Republican committeeman, and eventually United States congressman. Thompson also protected Negro underworld figures, winked at Negro gambling operations, and admonished his police force to treat Negroes fairly. At every opportunity, he sought to demonstrate that he was "the Negro's friend"; he took firm action against the showing of *The Birth of a Nation,* insisted that Negroes be included at political banquets, and caustically attacked political opponents who made racially prejudiced remarks.[29]

Most important, Thompson treated Negroes with respect and dignity. Unlike most white politicians, he did not regale Negro audiences with tales of his "dear old Mammy." He told them instead that he was making Negro appointments because the men he selected were the best qualified for the job. He did not hide Negro officeholders in the back rooms, but placed them in such conspicuous positions that his foes derisively referred to City Hall as "Uncle Tom's Cabin." He appeared frequently on the South Side, not just at political rallies but at civic functions and at the funerals of community leaders. In thus giving Negroes the recognition they had so rarely received from white politicians, Thompson won almost universal admiration on the South Side. To the incredulous dismay of his many white critics, he was hailed by Chicago Negroes as "the second Lincoln."[30]

Thompson's Negro constituents served him well. He won the 1915 Republican primary by only 3,500 votes, but his plurality in the Second Ward was over 6,000. In the general election, he carried the Second and Third wards by more than two to one.[31] The migration further strengthened his position on the South Side. By 1919, the Second Ward was over 70 per cent Negro and the southern migrants who had moved in since 1915 formed a politically conscious bloc of voters highly susceptible to Thompson's blandishments. Deprived of the vote in the South, they viewed the ballot box as a symbol of their new life in the North and went to the polls in larger numbers than white voters; 72 per cent of the

[29] Gosnell, *Negro Politicians,* pp. 46–47, 53; Wendt and Kogan, *Big Bill Thompson,* pp. 162–63, 167–68.

[30] Gosnell, *Negro Politicians,* pp. 55–57; Wendt and Kogan, *Big Bill Thompson,* pp. 167–68; *Defender,* February 10, 1923.

[31] Wendt and Kogan, *Big Bill Thompson,* pp. 95–96, 114.

eligible Negroes were registered, compared with 66 per cent for the city at large.[32] Thompson struck responsive chords among these new voters as he pointed to his own record on race relations and reminded the newcomers of the treatment they had received from Democrats in the South. As a result, Thompson ran even stronger in Negro districts in 1919 than he had in 1915; almost 60 per cent of his total plurality came from the Second Ward alone.[33]

Thompson's enemies attempted to use his alliance with Negroes as a weapon against him. State's Attorney Maclay Hoyne, running against Thompson in 1919, openly courted anti-Negro elements by portraying the mayor as a tool of his black supporters.[34] Hoyne also tried to destroy Thompson's Negro allies. In 1917, he brought bribery charges against Alderman Oscar De Priest, charging that the alderman had accepted payoffs from gambling lords in the Second Ward and had made "vassals and pawns" of the police officers in the district, forcing them to protect his underworld friends. In response, De Priest insisted that the alleged payoffs were campaign contributions, that he had no knowledge of a gambling syndicate, and that Hoyne's charges were racially and politically motivated. He sharply dissented from Hoyne's characterization of him as "King Oscar," holding that George Harding was still the real boss of the black belt and the beneficiary of any tie-in with a crime syndicate. Clarence Darrow and Negro attorney Edward Morris defended De Priest and won an acquittal. Hoyne planned a second trial on an additional indictment, but eventually dropped the charges. De Priest and his allies in City Hall viewed the trial as a great victory for the Thompson forces and a defeat for the reform elements that were trying to discredit the mayor.[35]

Despite the acquittal, the De Priest trial produced a schism within the Second Ward political organization. De Priest had not yet been cleared at the time of the 1917 municipal election and so decided not to seek reelection. Louis B. Anderson, an assistant

[32] Harold Gosnell, "The Chicago 'Black Belt' as a Political Battleground," *American Journal of Sociology* (Chicago), 39 (November, 1933): 330–31.

[33] *Tribune*, April 2, 1919.   [34] *Chicago Daily News*, March 5, 1919.

[35] *Defender*, June 9, June 16, 1917; *Tribune*, January 18, January 22, April 1, June 2, June 5, June 6, June 9, June 10, June 21, 1917; Wendt and Kogan, *Big Bill Thompson*, pp. 147–48.

corporation counsel in the Thompson administration and a long-time Negro Republican regular, received organization support and was easily elected.[36] A year later, the other Second Ward aldermanic seat became vacant and De Priest attempted a comeback; but Harding and Madden, who had broken with De Priest at the time of the trial, supported State Representative Robert R. Jackson. Although the white bosses could no longer force white candidates upon the predominantly Negro electorate, their support was still crucial in primary battles between Negro candidates. De Priest had wide popular support and ran a strong campaign, but Jackson won by three hundred votes.[37]

Encouraged by his showing, De Priest set up his own political organization, the People's Movement, and ran against Jackson in the general election. Again he did well, but could not quite overcome the strength of the regular organization.[38] In 1919, he tried again, this time for Anderson's seat, but fell below his 1918 strength.[39] De Priest's People's Movement used the rhetoric of race pride and Negro solidarity. De Priest depicted himself as a rebel against white control and assailed Anderson and Jackson as "hand-picked leaders" and "two monkeys." But his motives were primarily personal. He had shown no disinclination to accept white support before his feud with Harding, and late in 1919 he made peace with the regular organization at a well-publicized "harmony chicken dinner."[40]

Negroes came to dominate Second Ward politics not by rebelling against the regular organization but by using their leverage within it. De Priest's strong showing in 1918 indicated that Harding and Madden's days as bosses of the black belt were numbered. Having already increased their representation in the city council and the state legislature, Negro politicians demanded the leadership of the ward organization as well. In 1919, Congressman Madden agreed to step down as Republican committeeman in the Second Ward and allow a Negro to succeed him. With De Priest still in revolt, the natural choice for the post was Ed Wright, who

[36] *Defender*, February 3, March 3, 1917; Gosnell, *Negro Politicians*, p. 75.

[37] *Defender*, October 20, 1917, January 19, February 2, March 2, 1918.

[38] *Ibid.*, March 9, April 6, 1918; *Tribune*, March 14, April 3, 1918.

[39] *Defender*, February 22, March 1, 1918.

[40] *Whip*, January 31, 1920.

had worked in the city administration since 1915 and contributed significantly to Thompson's reelection in 1919. Wright's election as ward committeeman early in 1920 cemented Negro control of the Republican party in the black belt. To be sure, Madden held his seat in Congress for another eight years: he was an old man who could not be unceremoniously deposed. But it was generally understood that when he died a Negro would replace him. Wright, Anderson, Jackson, and, with his return to the fold, De Priest were now the actual as well as the titular leaders of the Second Ward Republican organization.[41]

By 1920, Negroes had more political power in Chicago than anywhere else in the country. They held more appointive and elective offices and exercised greater influence on the dominant political organization than their counterparts in New York, Philadelphia, or Baltimore. A rapidly growing and increasingly concentrated Negro population and the rise of a political machine dependent upon Negro votes to retain its power had given the Negro electorate and the politicians who dominated it enormous leverage. White political leaders could no longer ignore Negro sensitivities. Frank Lowden, the Republican candidate for Governor of Illinois in 1916, threatened to move his headquarters from a downtown hotel when the management discriminated against Negroes.[42] Negro protests over racial slurs in the motion pictures led not only to bans on specific films but to a new state law that prohibited "the exhibition, manufacture, or sale of any lithograph, moving picture, book or drama which tends to incite race or religious prejudice."[43] In 1919, the legislature strengthened the state's civil rights legislation by forbidding landlords, schools, and places of public accommodation to advertise a discriminatory policy.[44] When Illinois adopted a new constitution in 1920, it included a strong and explicit civil rights clause.[45]

[41] Defender, October 20, 1920; Whip, March 13, 1920; Gosnell, Negro Politicians, p. 157; interview with William E. King, Negro Republican leader, April 11, 1963.

[42] William Hutchinson, Lowden of Illinois (Chicago: University of Chicago Press, 1957), pp. 268–69.

[43] Illinois Legislative Reference Bureau, Legislative Digest, 1917, p. 206.

[44] Illinois Legislative Reference Bureau, Legislative Synopsis and Digest, 1919, p. 227.

[45] Defender, July 10, 1920; Whip, July 10, 1920.

Yet the gestures that the white political structure made toward the Negro community remained largely formal and ceremonial. They hardly touched the basic problems of the black belt: inadequate housing, inferior job opportunities, poverty, social disorganization, crime, and corruption. The Negro community paid a price for political recognition. Its leaders allied themselves with the least progressive, most corrupt element in Chicago politics. Under Thompson, prostitution and gambling flourished openly on the South Side, and underworld figures enjoyed not only protection but political power in their own right. At the same time, housing conditions grew worse, alleys and streets accumulated filth, zoning and health regulations were ignored.[46] In terms of their goals, the Negro political leaders probably had no choice but to make the decisions that they did. Yet it is hard not to agree with Ralph Bunche that their alliance with the Thompson machine gave Negroes "no little patronage and favor, a significant increase in recognition and influence, and a whole lot of bad government."[47]

The business-class leaders who had become prominent before the war continued to dominate Negro economic, political, and civic life. George Cleveland Hall, Robert Abbott, Jesse Binga, Anthony Overton, Ed Wright, and Oscar De Priest imprinted their racial ideology upon every community development. Many of the old elite were gone: Dan Williams had withdrawn from Negro affairs after he was forced out of Provident Hospital; John G. Jones was dead; James Madden and Reverdy Ransom had left Chicago. The Barnetts, Charles Bentley, Edward Morris, and Edward Wilson were still active, but no longer formed an effective and cohesive opposition. The new leaders had established themselves as the dominant force in the Negro community, ready to lead the South Side into an era of hopeful expansion and consolidation. The hospital and the YMCA, the new insurance companies and the Binga Bank, the large churches and the Negro political machine all stood as symbols of what Negro solidarity could accomplish. The migration had sealed the triumph of the self-help ideology.

[46] See, for example, *Defender,* September 25, 1926, January 26, 1929; and *Whip, passim,* 1919–21.

[47] Ralph J. Bunche, "The Thompson-Negro Alliance," *Opportunity* (New York), 7 (March, 1929): 80.

Yet, no sooner had the old opposition been silenced than two new schools of racial thought began to question the assumptions of the business-class leadership. On the one hand, the black nationalists, particularly the followers of the charismatic Marcus Garvey, argued that racial solidarity and self-help did not go far enough. The Negro community, they pointed out, was still dependent upon whites economically and politically and, since whites could never be trusted, Negroes had no choice but to remove themselves completely from American society. Moreover, the nationalists argued, Negroes must not only rebel against their economically and socially subservient position in white America, but must overcome the feelings of inferiority with which whites had indoctrinated them. To effect this change, the Garveyites preached a shrill chauvinism that glorified blackness and deprecated white culture.

Distinct from the nationalists, although often sympathetic with them, were the "New Negroes," whose major vehicle of expression in Chicago was the militant weekly newspaper, the *Whip*. The "New Negroes" borrowed part of their critique of the dominant business-class ideology from the old assimilationists; they opposed all forms of segregation and favored a broadside attack on injustice and oppression. But they combined this creed with a doctrine of economic radicalism, urging Negroes and lower-class whites to unite against their common foes—exploiting capitalists and corrupt political bosses. And while rejecting Garvey's message that Negroes should separate themselves from white society, they shared with the nationalists a strong sense of race pride—a tenet that frequently conflicted with their call for working-class solidarity.

Black nationalism had prewar roots in Chicago. Two self-styled Abyssinian Jews, who called themselves David Ben Itzoch and Henry Itzoch, tried to promote their International Peace and Brotherly Love Movement in 1913, holding that "the Negro is the right Jew" and should "confess his identity" and emigrate to Abyssinia. The movement had an early death a year later when David Ben Itzoch was exposed as a southern Negro who had never been within five thousand miles of Abyssinia.[48] At the same time, a mysterious white man, known only as "Jonah," began speaking on South Side street corners, arguing that "85% of the human race belongs to the brown [races] and that these same

[48] *Defender*, August 23, 1913, April 18, November 28, 1914.

brown races should combine against the white race and whip them off the earth." Protesting that Negroes were cheated by Jewish merchants, "Jonah" attempted to organize a cooperative store where "Negroes could buy and sell their own goods on square scales."[49] The project failed, but "Jonah" continued to promote nationalistic movements among Negroes in Chicago; he reappeared after the war as a leading figure in the so-called Abyssinian affair.[50]

The Garveyites made a more concerted effort to win a mass following in Chicago. Marcus Garvey made his first appearance in the city in 1919, addressing a rally at the Eighth Regiment Armory. By this time, he was already a national figure: his appeal to race pride, his vision of a Negro state in Africa, and his spectacular parades, splendid regalia, and pompous ritual had elicited an enthusiastic response in Harlem. His United Negro Improvement Association had a large membership, if considerably less than the two million claimed by Garvey, and its newspaper, the *Negro World*, boasted a circulation of over fifty thousand.[51] Garvey used his Chicago visit to bolster membership in the newly formed Chicago branch of the U.N.I.A. and to promote his latest scheme—an all-Negro steamship company that would link the black peoples of the world.

The Garvey movement faced serious difficulties in Chicago. Garvey's flamboyant nationalism had won him bitter enemies as well as enthusiastic supporters, and Robert Abbott, in particular, had waged a vigorous campaign against him since he first emerged as a national leader. When Abbott learned that Garvey planned to sell stock in his Black Star Line in Chicago, he engaged a private detective who trapped him into selling stock in violation of Illinois law. Garvey was fined and left Chicago ignominiously.[52]

[49] *Ibid.*, August 30, September 27, 1913, April 18, 1914.

[50] Chicago Commission on Race Relations, *The Negro in Chicago: A Study of Race Relations and a Race Riot* (Chicago: University of Chicago Press, 1922), p. 61.

[51] E. David Cronon, *Black Moses: The Story of Marcus Garvey and the United Negro Improvement Association* (Madison: University of Wisconsin Press, 1955), pp. 44, 45, 49.

[52] *Defender*, October 4, 1919; Report on Garvey in "The Negro in Illinois," a file of reports and interviews compiled by the Illinois Writers Project of the Works Progress Administration (George Cleveland Hall Branch of the Chicago Public Library), cited hereafter as Illinois Writers Project Files; Cronon, *Black Moses*, pp. 75-76; Ottley, *The Lonely Warrior*, pp. 216-17.

Abbott continued to press his attack, and soon he and Garvey were in court, each suing the other for libel. Both men won their suits, but Garvey was awarded six cents, Abbott $5,000. Abbott had clearly won the battle and made Garvey look exceedingly foolish.[53]

Garveyism received a second setback in Chicago in 1920 as a result of the so-called Abyssinian affair. The Star Order of Ethiopia and Ethiopian Missionaries to Abyssinia was a schismatic offshoot of the Chicago branch of the U.N.I.A. Influenced by the white promoter, R. D. Jonas, the man who had appeared in prewar Chicago as the mysterious "Jonah," two Negroes, Grover Redding and Joseph Fernon, gathered together a group of disgruntled Garveyites and proclaimed that according to biblical prophecy, all black men would return to their ancestral Ethiopia. In the summer of 1920, the Abyssinians held a parade and street corner rally. As a sign that blacks should no longer stay in the United States, one of the leaders, clad in elaborate African regalia, burned an American flag. When a white policeman tried to interfere, the Abyssinians fought back and before order was restored, they had shot two white men to death and wounded a third.[54] Negro leaders universally condemned the Abyssinians and aided the authorities in capturing their leaders and bringing them to trial. The *Defender* warned "all agitators, whether they be white or black . . . that we condemn their disloyalty and will do all in our power to aid the constituted authorities in crushing them."[55] The *Whip* called the Abyssinians "frenzied fanatics" and insisted that "patriotism, equality and justice must be the order of the day."[56] Despite its repudiation of the Abyssinians, the U.N.I.A. suffered from a general revulsion against nationalistic extremism.

Nevertheless, Garveyism flourished in Chicago for several years. As in Harlem, it reached lower-class Negroes, especially recent migrants, who were relatively untouched by the philosophy of

[53] *Defender,* June 26, 1920, May 21, 1921; report on Garvey in Illinois Writers Project Files; Cronon, *Black Moses,* pp. 75–76; Ottley, *The Lonely Warrior,* p. 217.

[54] *Defender,* June 26, July 3, 1920; *Whip,* June 26, 1920; Chicago Commission on Race Relations, *The Negro in Chicago,* pp. 59–64; Ottley, *The Lonely Warrior,* pp. 214–16.

[55] *Defender,* June 26, 1920.

[56] *Whip,* June 26, 1920.

the leadership class. These people found in Garvey's vision of a glorious Negro kingdom and in his elaborate ritual an escape from the frustrations and disappointments of life in the South Side ghetto. At the Chicago U.N.I.A.'s first annual mass meeting late in 1920, eighteen hundred people thrilled to "the choir in white robes and the Juvenile department arrayed in red, black and green, the black cross nurses robed in white veils and white dresses, the legions stepping with martial tread decorated with armlets of the colors marching to the tune of 'Onward Christian Soldiers.'" William Wallace, a prosperous baker who had closed a thriving business to devote full time to the U.N.I.A., told the rally that, unlike the traditional Negro leaders, Garvey offered a constructive program:

> The Garvey movement takes the children and trains them to love and respect their own and learn the history of their race, not to hate anybody, but to lift up their heads and look the world in the face. It takes the women and teaches them the duties of life and instills in them a hope for the future of their children. It takes the men and trains them to be manly and lawful, loyal to their race and country.[57]

Wallace claimed that the U.N.I.A. had four thousand members in Chicago in 1920, and two years later he claimed nine thousand.[58]

Even at its peak, however, Garveyism never became as potent a force on the South Side as it was in Harlem. The incidents of 1919 and 1920 and Abbott's continuing opposition crippled it at the start. Perhaps too the political participation and recognition that Chicago Negroes, unlike New York Negroes, enjoyed undercut the appeal of Garveyism. In any case, the movement's influence in Chicago was limited even during its peak years, and its decline was rapid. By the end of 1923, a violent schism in the local U.N.I.A. had produced two rival Garveyite groups. Their feud, marked by frequent shootings, dissipated whatever strength the movement had retained in Chicago.[59] Wallace used his Garveyite following as a base from which to launch a political

[57] *Ibid.*, October 23, 1920.

[58] *Ibid.*, December 11, 1920; Cronon, *Black Moses*, p. 206.

[59] *Defender*, March 8, 1924, February 27, 1926; report on United Negro Improvement Association in Illinois Writers Project Files.

career that eventually took him to the state senate. But Garveyism had declined sharply by the mid-1920's.

The "New Negroes" voiced an even more virulent and at the same time more sophisticated dissent from the self-help ideology. Led by a group of college-trained intellectuals who wrote for the *Chicago Whip*, the "New Negroes" attacked the institutions and leaders of the South Side in a vitriolic style reminiscent of Julius Taylor and "Indignation" Jones. The leaders of the Second Ward Republican organization were "big-fake politicians who for a 'mess of pottage' have preached submissiveness to the black masses." The Wabash Avenue YMCA was a "segregated, Jim Crow institution [which] catches all the black Blue Stockings or better styled cod fish aristocracy of the race," and the *Defender* advanced "the same insidious propaganda that Vardaman, Blease and Bilbo preaches." Jesse Binga was a "Black Capitalist . . . very much disliked by the black constituency," Ed Wright a "demagogue" with an "arrogant disposition and self-conceited attitude," and the prestigious Appomattox Club included "the biggest gamblers in town."[60]

The *Whip*, however, styled itself as more than a sharp-tongued gadfly; it also articulated a positive philosophy of racial protest. "Pacifism and patience," it insisted, were "not the medicine for all racial ailment. . . . This is no time for pussy-footing and watchful waiting, but for intelligent concerted attack on existing evils with all necessary methods."[61] The "New Negroes," the *Whip* contended, would not accept "a back seat and half a loaf," but insisted on an "end to Jim Crow, preferably by legislation, [but] if not, through more drastic means."[62] Together with its racial militancy, the *Whip* supported labor unions and urged working-class solidarity. "We assert that it is to the Negro's decided advantage to join the A.F. of L.," the *Whip* declared during the organizing campaigns in the stockyards and steel mills.[63] Two months later, the *Whip* called economic radicalism "the incipient ingredient in progress" and "the hope of the Negro."[64] The *Whip*

[60] *Whip*, June 24, October 4, 1919, March 13, June 26, 1920, September 10, 1921.

[61] *Ibid.*, January 10, 1920.

[62] *Ibid.*, June 24, 1919, January 17, 1920.

[63] *Ibid.*, October 11, 1919.   [64] *Ibid.*, December 13, 1919.

opened its columns to union organizers and excoriated church and civic leaders who thwarted the union's efforts.

Joseph Bibb, William Linton, and A. C. MacNeal, the young editors of the *Whip*, like A. Philip Randolph and Chandler Owen who edited the radical Negro magazine, the *Messenger*, in New York, had been influenced by socialism and saw the Negro problem as basically an economic problem.[65] Yet at the same time they were attracted by the racial chauvinism that motivated the Garveyites. Unlike the old integrationists, they rejected the notion that racial solidarity leads to segregation. "Race solidarity," declared the *Whip*, ". . . binds the race together politically and economically. . . . Segregation . . . is not even tangent to race solidarity."[66] More revealing was the editors' ambiguous attitude toward Garveyism. On the one hand, they rejected the idea of an independent Negro state and ridiculed Garvey's "predilection for red robes and gorgeous tassels and other ungainly paraphernalia." Yet Garvey was "doing wonderful work . . . waking up Negroes to new opportunities and greater business attitudes." Furthermore, the *Whip* called Garvey "the first [leader] in the history of the Black People of America who has been made great by his own people," and praised him for "awakening a new race consciousness and creating a new race solidarity." "All of those who love their kind" should "at least be open-minded on the Garvey movement."[67]

In addition to formulating an ideological position, the "New Negroes" organized politically and challenged both the regular Second Ward Republican organization and Oscar De Priest's quasi-independent People's Movement. The Independent Non-Partisan Political League, formed late in 1919, accused the old-line politicians of "vote profiteering," "vice immunity and political graft," "boss rule," and "sycophancy" before white leaders. Its platform called for not only the eradication of all forms of discrimination, but public ownership of utilities, civil service reform, women's suffrage, a children's welfare service, and the

[65] Bibb, for instance, had belonged to a socialist club in college. He maintains, however, that despite the similarity in outlook there was no direct contact between the *Whip* group in Chicago and the *Messenger* group in New York. Interview with Bibb.

[66] *Whip*, October 2, 1920.

[67] *Ibid.*, August 28, 1920, January 1, March 5, March 12, 1921.

"organization of labor into One Union."[68] The "New Negroes" demanded an end to politics based on personal loyalties and party factionalism and asked for a program that would improve the economic and social status of Negroes in Chicago. The League ran a full slate of candidates in the 1920 Second Ward Republican primary. The regular Republicans regarded them with scorn, accused them of being "Reds," and assured themselves that "it takes more than talk to launch a movement which will amount to anything." None of the League's candidates was successful, but several made respectable showings, and the *Whip* hailed the election as a "big victory."[69]

Rejecting the elitism of the old aristocracy, the moderation of the business class, and the complete separatism of the nationalists, the "New Negroes" worked toward a racial ideology based on militancy, race pride, and economic and social reform with a decidedly socialist cast. They more nearly approached the temper of the Negro Revolt of the 1960's than any other Negro spokesmen of their time. They believed that the white leadership perpetuated Negro subservience by controlling the political and economic life of the Negro community. They expressed a distrust of white liberals, such as Congressman Madden, who, according to the *Whip*, had cleverly deceived [his Negro constituents] into the belief that he is fighting tooth and nail for their interests."[70] They flirted with Garveyism, much as latter-day militant Negro leaders expressed a grudging admiration for the Black Muslims. And alone among their Negro contemporaries, they insisted that Negro advancement must be accompanied by general economic and social reform. By the late 1920's, Chicago's "New Negroes" were experimenting with direct action techniques. The "Don't Spend Your Money Where You Can't Work" campaign, promoted by the *Whip* in 1929, was a pioneer attempt to advance Negro interests through economic pressure.[71]

Neither the Garveyites nor the "New Negroes" seriously challenged the business-class leadership during the migration years. The migration had solidified the already strong position of the

[68] *Ibid.*, December 27, 1919, January 3, 1920.

[69] *Ibid.*, January 31, February 7, 1920.

[70] *Ibid.*, May 1, 1920.

[71] *Whip*, July 6, 1929; interview with Bibb.

new leaders, and the prosperity and business climate of the 1920's further contributed to their preeminence. But the halcyon days would not last forever; and when the Great Depression destroyed the middle-class dream of a self-sufficient, economically viable "Black Metropolis" on the South Side, the advocates of radicalism and militancy would find receptive audiences among Chicago's Negroes.[72]

[72] The effect of the depression on the dream of a self-sufficient black belt is a major theme of St. Clair Drake and Horace Cayton, *Black Metropolis* (New York: Harcourt, Brace & Company, 1945).

CHAPTER 11

THE IMPACT OF THE MIGRATION: THE WHITE RESPONSE

White hostility to Negroes had been mounting in Chicago since the 1890's. Although segregation was never formalized, increasing interracial contacts had created a pattern of pervasive discrimination. Moreover, rising racial tension had been accompanied by periodic outbursts of violence: the 1905 teamsters strike had led to anti-Negro rioting; frequent melees had grown out of housing disputes; and the Springfield race riot of 1908 had provoked violence among whites in Chicago.[1] Nevertheless, the Negro community was too small to appear as a major threat before the war; only the few whites who had frequent and direct confrontations with Negroes expressed violent hostility.

The migration sharply altered this pattern. As the black belt grew, Negroes began competing for jobs and homes and exercised an often decisive influence in politics. Open hostility to Negroes was no longer confined to a few families in Hyde Park or to striking teamsters. Now many whites—especially the Irish and Poles who lived west of the black belt and the old stock middle-class families who lived to the south and east—felt threatened by Negroes. They responded by attempting to tighten the color bar in housing, schools, and public accommodations. Failing that, some resorted to terrorism. The occasional skirmishes of the pre-war period gave way to organized guerilla warfare. Between 1917 and 1919, white "athletic clubs" assaulted Negroes on the streets, and "neighborhood improvement societies" bombed Negro homes. During the summer of 1919, the guerilla warfare in turn gave way to open-armed conflict—the South Side of Chicago became a battleground for racial war.

The migration alarmed most white Chicagoans. At the very outset, a few voices welcomed the newcomers: Henry M. Hyde, for

[1] See chaps. 1 and 2.

instance, a reporter for the *Tribune*, wrote in the summer of 1916 that "in the long run, if the Negro hegira continues, . . . the effects will probably be good."[2] But by the following spring, the continuing influx of southern Negroes had conjured up images of epidemics, crime, and chronic unemployment. The city health commissioner expressed his fear "that an epidemic of contagious diseases, especially tuberculosis, may strike."[3] The *Tribune* portrayed the newcomers as lazy, shiftless ne'er-do-wells, sure to be burdens on the city: "In a house at Thirty-second and Wabash eight or ten Negroes were lying about on the floor, and one was picking a banjo and singing a song the chorus of which ended 'Mo' rain, mo' rest, / Mo' niggers sleep in de nest.' Today's the day, not tomorrow, with them."[4] Labor leaders, fearing job competition once the wartime boom receded, were particularly alarmed. Some advocated legislative restriction on migration, a proposal so extreme that even the *Tribune* labeled it as a "demand for serfdom."[5]

Hysteria over the migration reached its peak in the summer of 1917 when almost fifty people died in race riots at East St. Louis, Illinois. "Black man, Stay South!" cried the *Tribune*. The entire migration, the paper editorialized, was a "huge mistake," and the East St. Louis outbreak proved that Negroes did not really enjoy the "liberties of the north" but were "happiest when the white race asserts its superiority."[6] The secretary of the Illinois Federation of Labor warned Chicago to expect riots unless the migration was halted, and he attacked employers who imported Southern Negro laborers.[7] A state labor commission recommended curbs on labor agents, holding them entirely responsible for the influx.[8] A few white spokesmen were more sympathetic: Sophonisba Breckinridge of Hull House, for example, urged whites to welcome the migrants and "give them a chance to make Chicago a better home than they could find in the South"; and Edgar Blake, a prominent Methodist minister, argued that whites should "do something for

[2] *Chicago Tribune,* July 25, 1916.

[3] *Ibid.*, March 5, 1917. [4] *Ibid.*, March 15, 1917.

[5] *Ibid.*, June 9, July 1, 1917.

[6] *Ibid.*, May 30, 1917; for a general account of the East St. Louis riot, see Elliott M. Rudwick, *Race Riot at East St. Louis* (Carbondale: Southern Illinois University Press, 1964).

[7] *Tribune,* July 4, 1917. [8] *Ibid.*, July 1, 1917.

these Negroes, . . . provide for them better."[9] But these were the voices of a small, liberal minority. Most Chicagoans wanted the newcomers to return South.

Several white groups made concrete efforts to turn back the Negro tide. During the East St. Louis riots, the *Tribune* offered financial aid to Negroes who would leave Chicago.[10] Two years later, the Chicago Association of Commerce sent telegrams to chambers of commerce throughout the South, informing them of a "large surplus" of Negro labor in Chicago and urging them to "send a responsible party to interview Negroes and make suitable selection and arrangements for locating them in your section."[11] At the same time, white civic leaders tried to persuade Urban League officials to advise Negroes to return South. The League resisted the pressure, affirming the right of every man to seek opportunity wherever he chose.[12] Southern whites cooperated with these efforts. A group calling itself the Mississippi Welfare League took three Chicago Negroes on a tour of the South and sent them back with glowing reports of good treatment, Negro prosperity, and amicable race relations. The Urban League and other Negro groups impugned the accuracy of the report and denounced the Mississippians and their Negro pawns.[13] The attempt to reverse the migration met with scant success. A few migrants returned during the economic recession of 1919–20, but most became permanent residents of Chicago. In fact, the migration, though slowed down after 1919, continued throughout the 1920's.

Unable to turn back the Negro influx, some whites hoped to minimize contacts with Negroes by strengthening Chicago's informal pattern of segregation and discrimination. One target for hostile whites was the school system, which had registered a sharp rise in the number of Negro students during the migration years. Before the war, only two or three schools had been predominantly Negro; by 1920, ten elementary schools and one high

[9] *Ibid.*, May 30, 1917, April 4, 1918.   [10] *Ibid.*, July 12, 1917.

[11] *Chicago Defender*, May 17, 1919.

[12] L. Hollingsworth Wood to T. Arnold Hill, May 19, 1919, Julius Rosenwald Papers (University of Chicago Library), cited hereafter as Rosenwald Papers.

[13] *Defender*, September 27, 1919; *Chicago Whip*, September 27, 1919; Robert Kerlin, *The Voice of the Negro* (New York: E. P. Dutton, 1920), pp. 132–35.

school—Wendell Phillips—were over 50 per cent Negro.[14] Moreover, many of the new children, recently arrived from the South, stood out from their classmates. Their inferior educational and cultural background retarded their scholastic achievement and frequently created disciplinary problems.[15]

Some white spokesmen revived the old proposal for a segregated school system, which Negro leaders thought they had laid to rest a decade earlier. Max Loeb, a member of the Chicago school board, sent a letter to several prominent Negroes in the city. He wrote:

> The colored population has increased largely since the war. . . . Colored attendance in the public schools has grown accordingly. How best can the Race antagonisms be avoided which so often spring up when the two races are brought into close juxtaposition? . . . Do you think it wiser when there is a large Colored population, to have separate schools for white and colored children? . . . How in your opinion should a separation movement, if under any circumstances it is wise, be begun?[16]

Although Loeb's letter was phrased in the form of questions, Negro leaders interpreted it as an indication that the school board was considering segregation. They responded with indignation. "I must confess," replied Beauregard Moseley, "your letter astonishes me and almost made me feel I had been insulted."[17] Robert Abbott advised those who had received the letter to ignore it. "Separate schools may be desired by a few traitorous Negroes," he said, ". . . but for the great mass of our people—NEVER."[18] Loeb's inquiry was quickly and quietly forgotten.

If formally segregated schools remained as unattainable as before, whites turned to less direct means of separating Negro

[14] Chicago Commission on Race Relations, *The Negro in Chicago: A Study of Race Relations and a Race Riot* (Chicago: University of Chicago Press, 1922), p. 242; Frederick Robb, ed., *Intercollegian Wonder Book, or, The Negro in Chicago, 1779–1927* (Chicago: Washington Intercollegiate Club, 1927), p. 45.

[15] Chicago Commission on Race Relations, *The Negro in Chicago*, pp. 239, 256–57.

[16] *Defender*, August 17, 1918.

[17] *Broad Ax* (Chicago), August 17, 1918.

[18] *Defender*, August 17, 1918.

and white students. Several school principals made no secret of
their preference for racial segregation and employed various sub-
terfuges to keep the races apart. One principal placed as many
Negroes as possible in a branch school, which was under his
jurisdiction; as a result, he kept the proportion of Negroes in the
main building below 20 per cent, while the substandard branch
was 90 per cent Negro.[19] Many parents also expressed their preference for racially separated schools. A delegation of white parents in the Wendell Phillips school district petitioned the school
board for a new junior high school just south of the black belt.
Although they ostensibly objected to the Phillips school because
of "immoral conditions" surrounding it, they admitted under
questioning that "the Phillips school is two-thirds colored and
white children should not be compelled to sit with colored children."[20]

Within the schools, racial conflict was infrequent. Teachers in
racially mixed elementary schools, questioned by the Race Relations Commission in 1920, reported "little friction so far as school
work was concerned, even when it meant sitting next to one
another or in the same seat."[21] In high schools, whites and Negroes did not share in social activities, but Negroes participated
in athletic, musical, and literary societies without friction.[22] A proposal to establish segregated military units at Wendell Phillips
met with opposition from both the principal and the student
body.[23]

Parks, playgrounds, and beaches were far greater sources of
racial conflict. Although formally operated on a non-discrimina
tory basis, recreational areas were often unofficially segregated.
Certain playgrounds and parks on the fringe of the black belt
were limited to whites by a tacit understanding, and the recreational directors, influenced by the whites in the neighborhood,
made Negroes feel unwelcome. In some cases, policemen kept
Negroes out of "white" parks. The Municipal Bureau of Parks im-
plicitly recognized this extralegal segregation. When the Negro
population in a neighborhood became so large that Negroes could

[19] Chicago Commission on Race Relations, *The Negro in Chicago*, p. 242.

[20] *Tribune,* April 6, 1917.

[21] Chicago Commission on Race Relations, *The Negro in Chicago*, p. 246.

[22] *Ibid.*, pp. 254–55.   [23] *Defender,* March 17, 1917.

no longer be barred from the parks and playgrounds, city authorities "turned over" the facilities to Negroes. They hired a Negro director and staff, indicating to the neighborhood that the recreational areas were now reserved for Negro use. Segregation on the beaches was even more rigidly maintained. Although three beaches lay adjacent to the black belt, only one—a small and unattractive beach between Twenty-sixth and Twenty-ninth Streets —was open to Negroes. Policemen and attendants barred Negroes from other South Side beaches.[24]

When whites were unable to enforce segregation in the parks by non-violent means, overt racial clashes often erupted. White gangs terrorized Negroes who attempted to use Fuller Park and the Armour Square recreation center—in the Irish and Polish district just west of Wentworth Avenue. Washington Park—a large recreational area that separated the black belt from Hyde Park and Woodlawn—was a scene of racial violence throughout the migration era. Several of the white gangs that precipitated these outbreaks operated ostensibly as athletic clubs. The most notorious of them—Ragan's Colts, a band of Irish youths, ranging in age from seventeen to twenty-two—was sponsored by an alderman and reputedly enjoyed police protection. During the summer of 1919, the Colts and other young white hoodlums regularly attacked Negro boys who attempted to use the baseball diamonds in Washington Park. Negro groups that ventured into Fuller Park or Armour Square were assaulted even when accompanied by adult leaders.[25]

Places of public accommodation continued to discriminate against Negroes, but as before the war, their policy was erratic.[26] Downtown restaurants, hotels, theaters, and stores employed a variety of tactics to discourage Negro patronage without violating the Civil Rights Act. Restaurant owners frequently instructed waiters to ignore Negro customers, serve them spoiled food, or overcharge them. Theaters tried to seat Negroes in the balcony or in inconspicuous side sections. Marshall Field's reportedly

[24] Chicago Commission on Race Relations, *The Negro in Chicago*, pp. 272–80; *Tribune*, August 24, 1916.

[25] Chicago Commission on Race Relations, *The Negro in Chicago*, pp. 12–14, 288–95; *Defender*, July 12, 1919.

[26] See chap. 2.

ordered its clerks to treat Negroes with indifference and to direct them to the basement "as the most likely place where they were to find the articles they desired to purchase."[27] Yet, as before, some white establishments served Negroes with courtesy, and many places had no policy at all but simply allowed individual clerks to follow their own inclinations. As a result, Negroes who patronized firms outside the black belt could never be certain when they might be embarrassed or humiliated by discriminatory practices.[28]

Even when the Civil Rights Act had been clearly violated, Negroes found it difficult to obtain proper relief. A civil suit usually resulted in a nominal award for damages; the amount was rarely large enough either to meet the plaintiff's court costs or to deter the defendant from future violations. A criminal suit required a jury trial, and Chicago juries invariably refused to convict violators of the Civil Rights Act. To solve this dilemma, Alderman Oscar De Priest sought passage of an ordinance giving the mayor the right to revoke the license of any establishment that discriminated on the basis of race.[29] The press loudly ridiculed De Priest's proposal and even some Negro spokesmen thought it unrealistic. The *Tribune* headlined its story on the ordinance, "Negro Alderman Asks Law Forcing Society of Races." The Civil Rights Act was not effectively enforced, the *Tribune* admitted,

> and will not be in this generation. . . . In fact, modus operandi in Chicago is as nearly perfect as human nature will permit it to be. It is a fiction that a Negro has full civil, meaning full social, rights in any American community. . . . The social relations in which the white and black parts of our population stand with regard to each other never will be determined by the enactment of law or ordinance. They will be established by custom.[30]

27 *Defender*, June 10, 1916.

28 Chicago Commission on Race Relations, *The Negro in Chicago*, pp. 309–23.

29 City of Chicago, *Journal of the Proceedings of the City Council, 1916–17*, p. 648.

30 *Tribune*, June 13, June 14, 1916; see also "The DePriest Ordinance," *Champion Magazine* (Chicago), 1 (September, 1916): 10.

The De Priest ordinance was tabled by the city council and promptly forgotten.[31]

Thus racial hostility was mounting on many fronts. Whites responded with fear and alarm to a large influx of strange, uncouth Negroes, whose appearance and behavior often confirmed their harshest prejudices. Schools, parks, and public places that whites had formerly regarded as their own were now frequented by Negroes. The political situation further aroused the resentment of many whites: anti-Thompson forces pointed out that Negroes were exerting a decisive influence in municipal elections and, as a result of bloc voting, were receiving unprecedented recognition from the city administration. While job competition was not severe so long as the wartime boom lasted, many workers were laid off in the recession of 1919 and whites began to view Negroes as a permanent threat to their economic well-being. And the policies of the meat packers and the steel magnates demonstrated that the old practice of using Negro strikebreakers was still potent. Moreover the southern migration was not limited to Negroes; an estimated twenty thousand Southern whites moved to Chicago during the war years, bringing with them traditional anti-Negro prejudices that further contributed to the city's racial unrest.[32] But by far the most crucial area of racial conflict was housing. White reaction to the Negro's search for better housing precipitated a wave of violence that, together with the terrorism of the "athletic clubs," led directly to the riot of 1919.

Organized white resistance to Negro residential expansion was nothing new in Chicago. Whites had used coercion, boycotts, and violence to keep Negroes out of their neighborhoods throughout the prewar period.[33] But the migration added a new dimension to the housing problem. Before the war, the black belt had grown gradually, usually expanding into districts that whites were vacating. Although individual Negro families occasionally sought

[31] City of Chicago, *Journal of the Proceedings of the City Council, 1917-18*, p. 273.

[32] Walter White, "Chicago and Its Eight Reasons," *Crisis* (New York), 18 (October, 1919): 293–94; [Carter G. Woodson], review of *The Negro in Chicago*, by the Chicago Commission on Race Relations, *Journal of Negro History* (Washington), 8 (January, 1923): 114.

[33] See chap. 1.

homes in white neighborhoods and evoked a hostile reaction, these incidents rarely presaged a mass "invasion." Once the migration began, however, the black belt was no longer large enough to accommodate the rapidly growing Negro population. To be sure, the newcomers first displaced the whites in the formerly mixed areas of the black belt. But sheer numbers caused an overflow into the neighborhoods east of Cottage Grove Avenue and south of Fifty-fifth Street. Whites in these areas, confronted with the prospect of Negro neighbors, found it difficult to move elsewhere because war had halted home construction and housing was scarce. The middle-class whites who lived in Kenwood, Hyde Park, Woodlawn, and the Grand Boulevard district, then, faced the choice of living in a racially mixed community or resisting the Negro "invasion" by any means possible. They chose to resist.

The housing problem emerged as a major issue in the spring of 1917. The Chicago Real Estate Board noted with alarm that Southern Negroes were "pouring into Chicago at the rate of ten thousand a month" and that they would "do more than $250,-000,000 damage" to property in the city. Board members charged that Negro real estate dealers had conspired to "ruin" white residential districts by obtaining leaseholds on one building in every block and renting the property to Negroes. The Board appointed a committee to study the problem and if necessary recommend a residential segregation ordinance to the city council.[34] A week later the Board met with a committee of Negro leaders and reported that the Negroes were "anxious to confine [themselves] to [their] own community life, social affairs, and business" and did not "want to live in the same block with whites." The Negroes angrily declared that they had been misquoted.[35] When the Board's specially appointed committee submitted its report, it made no mention of legal segregation in housing, but suggested, in conciliatory terms, that "modern houses and apartments should be built and rented to Negroes in desirable neighborhoods," "agents and owners in predominantly Negro sections should sell and rent to Negroes," and "conservative loans and renewals should be made to Negroes." A delegation of Negroes attending

[34] *Tribune,* April 5, 1917; *Defender,* April 14, 1917.

[35] *Tribune,* April 10, 1917; *Defender,* April 21, 1917.

the meeting objected strenuously to the report, arguing that the Board had no right or authority to determine which neighborhoods were "desirable" for Negroes.[36]

As the migration continued and the black belt began to overflow, white real estate agents and property owners turned from conferences and committee reports to organized action. Late in the summer of 1917, a businessmen's association in the Far South Side community of Morgan Park obtained an injunction forbidding a real estate dealer from renting apartments to Negroes until "unhealthful" conditions were remedied.[37] The following year, the Kenwood and Hyde Park Property Owners' Association announced its intention to "make Hyde Park white." Originally organized for the improvement of civic conditions in the neighborhood—cleaner streets, better lighting, neater lawns—the Association fell under the control of real estate dealers resolved not only to prevent a Negro "take-over" of Hyde Park, but to evict Negro families that had moved in since the beginning of the war. Whites "won't be driven out," the group's leaders declared, but would keep Kenwood and Hyde Park "clear of undesirables . . . at all cost."[38]

The first task of the Kenwood and Hyde Park Property Owners' Association was to convince the community that the Negroes depreciated property values. At weekly meetings, in a neighborhood newspaper, and in frequent broadsides, the Association's leaders argued that the Negro influx resulted in a financial loss for every white property owner: "The depreciation of our property in this district has been two hundred and fifty millions since the invasion. If someone told you that there was to be an invasion that would injure your homes to that extent, wouldn't you rise up as one man and one woman, and say as General Foch said: 'They shall not pass'?"[39] The Association's methods, its leaders confidently declared, would be "effective and legal." A white Hyde Park could "be obtained through conciliation rather than antagonism," they argued, for if Negroes had a "place to go" they would "segregate themselves." The Association therefore urged whites to

[36] *Chicago Daily News*, April 30, 1917.

[37] *Tribune*, August 2, 1917; *Broad Ax*, October 20, 1917.

[38] Chicago Commission on Race Relations, *The Negro in Chicago*, p. 118; *Tribune*, June 28, 1919.

[39] Chicago Commission on Race Relations, *The Negro in Chicago*, p. 119.

give Negroes "reasonable loans at reasonable rates of interest" so that they might buy homes in their own neighborhoods.[40] But come what may, the Association vowed to keep Hyde Park "desirable for ourselves." To this end, it appointed thirty-five block captains and instructed them to apply pressure to any property-owners who considered selling or renting to Negroes. The twenty real estate dealers who formed the nucleus of the organization tried to persuade the mortgage holders of all property owned by Negroes east of Cottage Grove Avenue to squeeze out the owners when the mortgages fell due.[41]

When, in spite of conferences and organizational efforts, Negroes continued to move into Kenwood and Hyde Park, hostile whites turned to a third tactic—violence. Between July 1, 1917, and March 1, 1921, there were fifty-eight racially-inspired bombings in Chicago. Two persons died in the explosions, several more were injured, and property valued at over $100,000 was destroyed. Most of the bombings took place in disputed residential areas and were directed at the homes of Negroes.[42] In some cases, the Negro families were warned that unless they moved out of the community, their homes would be bombed. Negro tenants on Vincennes Avenue received a letter: "We are going to BLOW these FLATS TO HELL and if you don't want to go with them you had better move at once"; within the next two weeks, three bombs exploded in the neighborhood.[43] Jesse Binga, who not only lived in a disputed area but handled many real estate deals in the district, was a special target for the bombers: his home and office were bombed seven times.[44] Most of the bombings outside of Kenwood, Hyde Park, and the Grand Boulevard area were aimed at real estate dealers who rented to Negroes and bankers who made loans on Negro property. A luxurious home in an exclusive Lake Shore Drive neighborhood was bombed because its owner, a wealthy white businessman, had rented property to Negroes in

[40] *Tribune,* June 28, 1919.   [41] *Whip,* June 24, 1919.

[42] Chicago Commission on Race Relations, *The Negro in Chicago,* pp. 122–23; "The Inter-Racial Situation in Chicago," Bulletin Number 1, Chicago Survey Division, Industrial Relations Department, Interchurch World Movement, Chicago [1920].

[43] *Defender,* September 28, 1918.

[44] *Tribune,* April 7, 1919; *Defender,* June 26, 1920, September 3, 1921; Chicago Commission on Race Relations, *The Negro in Chicago,* p. 123.

the Grand Boulevard district.[45] Despite numerous pleas from Negro groups for stricter law enforcement, the police provided scant protection for families that had been threatened. Nine men were finally arrested for planting bombs in 1921, but the failure of the police to make any arrests for four years—and frequent cavalier statements by the Chief of Police and State's Attorney Hoyne—undermined the Negro community's confidence in the law enforcement agencies.[46]

No one ever proved that the Kenwood and Hyde Park Property Owners' Association was directly responsible for the bombings. The *Defender* said that the Association was "back of the attempted assault and murder" and later called for an "effort to discover the relationship existing between the 'bombing trust' and the various South Side improvement associations."[47] Many of the bombings—particularly those designed to intimidate real estate dealers—seemed to be part of the Association's coordinated plan to stop the Negro "invasion." But the evidence was circumstantial. In any case, the Association's vow to make its community white "at all cost" had prepared the way for violence. Sensing this, some whites criticized the Association's extremist tactics and statements. The *Tribune,* while still maintaining that racial adjustment in Chicago must be based on residential segregation, attacked the Association's classification of Negroes as "undesirables."[48] White ministers in Hyde Park condemned the Association for encouraging disorder, and a neighborhood newspaper called the "improvement" groups unlawful conspiracies and urged its readers to avoid them.[49]

In the spring of 1919, the bombing of Negro homes and assaults on Negroes in the streets and parks became almost everyday occurrences. In March, a bomb exploded in Binga's real estate office. In April, another realty office and a home on Ellis Avenue were bombed, and a melee between Negroes and whites erupted in the vicinity of Fortieth Street and Vincennes Avenue—a center

[45] *Tribune,* June 17, 1919.

[46] Chicago Commission on Race Relations, *The Negro in Chicago,* pp. 123-24; *Defender,* May 28, 1921.

[47] *Defender,* June 1, 1918, May 28, 1921.

[48] *Tribune,* June 30, 1919.

[49] Chicago Commission on Race Relations, *The Negro in Chicago,* pp. 129-31.

of the housing struggle.[50] In May, two explosions rocked a building occupied by Negroes on Grand Boulevard, and a gang of white youths, reputedly members of Ragan's Colts, attacked and beat a Negro who entered a "white" saloon on State Street.[51] June brought warm weather and more frequent interracial contacts in the streets and parks. The white "athletic clubs" became bolder and habitually assaulted Negroes along the western boundary of the black belt and in Washington Park. Early in the month, a riot was narrowly averted on a State Street car when a white sailor slapped a Negro woman who had asked him not to step on her children's toes.[52] On the night of June 21, gangs of young hoodlums murdered two Negro men for no more apparent reason than their desire to "get a nigger." Although there were witnesses to the crimes, the police made no arrests, strengthening the suspicion that the gangs were protected by white politicians.[53] A week later, rioting erupted in a West Side neighborhood recently "invaded" by Negroes; one man died and six were injured.[54] The white gang leaders threatened still more violence; they posted notices along the boundaries of the black belt threatening to "get all the niggers" on the Fourth of July.[55]

Both Negro and white civic leaders realized that the racial situation was deteriorating rapidly and that unless immediate action were taken a full-scale riot was imminent. But no one seemed to know what to do, and the Thompson administration simply failed to act. As early as April, Beauregard Moseley advised the white community that Negroes would not tolerate assaults and bombings indefinitely, that many were "resolved to meet force with force, and [that] the situation will become more and more acute if this threat eventuates into reality."[56] After the June disorders, Ida Wells-Barnett warned:

> Just such a situation as this . . . led up to the East St. Louis riot. . . . Will the legal, moral and civic forces of this town

[50] *Tribune*, April 7, April 23, 1919; *Defender*, April 26, 1919.

[51] *Tribune*, June 17, 1919; Chicago Commission on Race Relations, *The Negro in Chicago*, p. 54.

[52] *Defender*, June 7, 1919.

[53] Chicago Commission on Race Relations, *The Negro in Chicago*, pp. 55–57.

[54] *Tribune*, July 1, 1919.

[55] Chicago Commission on Race Relations, *The Negro in Chicago*, p. 57.

[56] *Tribune*, April 26, 1919.

stand idly by and take no notice of these preliminary outbreaks? . . . I implore Chicago to set the wheels of justice in
motion before it is too late and Chicago be disgraced by some
of the bloody outrages that have disgraced East St. Louis.[57]

The *Tribune* urged city officials and industrialists to take the lead
in providing adequate housing for Negroes: "Will we undertake
[remedial measures] now or will we wait until some shocking
tragedy stirs us into belated action?"[58]

Chicago did not have long to wait. On a blisteringly hot Sunday
afternoon, July 27, 1919, Eugene Williams drowned at the Twenty-ninth Street beach, touching off the calamity that had so long
been feared.[59] The rioting began on the beach when the police,
ignoring Negro charges that Williams had been stoned by whites,
refused to make any arrests. The Negro crowd attacked several
white men, and impassioned accounts of a general racial war
quickly flashed through the South Side. After dark, the white
gangs west of Wentworth Avenue retaliated by beating, stabbing,
or shooting thirty-eight Negroes who had accidentally wandered
into white districts. Two people died the first day and over fifty
were injured, but the South Side was calm on Monday morning,
and most Chicagoans were able to view Sunday's disorders as
merely the latest in the series of minor racial outbreaks that had
plagued the city all year. The *Tribune* did not even give the riot
a banner headline.

But by Monday night, Chicago knew that the catastrophe had
come. Rioting resumed in the late afternoon as white gangs
assaulted Negro workers leaving the stockyards. Mobs pulled
streetcars from their wires and dragged out Negro passengers,
kicking and beating them. Negro mobs retaliated, attacking whites
who worked in the black belt. As the night wore on, the white

[57] *Ibid.*, July 7, 1919.   [58] *Ibid.*, July 2, 1919.

[59] The following account of the riot, unless otherwise documented, is based
on Chicago Commission on Race Relations, *The Negro in Chicago,* pp. 1–52;
Tribune, July 28–August 4, 1919; and *Defender,* August 2, 1919. See also
Arthur I. Waskow, *From Race Riot to Sit-In: 1919 and the 1960's* (New York:
Doubleday & Company, 1965), pp. 38–104. Waskow analyzes the Chicago
riot within the context of the national pattern of racial violence that developed
in the summer of 1919. Chicago's was the most serious of over twenty riots or
racial incidents that erupted throughout the country. Several of the others, as
Waskow demonstrates, resulted from conditions remarkably similar to those
in Chicago.

rioters became bolder: they raided Negro neighborhoods, firing shots into Negro homes from automobiles. During this night of terror—the worst period of the riot—twenty people were killed and hundreds injured.

With the renewal of violence on Monday, it had become clear that the police were unable to handle the situation. Not only were their forces insufficient, but many policemen sided with the white rioters and fired indiscriminately into Negro crowds. Several newspapers and many civic leaders demanded that Mayor Thompson ask Governor Lowden for a detachment of the state militia. The governor, responding promptly to the outbreak, ordered the mobilization of several companies of the militia and stationed them at nearby armories, but he could send them into the streets only at the mayor's request. Throughout Monday night and all day Tuesday, both the mayor and the chief of police insisted that the local forces were "in full command" and that no outside assistance was necessary.[60] Negro leaders tarried in voicing demands for the militia; they recalled that state forces had supported the white mobs in East St. Louis.[61]

Rioting continued on Tuesday and spread beyond the South Side. A white mob raided the Loop, killing two Negroes and robbing several others. A crowd of Italians on the West Side, aroused by a rumor that Negro rioters had killed an Italian child, brutally murdered an innocent Negro. By Wednesday, the riot began to wane, although skirmishes continued along the Wentworth Avenue boundary line. Finally, at 10:30 on Wednesday evening, with the worst already over, Mayor Thompson asked Governor Lowden to send in the militia. Unlike the guardsmen used at East St. Louis, the troops that entered Chicago were especially trained for riot duty and performed well. They efficiently and fairly maintained order and prevented the formation of mobs and marauding parties. Rain and cooler temperatures on Thursday and Friday, together with the work of the militia, quelled the riot. Early Saturday morning, incendiary fires de-

[60] Lloyd Wendt and Herman Kogan, *Big Bill Thompson* (Indianapolis: Bobbs-Merrill & Company, 1953), pp. 173–74.

[61] E. O. Brown, G. C. Hall and others to the Chief of Police, City of Chicago, July 28, 1919, Rosenwald Papers; Guido A. Dobbert, "A History of the Chicago Race Riot of 1919," unpublished master's thesis, University of Chicago, 1957, *passim*.

stroyed forty-nine houses in the stockyards district, but despite angry accusations that Negroes were responsible, rioting did not resume.

The governor never imposed martial law during the Chicago riot, but in other respects the South Side resembled a besieged city. Most Negroes were unable to go to work as a streetcar strike, unrelated to the riot, began on Tuesday, and to venture outside of the black belt on foot would have been foolhardy. Even the black belt itself was unsafe after dark, and Negro leaders urged everyone to stay off the streets. Moreover, white deliverymen and shopkeepers, fearing retaliation, refused to enter the black belt, and in many areas the food supply was nearly cut off. To meet these exigencies, the Red Cross and Urban League distributed food to needy families, and the packing companies set up pay stations on the South Side so that Negro employees, unable to go to the yards, would not be without funds.

The Chicago riot was a two-sided conflict and members of both races committed acts of wanton cruelty. Nevertheless, all objective observers agreed not only that whites were responsible for the violent incidents that led to the riot, but that they were, for the most part, the aggressors during the riot itself. Negroes, to be sure, killed and maimed innocent white men who entered the black belt. But unlike the white gangs that invaded Negro neighborhoods, Negroes rarely entered white districts to commit violence. The charges that Negroes burned the houses near the stockyards were never substantiated, and several witnesses reported having seen white men with blackened faces in the district at the time of the fire. Furthermore, Negro violence generally took the form of individual attack; there were no organized Negro gangs—comparable to the white "athletic clubs"—bent on furthering racial conflict. The final casualty figures also indicated that Negroes had been more the victims than the attackers: 23 Negroes and 15 whites died; 342 Negroes and 178 whites were injured. The grand jury that investigated the riot concluded that "the colored people suffered more at the hands of the white hoodlums than the white people suffered at the hands of the black hoodlums."[62]

Yet, many whites reacted to the riot, not by reproaching the anti-Negro elements, but by urging stricter racial segregation. The *Tribune* editorialized:

[62] Chicago Commission on Race Relations, *The Negro in Chicago*, p. 35.

Despite the possible justice of Negro demands, the fact is that the races are not living in harmony. . . . Shall there be separate bathing beaches for the white and colored? . . . How long will it be before segregation will be the only means of preventing murders? . . . How long will it be before public policy and the protection of life and property makes necessary another system of transportation?[63]

Five days later, the *Tribune* stated that "so long as this city is dominated by whites . . . there will be limitations placed on the black people. . . . A rebellion by Negroes against facts which exist and will persist will not help."[64] A white minister was even more explicit: "I believe in segregating the blacks for their own good as well as the good of the whites."[65] The Kenwood and Hyde Park Property Owners' Association responded characteristically with a demand for a conference to deal with the "promiscuous scattering of Negroes throughout white residential districts of our city."[66] When the mayor called a special meeting of the city council to investigate the causes of the riot, one alderman immediately introduced a resolution "to consider the question of seggregating the races within certain established zones."[67] Perhaps the most irrelevant response came from the Chicago Department of the U.S. Army Intelligence Office which, in a highly confidential report, blamed the riot on bolsheviks and anarchists.[68]

White authorities displayed a similar bias in the legal proceedings that grew out of the riot. Despite the casualty figures, twice as many Negroes were brought to trial and indicted for participation in the riot as whites. Prejudicial police action, resulting in a disproportionately large number of Negro arrests, partially accounted for this discrepancy. In addition, as the attorney general of Illinois later admitted, State's Attorney Maclay Hoyne, who had injected the racial issue into his unsuccessful mayoralty

[63] *Tribune*, July 29, 1919.

[64] *Ibid.*, August 3, 1919.

[65] *Ibid.*, August 4, 1919.

[66] *Ibid.*, August 6, 1919.

[67] City of Chicago, *Journal of the Proceedings of the City Council, 1919–20*, p. 1115. The Chicago Real Estate Board had suggested similar action in 1917, but in the interim the U.S. Supreme Court had ruled that a residential segregation ordinance in Louisville was unconstitutional (*Buchanan* v. *Warley*, 245 U.S. 60, 38 S. Ct. 16). Nevertheless, anti-Negro elements in Chicago and elsewhere expressed hope that the decision could be circumvented.

[68] Minutes of the Chicago Commission on Race Relations, December 4, 1919, copy in Rosenwald Papers; see also *Tribune*, August 2, 1919.

campaign earlier in the year, "tracked down Negroes more re-lentlessly than equally guilty whites."[69] The grand jury, incensed by Hoyne's obvious prejudice, suspended its hearings of crimes committed by Negroes "until the state's attorney submitted evidence concerning the various crimes committed by whites against blacks." Hoyne dismissed the grand jury's protest as a "tempest in a teapot" and charged that the jury had been swayed by "vicious black belt politics."[70]

Outraged by the state's discriminatory handling of the race riot cases, almost every Negro organization in Chicago banded together to form the Joint Committee to Secure Equal Justice for Colored Riot Defendants. "The courts," declared the Committee's secretary, A. C. MacNeal, "are alive to the need of meting out punishment and affording protection where discrimination occurs on the part of colored people against white people. . . . But where the discrimination is against the colored people there is not the same certainty of clear justice and able defense."[71] With the support of leading white liberals, the Committee engaged two prominent lawyers to defend "colored persons whom investigation shows to have been unjustly indicted." The Committee participated in about fifty cases and won acquittals for several of the more obvious victims of prejudicial treatment.[72]

Only one public official took constructive action in the wake of the riot. Governor Lowden, in compliance with a request submitted by eighty-one civic leaders, appointed a commission to "study and report upon the broad question of the relations between the two races."[73] The commission, made up of six Negroes and six whites, chose Graham Romeyn Taylor, a journalist and sociologist and the son of the director of the Chicago Commons settlement house, to serve as executive secretary. Taylor's assistant was Charles S. Johnson, a young Negro sociologist who had

[69] William Hutchinson, *Lowden of Illinois* (Chicago: University of Chicago Press, 1957), pp. 405–6.

[70] Chicago Commission on Race Relations, *The Negro in Chicago*, pp. 35–36; *Tribune*, August 7, 1919.

[71] A. C. MacNeal to Julius Rosenwald, November 18, 1919, Rosenwald Papers.

[72] A. C. MacNeal to William Graves, April 3, 1920, Rosenwald Papers.

[73] Chicago Commission on Race Relations, *The Negro in Chicago*, p. xvi.

recently headed the research department of the Chicago Urban League.[74] The Commission assembled a staff of fifteen and spent eighteen months investigating every aspect of race relations in Chicago.

The report of the Chicago Commission on Race Relations, published in 1922, was a monumental compendium of facts, surveys, and recommendations. Rejecting easy explanations of the riot, the report analyzed the entire complex of factors that led to the tragic events of July, 1919: the migration, population growth, Negro entry into industry, the housing conflict, discrimination in public places, and the rising tide of violence. Similarly, the report provided no easy answers; but its fifty-nine recommendations explicitly repudiated the notion that further segregation would lead to racial harmony. It urged instead that Negroes be assured equal rights and opportunities.[75] Marked by balanced treatment and judicious analysis, the report was the one achievement of interracial cooperation to come out of these years of racial strife.[76]

The months following the riot were less hopeful in other respects. The continuing struggle over housing indicated that the riot had effected few changes: like the Bourbons, white Chicago had learned nothing and forgotten nothing. In November, 1919, the Kenwood and Hyde Park Property Owners' Association called for "segregation by mutual consent" and asked Negroes to keep out of white neighborhoods for the sake of racial harmony.[77] Negro leaders understandably rejected any proposal to cooperate in maintaining segregation, and the new year ushered in the most violent series of bombings that the South Side had yet seen. Between January 1 and March 1, eight bombs exploded: bombers

[74] *Ibid.*, pp. xviii, 653; see also Mabel Hawkins to William Graves, November 21, 1919, and Paul Kellogg to Graves, November 23, 1919, Rosenwald Papers.

[75] Chicago Commission on Race Relations, *The Negro in Chicago*, pp. 640–51.

[76] Waskow, however, perceptively points out in his excellent analysis of the Chicago Commission on Race Relations and its work that the report suffered from a fatal weakness: it failed to indicate how those in power could be induced to make the changes recommended by the Commission. As a result, the report was much admired, but had little practical impact. Waskow, *From Race Riot to Sit-In*, pp. 97–104.

[77] *Defender*, November 1, November 29, 1919; *Whip*, November 1, 1919.

struck at Jesse Binga's home for the fourth time and at a building newly purchased by the Appomattox Club.[78]

The Property Owners' Association became increasingly shrill during these months. It commenced publication of a newspaper, the *Property Owners' Journal,* which it filled with inflammatory articles and statements. The *Journal* declared:

> To damage a man's property and destroy its value is to rob him. The person who commits this act is a robber. Every owner has the right to defend his property to the utmost of his ability, with every means at his disposal. . . . As the negro has increased his invasion and is looking for the opportunity to deliver the final paralysing blow at property values, he is attempting to justify his actions by vague phrases, placed in his mouth by cheap politicians . . . and, as a result, negroes, whose knowledge of the constitution is about as comprehensive as their understanding of the fourth dimension, are shouting "constitutional rights."[79]

Three weeks later, the *Journal* argued that "every colored man who moves into Hyde Park . . . is making war on the white man. Consequently he is not entitled to any consideration and forfeits his right to be employed by the white man." In February, the *Journal* turned from analysis of the housing problem to a general discussion of the Negro's character:

> There is nothing in the make-up of a Negro, physically or mentally, which should induce anyone to welcome him as a neighbor. The best of them are insanitary, . . . ruin alone follows in their path. They are as proud as peacocks, but have nothing of the peacock's beauty. . . . Niggers are undesirable neighbors and entirely irresponsible and vicious.[80]

By 1920, the campaign to keep Hyde Park and Kenwood white had begun to show results. The Property Owners' Association boasted that a year of "ruthless campaigning" had forced Negroes out of the neighborhoods east of Cottage Grove, and the Chicago

[78] *Whip,* February 14, 1920; Chicago Commission on Race Relations, *The Negro in Chicago,* p. 123.

[79] Excerpts from the *Property Owners' Journal* appear in the Minutes of the Chicago Commission on Race Relations, January 8, 1920, copy in Rosenwald Papers; and in Chicago Commission on Race Relations, *The Negro in Chicago,* pp. 121–22, 123–24.

[80] *Ibid.*

Real Estate Board congratulated the Association on its "prog-ress."[81] Violence and inflammatory propaganda had intimidated Negroes who sought homes in the area and prevented landlords and real estate dealers from selling or renting to them. Moreover, the wartime housing shortage had ended, and whites in the district between State and Cottage Grove had begun to move out, leaving this neighborhood almost exclusively Negro. Hence the line became sharply drawn along Cottage Grove Avenue: to the west was the solid black belt, to the east lily-white Hyde Park and Kenwood. Whites successfully defended this line for another generation. In the mid-1920's they strengthened their fortifications by adopting the most potent defensive weapon yet devised, the restrictive covenant.[82]

The riot and the continuing hostility of large segments of the white community strengthened the conviction of Negro leaders that the Negro community should become increasingly self-sufficient. On the one hand, Negroes rejected any humiliating agreement with white real estate interests to encourage segregated housing, and organized an association of their own, the Protective Circle of Chicago, to fight terrorism in Hyde Park and Kenwood.[83] At the same time, however, the newly organized Liberty Life Insurance Company reminded Negroes that during the riot "you could not buy a loaf of bread or a bottle of milk, because the white people, who own or control 99% of all business places, closed their doors and left the Negroes to sink or swim."[84] Lacey Kirk Williams told his large Olivet Baptist congregation on the Sunday following the riot that "we should hasten to build up our own marts and trades so we can give employment and help to provide against such a day as we are now experiencing."[85]

The riot of 1919 destroyed whatever hope remained for a peacefully integrated city. The migration had reinforced the internal pressure for a self-contained Negro community by creating new

[81] *Whip*, January 24, 1920; Minutes of the Chicago Commission on Race Relations, January 8, 1920, copy in Rosenwald Papers.

[82] For the adoption of restrictive covenants, which were not used in Chicago in the migration era, see *Defender*, October 22, 1927, June 30, 1928, July 20, 1929; and Louis C. Washington, "A Study of Restrictive Covenants in Chicago," unpublished master's thesis, University of Chicago, 1948.

[83] *Defender*, February 7, 1920.

[84] *Ibid.*, September 20, 1919.   [85] *Tribune*, August 4, 1919.

demands for services and institutions in the black belt. Now the riot and the activities of the neighborhood associations strengthened the external pressure, thwarting the expansion of the black belt and forcing it to rely more exclusively on its own resources. The black belt of 1920 had clearly delineated boundaries—Twenty-second and Fifty-fifth Streets, Wentworth and Cottage Grove Avenues. While the black belt had once included racially mixed neighborhoods, it was now becoming exclusively Negro. At the same time, the neighborhoods surrounding it remained exclusively white. Within the ghetto walls, Negroes attempted to solidify their economic and civic institutions and create a meaningful and satisfactory community life apart from White Chicago. During the next decade, the black belt became the "Black Metropolis." The prosperity of the 1920's made the dream of a truly self-sufficient Negro city seem close at hand. The South Side's halcyon days had arrived.

CONCLUSION

In the summer of 1966, Chicago's racial problems were front-page news throughout the country. Martin Luther King and his followers dramatized the persistence of segregation and discrimination in the city by marching into white neighborhoods, where they were greeted by taunts, insults, and physical violence. King's activities in Chicago, coupled with the riots that have erupted in a score or more American cities since 1964, shifted the focus of the race problem in the United States from the South to the North. By 1966, no domestic problem seemed more complex, more fraught with danger to the social fabric of the nation, than the confrontation in our major cities between Negroes, frustrated by generations of oppression, and whites, battling against what they conceive to be a threat to their way of life. Chicago, with its seething ghetto and its rigid pattern of housing segregation, had come to exemplify the urban racial conflict of the 1960's.

At first glance, Chicago's racial problem in 1966 seemed vastly different from the problems of the late nineteenth and early twentieth centuries. Quantitatively there had been enormous change. Over ten times as many Negroes lived in Chicago in 1966 as in 1920; instead of 4 per cent of the population, they now constituted almost 30 per cent. The ghetto occupied large sections of the city that had been all-white just two decades before. The Cottage Grove Avenue and Fifty-fifth Street boundary lines, successfully defended for a generation, fell after World War II, as Negroes, their ranks swelled by continued migration from the South, moved east into Kenwood and Hyde Park, south into Woodlawn, Park Manor, and Chatham, and southwest into Englewood. In the 1950's, the formerly Jewish section of Lawndale became solidly Negro, and a ghetto grew on the West Side soon to rival in size the South Side black belt.

On the surface, too, white attitudes toward the Negro's struggle seemed far different in 1966 from what they had been early in the century. Between 1890 and 1920, Negroes had fought against an almost solid wall of white resistance; white Chicagoans had stood virtually united in their belief in Negro inferiority and their conviction that Negroes must forever occupy a subordinate status in the city's social structure. The conflict in the summer of 1966, on the other hand, came in the wake of ten years of almost continual civil rights activity. Nationally, the Negro plight had been recognized as the country's most pressing domestic problem. The President had committed himself to the Negro Revolt, the Supreme Court had upheld the legitimacy of the Negro's claim to full citizenship rights, and the Congress had passed four civil rights bills in eight years. On the local level, too, Chicago's politicians, newspapers, clergymen, and civic leaders had proclaimed their support of the Negro's struggle for equality. Unlike the situation fifty years earlier, Chicago's Negroes seemed to be moving with the wind at their backs.

Nevertheless, in many significant ways, remarkably little had changed since 1920. Increased numbers had vastly expanded the ghetto, but had not changed its basic structure. Negroes were still unable to obtain housing beyond the confines of the ghetto, and within the black belt the complex of separate institutions and organizations that had first developed between 1890 and 1920 continued to serve an isolated Negro populace. The same restrictions that had limited Negro opportunities in the early twentieth century still operated in 1966. In fact, four civil rights bills, dozens of court decisions, and thousands of brave words about Negro rights had barely touched the life of Chicago's Negroes. It remained as constricted as it had been two generations earlier. And the bitter hostility of the residents of Gage Park, Belmont-Cragin, and Cicero toward Dr. King's marches demonstrated that thousands of white Chicagoans were still determined to preserve the status quo.

No other ethnic enclave in Chicago had changed so little over the past fifty years. While the city's Irish, Polish, Jewish, and Italian sections had broken down or developed new forms in the suburbs, the Negro ghetto remained much as it had been—cohesive, restrictive, and largely impoverished. Some historians and sociologists have suggested that the persistence of the Negro ghetto is simply the result of the steady influx of Southern Negroes into the city. While European immigration almost ceased in the

1920's, Negro migration continued, augmenting the ghetto and strengthening its internal structure. In its inception, they have argued, the Negro ghetto was no different from other ethnic neighborhoods; only the difference in population patterns over the past fifty years has made it so. Oscar Handlin, for instance, maintains that the Negroes of the urban North, like the Irish, Germans, Italians, and Yankees, "chose . . . to live in communities of their own because they could thus best satisfy their social and cultural needs." In his view, the Negro ghetto, like the immigrant enclaves, was established "by adjustment—largely voluntary— . . . to the conditions of metropolitan life."[1]

Much of the rhetoric that accompanied the rise of the Chicago Negro ghetto in the early twentieth century seems to support Handlin's contention that Negroes voluntarily chose separate development as a positive good. Both Negro and white leaders extolled the move toward separatism. Many Negroes spoke proudly of self-help, Negro achievement and racial solidarity. White leaders hailed the growth of a self-sufficient Negro community as proof that Negroes not only recognized the realities of a biracial society, but preferred to be "with their own." In brief, the growth of the Negro ghetto often seemed, from the statements of both Negro and white leaders, less a manifestation of proscription than a mark of Negro progress.

The rhetoric contained a certain degree of truth. Separate community development in the urban North provided Negroes with new opportunities for independent action. In the rural South, despite legal segregation, Negroes did not really act on their own. The white landowner told them what crops to plant and when to plant them, provided them with tools and living quarters, gave them what few welfare benefits they might expect, and possessed sole political power. Only in their churches and lodges did the rural southern Negroes manage their own affairs. In Chicago, on the other hand, Negroes acted independently in many ways. They were on their own in seeking homes and jobs, and their employers exercised no control over their lives once they left the factories and yards. They supported Negro civic institutions and a Negro hospital, read Negro newspapers, and participated in a Negro political organization headed by Negro politicians. Para-

[1] Oscar Handlin, *Fire-Bell in the Night* (Boston: Little-Brown & Company, 1964), p. 97.

doxically, Negroes were more independent of whites in the integrated North than in the segregated South.

The importance of this self-sufficiency should not be minimized. First, it provided Negroes with opportunities for leadership that hitherto they had never enjoyed. In the rural South, only the church and the fraternal orders provided training for Negroes with leadership ambitions. Chicago's black belt, on the other hand, afforded Negroes the opportunity to become leaders in politics, business, journalism, and civic life. Second, the idea of an independent black belt provided Negroes with a new sense of pride. Whatever the real achievements of Negro businessmen, politicians, and civic leaders, the sight of Negroes participating independently in fields that had previously been monopolized by whites became a source of race pride. Jesse Binga, Oscar De Priest, and George Cleveland Hall were more than Negro leaders; they became race heroes. Their accomplishments seemed to prove that Negroes could succeed, just as whites had succeeded, even with the odds arrayed against them.

Most important, even the man who could never hope to own a bank, go to Congress, or run a hospital could attain a degree of self-respect in Chicago that was often impossible in Natchitoches, Louisiana, or Macon County, Alabama. In Chicago, there was no omnipresent white man demanding obeisance. "The man," to be sure, was still there—the boss on the job, the cop on the beat, the Jew that ran the clothing store, but he was further removed from the intimacies of everyday life. Moreover he was an impersonal figure who, unlike the southern white, expected no fealty from "his niggers." In an almost all-Negro community, with no white man supervising every decision, manifesting his superiority in status at every opportunity, the northern Negro was able to develop a new sense of self-reliance and, to some degree, self-respect.

Nevertheless, much of the rhetoric of Negro achievement rings false when compared with the reality of Negro life in Chicago. The advantages of separate development were far outweighed by the disadvantages. In the first place, the Negro community was never truly independent. Only a handful of Negroes worked for Negro firms. The vast majority continued to rely upon white employers for their livelihood. The Negro civic institutions were run by Negroes, but white philanthropists provided them with the necessary financial support. White merchants controlled most of

the retail businesses in the black belt, and even the most successful Negro businessmen often operated at the sufferance of white
interests. This was most graphically illustrated in the late 1920's
when Jesse Binga became a vassal of Samuel Insull, the utilities
magnate, and the Binga State Bank became the first in Chicago to
fall in the wake of the stock market crash, because Insull, pre-
occupied with his own interests, was unable to help.[2] Negro politicians came closest to exercising truly independent power. With
Edward Wright's election as ward committeeman in 1920, Negroes gained control of the Second Ward Republican machinery.
Still, the Thompson organization could break the Negro politicians, as Wright ruefully learned later in the decade.[3]

Second, no amount of rhetoric could obscure the inferiority of
Negro community institutions and facilities. Probably the only
Negro venture with a solid claim to excellence was Provident Hospital in its early days under Daniel Hale Williams; but once Williams and his white associates resigned, Provident could no longer
compete with other hospitals in quality of medical care. Although
Negro leaders were reluctant to recognize it, the indisputable fact
remained that they had neither the experience nor the resources
to create an adequate community life of their own. Moreover
whites stood in their path at every turn. The inability of Negro
businessmen to obtain credit from white banks, the inferior
municipal services provided by the city to Negro districts, and the
refusal of many white agencies to take Negro community projects
seriously all made the task of creating a separate but equal Negro
community nearly impossible. Negro businesses were, by white
standards, small, unstable, and underfinanced. The Wabash Avenue YMCA was but a shadow of the superbly equipped, lily-
white YMCA in the Loop, and Negro welfare organizations were
inadequate to meet the needs of the underprivileged and malad-
justed. The Second Ward political organization could determine
the outcome of a mayoralty election, but it had neither the talent
nor the will to face realistically the black belt's most pressing

2 "A Negro Bank Closes Its Doors," *Opportunity* (New York), 8 (September, 1930): 264; W. E. B. DuBois, "Binga," *Crisis* (New York), 37 (December, 1930): 425–26; *Chicago Defender,* April 6, 1935; interview with Joseph
D. Bibb, March 29, 1963.

3 Lloyd Wendt and Herman Kogan, *Big Bill Thompson* (Indianapolis:
Bobbs-Merrill & Company, 1953), pp. 249, 256–57.

problems. In sum, the idea of a Negro city on the South Side, providing its inhabitants with all of the facilities from which they were excluded in the white community, remained a dream. Instead, the South Side was no more than a woefully inadequate, vastly inferior version of White Chicago.

Finally, despite their emphasis on the positive aspects of separate development, Negro leaders did not make a free choice when they opted for separatism. Their action was necessitated by white hostility and oppression. They built the institutional ghetto only after whites had created the physical ghetto, after Negroes had been barred from white neighborhoods and from the facilities of white Chicago. The architects of the "black metropolis" merely made the best of a bad situation. Many of them realized this and expressed an ambiguous attitude toward the developments they themselves encouraged. A few, perhaps, may have been wholeheartedly committed to the idea of a Negro metropolis on the South Side. Some probably saw an immediate advantage—both for themselves and for the Negro community—in separate development and never considered long-range objectives. Others saw no alternative, given the hostility of white Chicagoans. And still others looked upon separatism as merely a temporary expedient, never losing sight of the ultimate goal of an integrated society. In Drake and Cayton's analysis, "the very preachers, editors and politicians who did the most to keep the dream of Black Metropolis alive only half believed in its ultimate realization."[4]

The Chicago experience, therefore, tends to refute any attempt to compare Northern Negroes with European immigrants. Unlike the Irish, Poles, Jews, or Italians, Negroes banded together not to enjoy a common linguistic, cultural, and religious tradition, but because a systematic pattern of discrimination left them no alternative. Negroes were tied together less by a common cultural heritage than by a common set of grievances. Even those who made a major effort to emphasize the positive aspects of separate Negro development were hard-pressed. The Garveyites, for instance, were forced to glorify an African past that had no relationship to the historical experience of American Negroes. Racial solidarity was a response rather than a positive force. It was an

[4] St. Clair Drake and Horace Cayton, *Black Metropolis* (New York: Harcourt, Brace & Company, 1945), p. 82.

attempt to preserve self-respect and foster self-reliance in the face of continual humiliations and rebuffs from white society.

The persistence of the Chicago Negro ghetto, then, has been not merely the result of continued immigration from the South, but the product of a special historical experience. From its inception, the Negro ghetto was unique among the city's ethnic enclaves. It grew in response to an implacable white hostility that has not basically changed. In this sense it has been Chicago's only true ghetto, less the product of voluntary development within than of external pressures from without. Like the Jewries of medieval Europe, Black Chicago has offered no escape. Irishmen, Poles, Jews, or Italians, as they acquired the means, had an alternative: they could move their enclaves to more comfortable environs or, as individuals, leave the enclaves and become members of the community at large. Negroes—forever marked by their color—could only hope for success within a rigidly delineated and severely restricted ghetto society. No physical wall has encircled the black belt. But an almost equally impervious wall of hostility and discrimination has isolated Negroes from the mainstream of Chicago life. Under such conditions, Negroes have tried, often against impossible odds, to make the best of their circumstances by creating a meaningful life of their own. But they have done so, not out of choice, but because white society has left them no alternative.

A NOTE ON SOURCES

The following note makes no attempt to be comprehensive. It includes only those sources that were the most useful to me in preparing this book.

MANUSCRIPT COLLECTIONS

Despite a major effort, I could locate no extant manuscript collection left by a Chicago Negro dealing with the period covered by this study. Two personal collections, however, were extraordinarily useful. The Julius Rosenwald Papers at the University of Chicago Library contain significant material on nearly every major Negro organization and institution. Of particular value were the memoranda prepared by Rosenwald's secretary, William C. Graves, informing the philanthropist of the programs and activities of organizations to which he might contribute. The Booker T. Washington Papers at the Library of Congress are a source that no student of early twentieth-century Negro history, regardless of his special interest, can ignore. Washington's correspondence with S. Laing Williams, in particular, provides a running account of the leadership struggle in Chicago between 1900 and 1912. Of less value, but containing some pertinent material were the Mary McDowell Papers at the Chicago Historical Society, the Graham Taylor and Victor Lawson Papers at the Newberry Library, and the Frank O. Lowden Papers at the University of Chicago Library. The Jane Addams Papers, available on microfilm at the Chicago Historical Society, were disappointing.

The file of the Illinois Writers Project on "The Negro in Illinois," located in the George Cleveland Hall branch of the Chicago Public Library, is an important source that defies classification. The project was conducted in the late 1930's by the Works Progress Administration and employed students, social workers, and clerical workers whose task was to assemble material for a sociohistorical study of Negroes in Illinois. The study, as originally conceived, was never written, but the files contain invaluable material—clippings, transcripts of interviews, and notes on organizations, churches, and community leaders written by the project workers.

NEWSPAPERS

The files of the Chicago Negro press provided the one most important source for this study. There are no complete files of any Chicago Negro newspaper before 1899, but the *Appeal* (St. Paul) regularly carried Chicago news and its files are relatively complete from 1889 through its demise in the 1920's. The *Broad Ax* commenced publication in Chicago in 1899 and files for this paper are complete through 1931. Although its editor, Julius Taylor, presented a highly individualistic view of Negro affairs, the *Broad Ax's* news columns are an invaluable source for early twentieth-century community life. The *Defender* first appeared in 1905 and has relatively complete files beginning in 1909. From this date on, its pages provide the fullest account of Negro life in Chicago. For the last two years of the period covered in this study, the files of the *Whip* were an important supplement to the *Defender*. Scattered copies of two other Chicago Negro papers, the *Conservator* and the *World,* are also available. A general account of the Negro press in Chicago appears in Ralph N. Davis, "Negro Newspapers in Chicago" (master's thesis, University of Chicago, 1939).

The white press was of particular importance in understanding interracial relations and white attitudes toward Negro life. The *Tribune,* although generally anti-Negro, provides the most complete coverage, but between 1900 and 1912 the *Record-Herald* is indexed and thus the most convenient paper to use. Also of interest for the period before 1914 is the *Inter-Ocean,* published by the reform-minded H. H. Kohlsaat, the one daily newspaper in Chicago to cover Negro affairs with some sympathy.

STATISTICAL REPORTS AND PUBLIC DOCUMENTS

The decennial reports of the U.S. Census Bureau were basic in the compilation of statistics for this study. In addition to the regular census reports, the Bureau's special volume, *Negro Population in the United States, 1790–1915* (Washington: Government Printing Office, 1918), was particularly valuable. Simon Kuznets, and others, have refined the census data to provide more detailed statistics on migration; see their *Population Redistribution and*

Economic Growth, United States, 1870–1950, 2 vols. (Philadelphia: American Philosophical Society, 1957). Statistics for Chicago based on otherwise unpublished data can be found in Ernest W. Burgess and Charles Newcomb, *Census Data of the City of Chicago, 1920* (Chicago: University of Chicago Press, 1931). Professors Otis Duncan and Beverly Duncan of the Population Studies Center of the University of Michigan kindly provided me with unpublished census data for Chicago, 1910.

Public documents contained some information, but were disappointingly thin in Negro material. Of use were the reports of the Department of Public Welfare of the City of Chicago, the *Journal of the Proceedings of the Chicago City Council,* the Illinois Legislative Reference Bureau's *Legislative Digest,* and the report of the Vice Commission of Chicago, *The Social Evil in Chicago: A Study of Existing Conditions with Recommendations* (Chicago: Gunthorp-Warren, 1911).

GENERAL STUDIES OF CHICAGO

Bessie Louise Pierce's comprehensive *A History of Chicago,* 3 vols. (New York: Alfred A. Knopf, 1937, 1940, 1957), is a model of scholarship, but unfortunately Professor Pierce has, to date, carried her study only to 1893. For the later period, one must turn to less scholarly works: Lloyd Lewis and Henry J. Smith, *Chicago: The History of Its Reputation* (New York: Harcourt, Brace & Company, 1929), and Emmett Dedmon, *Fabulous Chicago* (New York: Random House, 1953). Ray Ginger, in *Altgeld's America* (New York: Funk and Wagnalls, 1958), interprets Chicago life between 1892 and 1905 with particular emphasis on reform activities. These works should be supplemented with several biographies and autobiographies of interest to students of Negro Chicago: Jane Addams, *Twenty Years at Hull House* (New York: Macmillan Company, 1910); William Hutchinson, *Lowden of Illinois,* 2 vols. (Chicago: University of Chicago Press, 1957); Claudius Johnson, *Carter Harrison I* (Chicago: University of Chicago Press, 1928); Graham Taylor, *Chicago Commons through 40 Years* (Chicago: Chicago Commons Association, 1936); Louise C. Wade, *Graham Taylor: Pioneer for Social Justice* (Chicago: University of Chicago Press, 1964); Lloyd Wendt and Herman Kogan, *Big Bill Thompson* (Indianapolis: Bobbs-Merrill, 1953); Wendt and Kogan, *Lords of the Levee* (Indianapolis: Bobbs-Merrill,

1943); and Howard E. Wilson, *Mary McDowell, Neighbor* (Chicago: University of Chicago Press, 1928).

Two general works on Negro life in Chicago were of major importance, not only in providing material but in suggesting a framework for this study. The report of the Chicago Commission on Race Relations, *The Negro in Chicago* (Chicago: University of Chicago Press, 1922) is discussed in Chapter 11. St. Clair Drake and Horace Cayton's sociological classic, *Black Metropolis* (New York: Harcourt, Brace & Company, 1945), an exhaustive analysis of Negro Chicago in the late 1930's, is still the best study of urban Negro life ever written and its insights must necessarily influence every student of the subject. Several earlier works also contain valuable material. Louise De Koven Bowen, *The Colored Population of Chicago* (Chicago: Juvenile Protective Association, 1913), and Junius B. Wood, *The Negro in Chicago* (Chicago: *Chicago Daily News,* 1916), are brief but informative accounts, while Richard R. Wright, Jr., "The Industrial Condition of Negroes in Chicago" (B.D. thesis, University of Chicago Divinity School, 1901), is broader than its title suggests. For comparative purposes, I found two studies of Negro life in other cities particularly useful: Gilbert Osofsky, *Harlem: The Making of a Ghetto* (New York: Harper & Row, 1965); and Elliott M. Rudwick, *Race Riot at East St. Louis* (Carbondale: Southern Illinois University Press, 1964).

The literature on Negro migration, particularly for the World War I years, is voluminous. Louise V. Kennedy and Frank Ross's *Bibliography of Negro Migration* (New York: Columbia University Press, 1934) is an invaluable guide to contemporary material. Particularly important in understanding the personal dimension of the migration are the "Letters of Negro Migrants of 1916–18," collected under the direction of Emmett J. Scott and published in the *Journal of Negro History* (Washington), 4 (July and October, 1919): 290–340, 412–75. Alternately hilarious and touching, these letters are an unrivalled source for the causes of the migration, the element of mass suggestion that propelled it and the initial reaction of the migrants to urban life. Two important contemporary accounts are U.S. Department of Labor, *Negro Migrations in 1916–17* (Washington: Government Printing Office, 1919), which contains the reports of several government investigators, and Emmett J. Scott, *Negro Migration During the War* (New York: Oxford University Press, 1920). Somewhat broader in scope are Thomas J. Woofter, Jr., *Negro Migration* (New York: W. D. Gray, 1920); Louise V. Kennedy, *The Negro Peasant Turns Cityward* (New York: Columbia University Press, 1930); Lionel C. Florant, *Negro Migration, 1860–1940* (manuscript prepared for the Carnegie Corporation of New York, 1942, copy in the Schomburg Collection of the New York Public Library); and Arna Bontemps and Jack Conroy's impressionistic but highly readable *They Seek a City* (Garden City, N.Y.: Doubleday, Doran and Company, 1945).

Some specific references to Negro migration to Chicago can be found in all of the above works, but the file of the *Defender* for the war years is the most valuable source. Three demographic studies of Chicago are also useful: Otis Duncan and Beverly Duncan, *The Negro Population of Chicago* (Chicago: University of Chicago Press, 1957); Paul Cressy, "The Succession of Cultural Groups in the City of Chicago" (doctoral dissertation, University of Chicago, 1930); and Stanley Lieberson, "Comparative Segregation and Assimilation of Ethnic Groups" (doctoral dissertation, University of Chicago, 1960). E. Franklin Frazier's *Negro Family in Chicago* (Chicago: University of Chicago Press, 1932) contains important material on migrant adjustment.

LEADERSHIP

The framework for my analysis of Negro leadership in Chicago depends heavily upon the work of August Meier, in particular *Negro Thought in America, 1880–1915* (Ann Arbor: University of Michigan Press, 1963); "Negro Racial Thought in the Age of Booker T. Washington" (doctoral dissertation, Columbia University, 1957); and two important articles, "Booker T. Washington and the Negro Press," *Journal of Negro History* (Washington), 38 (January, 1953): 67–90, and "Negro Class Structure and Ideology in the Age of Booker T. Washington," *Phylon* (Atlanta), 23 (Fall, 1962): 258–60.

My most important single source for the ideological struggle among Chicago's Negro leaders was the Booker T. Washington

Papers. In addition, a number of books and articles provided biographical data. Four Chicago Negro leaders of the late nineteenth and early twentieth centuries have been the subjects of full-length studies. Helen Buckler, *Doctor Dan* (Boston: Little-Brown and Company, 1954), is a gossipy but perceptive biography of Daniel Hale Williams. Roi Ottley, *The Lonely Warrior: The Life and Times of Robert S. Abbott* (Chicago: Henry Regnery & Company, 1955), and Joseph Logsdon, "The Reverend A. J. Carey and the Negro in Chicago Politics" (master's thesis, University of Chicago, 1961) are both competent studies, while Miles Mark Fisher, *The Master's Slave* (Philadelphia: Judson Press, 1922), a biography of the author's father, the Rev. Elijah J. Fisher, is less satisfactory but useful. Two memoirs in manuscript form provided biographical data on other leaders: Mrs. Alfreda Barnett Duster kindly gave me access to her unpublished memoir of her mother, Ida Wells-Barnett, while Miss Olive Diggs shared with me material from the memoirs of Anthony Overton, in her possession. Reverdy Ransom's autobiography, *The Pilgrimage of Harriet Ransom's Son* (Nashville, Tenn.: Sunday School Union, 1950[?]) contains a full account of his Chicago years. Brief biographical sketches of a number of leaders appear in "Some Chicagoans of Note," *Crisis* (New York), 10 (September, 1915): 239–40; I. C. Harris, *Colored Men's Professional and Business Directory of Chicago* (Chicago: I. C. Harris, 1885); Frederick H. Robb, ed., *1927 Intercollegian Wonder Book, or, The Negro in Chicago, 1779–1927* (Chicago: Washington Intercollegiate Club, 1927); and John H. Taitt, ed., *The Souvenir of Negro Progress: Chicago, 1779–1925* (Chicago: De Saible Association, 1925). Jesse Binga receives more ample treatment in Inez Cantey, "Jesse Binga," *Crisis* (New York), 34 (December, 1927): 239, 350, 352; and J. B. Massiah is discussed in "A Preacher of the Word," *Crisis* (New York), 11 (April, 1916): 290. Herbert M. Smith provides a fascinating portrait of the evangelist, Lucy Smith, in "Three Negro Preachers in Chicago: A Study in Religious Leadership" (master's thesis, University of Chicago Divinity School, 1935). The best approach to Fannie Barrier Williams is through her published articles and speeches: "The Club Movement among Colored Women in America," *A New Negro for a New Century*, ed. J. E. MacBrady (Chicago: American Publishing House, 1900[?]), pp. 409–21; "The Intellectual Progress of the Colored Women of the

United States since the Emancipation Proclamation," *The World's Congress of Representative Women,* ed. May Wright Sewall (Chicago: Rand, MacNally, 1894), pp. 696–712; "The New Negro," *Chicago Record-Herald,* October 9, 1904, pt. 7, p. 6; "Religious Duty to the Negro," *The World's Congress of Religions,* ed. J. W. Hanson (Chicago: W. B. Conkey, 1894), pp. 893–97; and "Social Bonds in the Black Belt of Chicago," *Charities* (New York), 15 (October 7, 1905): 40–44. Mrs. Williams' husband, S. Laing Williams, is best understood from his correspondence with Booker T. Washington. In addition, biographical data on all of the major Negro leaders appear periodically in the files of the Negro press, both in obituaries and in the brief sketches that the newspapers frequently published.

ORGANIZATIONS AND INSTITUTIONS

The one comprehensive account of Negro organizational life in Chicago is St. Clair Drake, *Churches and Voluntary Associations in the Chicago Negro Community* (Chicago. Works Progress Administration, 1940), mimeographed. On Negro churches, Robert E. Sutherland, "An Analysis of Negro Churches in Chicago" (doctoral dissertation, University of Chicago, 1930), although basically concerned with a later period, is useful. Many brief histories of individual churches and souvenir programs of church functions can be found in the files of the Illinois Writers' Project. The only full-length history of an individual church is Miles Mark Fisher, "History of Olivet Baptist Church" (master's thesis, University of Chicago, 1922). Benjamin E. Mays and Joseph E. Nicholson, *The Negro's Church* (New York: Institute of Social and Religious Research, 1933), provides a good analytical framework in which to understand Negro religious life.

Of the secular institutions, the Chicago Urban League has received the best treatment: Arvarh E. Strickland, "The Chicago Urban League, 1916–1956" (doctoral dissertation, University of Illinois, 1962), is an excellent study which has been recently published (Urbana: University of Illinois Press, 1966). Although the records of the League for the early years no longer exist, there is useful material in the Rosenwald Papers and in the League's published annual reports. The Chicago NAACP has left no local records, but there is information about the Chicago branch in the minutes of the Executive Board of the NAACP, in the New York office of the Association. Provident Hospital is best treated in Buckler's biography of Williams, although the author is unduly harsh on George Cleveland Hall. The minutes of the Executive Board of the Wabash Avenue YMCA exist, beginning with the early 1920's; for the earlier period, see Channing H. Tobias, "The Colored Y.M.C.A.," *Crisis* (New York), 9 (November, 1914):33; the Rosenwald Papers; and numerous accounts in both the Negro and white press. M. S. Stuart discusses Negro lodges, particularly their insurance function, in *An Economic Detour: A History of Insurance in the Lives of American Negroes* (New York: Wendell Malliet & Company, 1940); for the Negro Masons in Chicago, see the annual proceedings of The Most Worshipful Lodge Ancient, Free and Accepted Masons of the State of Illinois and Jurisdiction. Women's organizations are treated in Elizabeth Lindsay Davis, *The Story of The Illinois Federation of Colored Women's Clubs* (Chicago[?], 1922[?]). In addition, of course, the Negro press reported regularly on organizational activity.

LABOR AND EMPLOYMENT

There are several general treatments of Negro labor in America that have been useful in this study: Sterling Spero and Abram Harris, *The Black Worker* (New York: Columbia University Press, 1931); Horace Cayton and George Mitchell, *Black Workers and the New Unions* (Chapel Hill: University of North Carolina Press, 1939); Charles Wesley, *Negro Labor in the United States, 1850–1925* (New York: Vanguard Press, 1927); and Erie W. Hardy, "Relation of the Negro to Trade Unionism" (master's thesis, University of Chicago, 1911). On Negro labor in Chicago, Oscar D. Hutton, "The Negro Worker and the Labor Unions in Chicago" (master's thesis, University of Chicago, 1939), is the only general treatment. Negro workers in the stockyards have been the subject of two studies: the better is Alma Herbst, *The Negro in the Slaughtering and Meat Packing Industry in Chicago* (New York: Houghton Mifflin & Company, 1932); but see also Catherine E. Lewis, "Trade Union Policies in Regard to the Negro Worker in the Slaughtering and Meatpacking Industry of Chicago" (master's thesis, University of Chicago, 1945). Some interesting material on the 1904 stockyards strike can be found in the Mary McDowell Papers. Negroes in the steel industry of

Chicago have been less well treated; there is some material in William Z. Foster, *The Great Steel Strike and Its Lessons* (New York: B. W. Heubsch, 1920), and Interchurch World Movement, Committee of Inquiry, *Report on the Steel Strike of 1919* (New York: Harcourt, Brace & Company, 1920). Female labor receives special treatment in "Employment of Colored Women in Chicago," *Crisis* (New York), 1 (January, 1911):24–25, and Forrester B. Washington, "Reconstruction and the Colored Woman," *Life and Labor* (Chicago), 8 (January, 1919):3–7. Henry McGee surveys an important segment of Chicago's Negro labor force in "The Negro in the Chicago Post Office" (master's thesis, University of Chicago, 1961). Of the press treatment of Negro labor, the *Whip* provides the best coverage for the later years. The census reports are the major source of statistics on Negro employment in Chicago.

POLITICS

There is one important general study of Negro politics in Chicago, Harold Gosnell, *Negro Politicians* (Chicago: University of Chicago Press, 1935), as much a work of history as of political science. James Q. Wilson's *Negro Politics* (New York: Free Press, 1961) covers Chicago in a later period, but has many perceptive insights of relevance to the early years. Several articles also deal with Negro politics in Chicago: Gosnell, "The Chicago 'Black Belt' as a Political Battleground," *American Journal of Sociology* (Chicago), 39 (November, 1933):329–41; Ralph J. Bunche, "The Thompson-Negro Alliance," *Opportunity* (New York), 7 (March, 1929):78–80; and two articles by George Ellis, "The Chicago Negro in Law and Politics," *Champion Magazine* (Chicago), 1 (March, 1917):349, and "The Negro in the Chicago Primary," *Independent* (New York), 62 (April 25, 1912):890–91. There are numerous works on Chicago politics in general that are essential for an understanding of the framework within which Negro politicians operated. See in particular, Charles E. Merriam, *Chicago: A More Intimate View of Urban Politics* (New York: Macmillan Company, 1929), and the two engaging political biographies by Wendt and Kogan, listed above. The Negro newspapers were all politically oriented and provide a running account of the politics of Black Chicago.

HOUSING

All of the statistical and demographic works listed above are useful in understanding the Negro housing pattern in Chicago as is the report of the Chicago Commission on Race Relations. The many interracial incidents that grew out of housing competition are fully treated in both the Negro and white press. Special studies of Negro housing include Sophonisba Breckinridge, "The Color Line in the Housing Problem," *Survey* (New York), 29 (February 1, 1913):575–76; Alzada P. Comstock, "Chicago Housing Conditions: The Problem of the Negro," *American Journal of Sociology* (Chicago), 18 (September, 1912):241–57; and Alice Q. Rood, "Social Conditions among the Negroes on Federal Street between Forty-fifth and Fifty-third Streets" (master's thesis, University of Chicago, 1924).

THE RACE RIOT OF 1919

As the most dramatic incident in the history of Black Chicago, the 1919 riot has received much attention. It is fully treated in the report of the Chicago Commission on Race Relations; and Guido A. Dobbert, "A History of the Chicago Race Riot of 1919" (master's thesis, University of Chicago, 1957), adds nothing new. An excellent recent analysis appears in Arthur I. Waskow, *From Race Riot to Sit-In* (New York: Doubleday & Company, 1965). Waskow treats the Chicago riot within the context of the racial violence that swept the country in 1919. The book also includes a superb chapter on the workings of the Chicago Commission on Race Relations and a perceptive analysis of the Commission's report, based on papers in the Illinois State Archives. Contemporary accounts of the riot include, of course, full coverage in both the Negro and white press; see also Carl Sandburg, *The Chicago Race Riots* (New York: Harcourt, Brace & Howe, 1919); and Walter White, "Chicago and Its Eight Reasons," *Crisis* (New York), 18 (October, 1919):293–94.

INTERVIEWS

I interviewed nearly fifty persons in the Chicago Negro community, most of whom had lived in Chicago in the early part of the twentieth century. These interviews varied widely in usefulness and, in all cases, I attempted to verify the information that I received. Although many of the interviews provided me with valuable information and insights, five deserve special mention. Chester Wilkins, for many years Chief Red Cap at the Illinois Central Station, described in vivid detail the arrival of southern migrants in Chicago and their initial contact with city life. Joseph Bibb, in a long and wide-ranging interview, told me of the *Chicago Whip* and of the "New Negro" group of which he was a prominent member. Edward S. Gillespie provided me with useful information about Negro insurance companies in Chicago. And I learned a great deal about Negro Catholics in Chicago from Dr. Arthur Falls and about Republican politics from William E. King.

INDEX

Abbott, Edith, 103, 169

Abbott, Robert S.: biographical sketch, 81–82; business activities, 114–15, 116, 184–85; role in migration, 134–36, 146, 167; racial philosophy, 167, 194–95, 196, 204; civic activities, 170, 192; mentioned, 181, 186

Abolitionism. *See* Anti-Slavery Movement

"Abyssinian Affair," 194, 195

Accommodationism: Chicago leaders oppose, 56, 59, 60, 61–62, 65, 73, 167

Adams, Cyrus F., 80, 114

Adams, John Q., 80, 114

Addams, Jane: as Chicago civic leader, 3–4, 5, 103; relations with Negro community, 00, 86, 87; mentioned, 7, 45, 63

African Methodist Episcopal Church: activities in Chicago, 5, 91–93; mentioned, 94. *See also* individual churches

Afro-American Council, 59–60, 80

Afro-American League, 59

Alabama: migration from, 132, 139, 140, 141, 147

All Nations Pentecostal Church, 176

Alschuler, Samuel, 160

Amalgamated Association of Iron, Steel, and Tin Workers, 163–64

Amalgamated Meat Cutters and Butcher Workmen of North America: policy toward Negroes, 38, 159, 160; launches organizational drive, 159; Chicago Urban League supports, 173; mentioned, 166

Amanda Smith School, 102–3

American Federation of Labor, 165, 197. *See also* individual affiliated unions

American Giants (baseball team), 117, 183

American Unity Labor Union, 162

Anarchists, 27

Anderson, Louis B., 124, 189–90, 191

Anson, Cap, 116

Anti-Slavery Movement: Chicago Negroes in, 5–6, 55; legacy in later years, 51, 54, 56, 102–3

Appeal (St. Paul): activities in Chicago, 80, 114; quoted, 100

Appomattox Club: founded, 78; historical sketch, 109; mentioned, 79, 197, 220

Argo Corn Products, 157

Arkansas, 129

Armour, Philip, 98

Armour Company, 38, 151, 162

Armour Institute, 52

Armour Square, 206

Arthur, George, 174

Ashland Avenue Business Men's Association, 37

Assimilation. *See* Integration

Athletic Clubs, 201, 206, 213, 216. *See also* Ragan's Colts

Attorneys. *See* Lawyers

Avendorph, Julius, 65–66

Avendorph, Mrs. Julius, 72, 108

Baker, Ray Stannard: quoted, 7, 138

Baltimore, 138, 191

Banking, Negroes in, 74–75, 118

Baptist church: activities in Chicago, 91–93, 169, 174–75, 176, 177–78; mentioned, 76, 94. *See also* individual churches

Barber, J. Max, 74

Barbers, Negroes as, 31, 111, 112

Barnett, Ferdinand L.: quoted, 53; biographical sketch, 58–59, 60–61; political activities, 67, 68, 77, 119–20, 121; civic activities, 85, 100, 104, 107, 108, 192; mentioned, 62, 66, 68

Barnett, Ida. *See* Wells-Barnett, Ida

Baseball, Negroes in, 116–18, 183

Beaches. *See* Recreational facilities

Belmont-Cragin, 224

Bentley, Charles E.: biographical sketch, 57–58; civic activities, 85, 87–88, 108, 192

Bentley, Mrs. Charles, 72

Bethel A.M.E. Church: activities at, 73, 92; role in Chicago religious life, 91, 93, 95; mentioned, 63, 84

243